Born in London in 1968 Robert Howells has spent the last 20 years investigating the mysteries of Rennes-le-Château and the Priory of Sion. During this time he has built up an extensive knowledge and experience of secret societies, symbolism and esoteric thought.

He is described in *The Templar Revelation* (Bantam Press, 1997) as having 'an extraordinarily extensive knowledge of esoteric symbolism and whose research into Rennes-le-Château is scholarly, sane and far reaching.'

As manager for five years of Watkins Books in London, one of the oldest esoteric bookshops in Europe, he extended his research into transpersonal psychology, sacred geometry, Gnosticism and alchemy. He also came into contact with a number of secret societies during this time including the Priory of Sion, the Freemasons, the Order of Lazarus, various neo-Templar orders plus Sufis and other religious groups.

From 2003–2007 Robert Howells worked as lead consultant and researcher on *Bloodline – the Movie*, an independent documentary by 1244 Films which premiered in New York in 2008. He has since done talks and radio interviews in the USA and UK to promote this film.

During the making of *Bloodline* he acted as mediator between the producers of the film and the Priory of Sion. When contacting Sion he offered them the opportunity to put the record straight on the controversy sparked by *The Da Vinci Code*. In response the Priory of Sion imparted a wealth of information including over 300 emails, images and documentation and has continued to do so to this day. Along with his own research Robert Howells has compiled the information into this book, *Inside the Priory of Sion*.

Robert's other writings include a feature film script titled *Belief in an Age of Chaos* and a television series based on secret societies called *The Hidden*. He continues to write articles for magazines and take part in television and radio interviews about the Priory of Sion and is currently working on a second book.

Robert Howells is married with two children and lives in Kent, England.

INSIDE THE PRIORY OF SION

REVELATIONS FROM THE WORLD'S
MOST SECRET SOCIETY –
GUARDIANS OF THE BLOODLINE OF JESUS

ROBERT HOWELLS

WATKINS PUBLISHING
LONDON

This edition published in the UK 2011 by
Watkins Publishing, Sixth Floor, Castle House,
75–76 Wells Street, London W1T 3QH

1 3 5 7 9 10 8 6 4 2

Designed and typeset by Jerry Goldie Graphic Design

Printed and bound by Imago in China

British Library Cataloguing-in-Publication Data Available

ISBN: 978-1-78028-017-2

www.watkinspublishing.co.uk

CONTENTS

PART 4: OUTCOME

LIST OF PLATES

Asmodeus statue at Rennes-le-Château

Father Bérenger Saunière's cassock

St Anthony and St Paul in the Desert painting by David Teniers the Younger

Et in Arcadia Ego (The Shepherds of Arcadia) painting by Nicolas Poussin

Altar at Rennes-le-Château with landscape

Photo of Coustaussa, Pech Cardou and Blanchefort

Manuscript - *Splendor Solis*: 'Deliver me out of the mire…'

For Nicky, Aaron and Joanne
all that remains when the dust settles

ACKNOWLEDGMENTS

There are a number of people who have greatly helped my journey. Bruce Burgess and René Barnett for the documentary *Bloodline – the Movie,* which attracted me back to the mystery; Nicole Dawe, ever the sane researcher; and all those I met and travelled with in the Languedoc. Watkins Bookshop in London – the Internet may have more information but the staff at Watkins have wisdom. The staff of the British Library, Glasgow University Library, the Wellcome Institute and the Vatican Secret Archive for their help. There is also a debt of gratitude to many authors and researchers who came before me, some of whose works I have listed at the back of this book. Should you wish to travel further along these paths, more can be found on the website **http:www. robhowells.co.uk**.

Thanks to my agent Susan Mears, who understood and believed in what I was trying to do, and the Watkins Publishing imprint of Duncan Baird Publishers, helmed by Michael Mann and his excellent team, who were brave enough to run with this book. Additional thanks are due to my editor, Peter Bently for his diligence and sound advice.

Finally, there are Nicolas Haywood and the Priory of Sion, to whom I owe the greatest debt. Nic's knowledge and his willingness to bring Sion into the light inspired and underpinned this book.

Note: Unless otherwise stated all biblical quotations are from the Authorised (King James) Version of the Bible.

FOREWORD

BY NICOLAS HAYWOOD

It was with little surprise that I received Robert Howells' letter back in the summer of 2005. The manager of the antiquarian book section at Watkins Bookshop had already contacted me by telephone to see if I was prepared to accept Robert's correspondence. The manner in which I was approached seemed to me to be following the correct etiquette and displayed a marked respect for the order with whom he was seeking contact. Eventually we found ourselves immersed in a great deal of email, and his questions seemed endless.

From the outset many of Robert's questions required that I contact others in Sion's ranks in order to negate reprisals or even harsh words and arguments thereafter. If I was going to assist Robert then I was going to do so with Sion's blessing, or at least the blessings of those with whom I had developed a solid rapport over a period of almost forty years. Even then, things were not always to run as smoothly as any of us would have liked. There were some repercussions. Fallings-out, and a lot of explaining on my part.

Despite having been proclaimed 'a hoax' back in the 1980s, Sion had continued to flourish as it had always done, and the apparent secret they were said to be guarding – the Holy Bloodline – was and remains but one facet, one element of which they are the age-old custodians.

What many could not comprehend was how the notion of a Holy Bloodline could encounter such hostility and offence. Surely those who believed the collection of writings incorporated into the Bible, those who had read them, could not have missed the fact that many of Christ's disciples were said to have been married. Furthermore, many had families. Children. Surely their respective family trees could be traced, and if not traceable, then at least they were known to the families from whom they were the descended. In fact, the Roman Catholic Church even tried to kill all Jesus' relatives on the maternal side. The

Desposyni, or blood relatives, as Rome had called them, were to be expunged at all cost. Surely that act itself would be an act of Deicide. Why were those in Rome so worried? What did they fear sufficiently to justify murdering their own god's blood-family? Perhaps they feared the truth coming to light, and such a scenario could certainly not have been permitted. The rapidly growing new empire of the Roman Church stood to gain more than its predecessor, the secular Roman Empire, could ever have hoped: total obedience, but obedience based upon personal and spiritual guilt.

What had rendered the Church's task seemingly impossible was the fact that the third expulsion of Jews from France (and other countries) in the 13th century merely required that they convert to Catholicism or leave. This, Rome assumed, would cause any remaining members of Jesus' maternal bloodline to fall quietly into toeing the line. This would also have been the case for any descendants of the apostles. (However, Rome's behaviour, ancient though it now is, has left tell-tale marks in the fact that Rome appears to hold the Virgin Mother in greater esteem than the all-important Jesus Christ, and the same can be said of St Peter.) But the terms underpinning the third expulsion of Jews from France simply caused them, for example, to go into hiding, pretending to be members of a religion which, in reality, they despised. This explains why so many noble family escutcheons and arms display Judaic symbolism and what can also be taken for occult devices openly, almost in flagrant defiance of Rome's past edicts.

Even if there had been no marriage between Jesus and Mary of Bethany (Mary Magdalene), and no offspring, then surely the children of the apostles would have posed some sort of threat to Rome's new religion founded on a fusion of Mithras, Virgin birth and significant pagan and ancient Egyptian elements.

We know that the Celtic Church still clung most vehemently to the 'original' tenets of *true* Christianity. We also know that the major symbols of significance to the Celts were such things as an equal-armed cross as opposed to a cruciform cross; the circle and/or disc; a crescent-moon shape lying on its back; and a crook akin to that of a shepherd or those found in Egyptian religion, (they are also likely to have used a symbolic flail). They also used the endless knot (as found in Islamic art) and, perhaps most bafflingly, a shape that appears to be a stylized fish, but which could equally represent one half of the ancient symbol for eternity or even the orbit of a celestial body. Even if it is a representation of a fish it is unlikely to refer to Christ as the 'Fisher of Men'. More likely it was a far older symbol relating to an ancient global story of the union of a female human and a semi-aquatic creature. It may also have its basis in a crude or stylized ancient Egyptian hieroglyph.

Celtic Christians had no crucifixes on their altars or anywhere else, and they observed their Sabbath on a Saturday. They had a peculiar form of tonsure which divided the entire head of hair into two distinct and separate halves. They had statues akin to those of Isis on their altars, and Egyptian iconography painted on the church walls. All their places of worship would appear to have had ceilings painted with the stars and constellations much like those found in ancient Egyptian temples and the Great Pyramid at Giza. Isis also bore the name 'Queen of Heaven', later used by the Catholic Church as an address to the Virgin Mary.

Equally, the circle of stars frequently depicted surrounding the Virgin's head is reminiscent of the flag of the European Union. If, in Rome's eyes, the stars are meant to indicate the number of disciples then why is she at the centre? Why are they shown encircling *her* head? Perhaps because, when all said and done, Mary is also a disciple. Indeed, the main disciple. She was, according to the Church, the first to see the risen Christ.

However it is equally likely, if not more so, that Mary of Bethany played a pivotal role in the mystery school that Christ promulgated, and that she and Jesus were married and had a family of their own. It is likely that, failing an attempt to reinstate the royal house of David in Roman-occupied Judea, they fled using trade maps or part of a trading route already in regular use by merchants such as Joseph of Arimathea and the Egyptians before that. It may even be that they originally set out for the Iberian Peninsula, where Rome's reach did not fully extend, but for some reason instead made landfall in France, not far from the present-day Spanish border.

Several elements of the above may not have been previously known to all readers. In that respect through my contact with Robert Howells I have attempted to enlighten those who were hitherto uninformed or had missed the connecting threads, while recapping historical attitudes and events for others.

Back in the autumn of 2005 I was told to convey a simple message and I did so:

> 'It matters little whether Sion's reality is believed or not.... It really makes no difference. There will come a time when many will say [of what will ultimately be revealed in due course], "Oh, it's pretty much what we expected", etc. It will, hopefully, come as no real

surprise. It is all in the timing – the points at which information and proof are released.'

As my colleague Gino Sandri, Sion's Secretary General, has already aptly stated:

'The Priory of Sion has become a household name. A brand name if you will....'

This is in keeping with Sion's goal, much in the same way that, through carefully timed release, the majority of younger people believe there was a marriage between Jesus and Mary of Bethany, or at least have no problem or issue with the notion of it. Children, they seem to accept, would be a natural result of the union.

So Sion's current circuit is going according to plan, or has already done so, and the pace at which future material will be disseminated is very soon to gain rapidly increasing momentum.

We furnished a vast amount of material in our correspondences with Robert Howells. Only about ten percent was of any practical use in his role as a researcher for an American film company making a feature-length documentary, *Bloodline*. There was a vast amount which, we know, was not passed to the film's producers. It would have served no purpose. However, for Robert it acted as a supplement to the wealth of material and information already supplied.

When he stated that he wanted to write a book about Sion there was immediate approval from at least three of its members. Even Pierre Plantard's son – Thomas – seemed content with this notion. Robert, we knew, had been a seriously assiduous student of occult sciences and had spent many years researching secret societies and related symbolism. I knew that he could be trusted to use the material that was surplus to the documentary.

There were several reasons why we were so agreeable. Partly because Robert Howells had soon realized that there was far more to the so-called 'mystery of Rennes-le-Château' than merely embalmed corpses and golden treasures. He had already grasped that there was – and is – something uniquely important about the area itself. Something which others have failed to comprehend, but is of vital importance to the world? Do the environs of Rennes-le-Château hold an ancient secret? Yes. Is it geographical in nature? Yes. A secret with relevance for the future? Certainly!

The author desperately wanted us to furnish him with additional documents and manuscripts. I was in favour of such a request, but others were not. Nonetheless, further documents and images were eventually supplied, and general information has been given with the consent of a handful of Sion's members. Had the edict of the 'old guard' been observed then little, if anything, would have been forthcoming. Fortunately, in the early years, back in 2005, I had 'slipped in' additional information by way of steers, snippets and references that I knew would provide – in part – some intriguing answers if followed up.

As to the machinations and structure of the Order of the Priory of Sion (or 'Sion' for the sake of brevity), I have only furnished paperwork for which I sought permission. At least one other high-ranking member had done likewise, and we have attempted to answer academic questions directly. However, Sion seldom speaks plainly and when it does so it is most on its guard. This does not seem to impede our author's ability to comprehend, and he possesses both the knowledge and the mindset with which to perform the exacting task he has set for himself.

Nicolas Haywood

January 2011

London

THE UNDERGROUND STREAM

In December 2005 I received a Christmas card from a representative of the secret society or order called the Priory of Sion. It was inscribed with a Latin abbreviation – L.V.A.A.T. – and stamped for release as a legitimate Priory of Sion document. The card depicted the Three Wise Men following the Star of Bethlehem.

The significance of the three men following the stars – astrologers perhaps – was not lost on me. For nearly six months I had been mediating between the Priory of Sion and 1244 Films, who were producing a documentary on the heretical notion that Jesus had fathered children.

My introduction to this mystery began long before the documentary. I had researched both the Priory of Sion, and the idea of the bloodline of Jesus, for fifteen years prior to 1244's invitation. My interest during this time centred on the mystery of Rennes-le-Château, a small village in southern France where a priest had become suddenly very wealthy at the end of the 19th century and had spent the money on modifying his church to include an array of unorthodox symbols.

Some twenty years ago a book called *The Holy Blood and the Holy Grail* had sparked my interest. Published in 1982, this was the first English account of the Rennes-le-Château mystery. The authors, Michael Baigent, Richard Leigh and

Henry Lincoln, briefly outlined the mystery and then introduced one Pierre Plantard as the current Grand Master of a secret society called the Priory of Sion.

In 1956 Plantard registered the Priory of Sion (la Prieuré de Sion) as an official organization in France and it later emerged that at around this time documents were deposited in the French National Library in Paris under the title *Dossiers Secrets*. These *Dossiers Secrets* contained a collection of esoteric cuttings, genealogies and a list of Grand Masters of the Priory of Sion over the centuries. Then in 1967 two encoded parchments appeared in a publication called *The Accursed Treasure of Rennes-le-Château* by Gérard de Sède, who was also influenced by Plantard. This in turn inspired Henry Lincoln and the writing of *The Holy Blood and the Holy Grail*. Sion were beginning to go public.

In *The Holy Blood and the Holy Grail* Plantard claimed that the key to the mystery of Rennes-le-Château was that Jesus and Mary Magdalene were married and had children. At the time this was a shocking revelation and I commend the authors on their bravery for bringing this idea into the public domain.

However, I had read many antiquarian books on secret societies, and I had never encountered the name Priory of Sion. I did not trust Pierre Plantard and I suspected that the authors of *The Holy Blood and the Holy Grail* had been led away from the truth, so I began my own quest to unravel the mystery of Rennes-le-Château.

By 1994 I had joined Watkins Bookshop in London. As one of the oldest and largest esoteric bookshops in Europe, Watkins attracts people from many religions and disciplines and during my time there I met Templars (English and European), Freemasons (English and European), Sufis, astrologers, occultists, members of the Order of Lazarus, the Golden Dawn, Gnostics, academics and archaeologists, and many authors on the subjects surrounding these mysteries.

During this time I was visiting Rennes-le-Château at every opportunity and was reasonably well equipped to interpret the symbols for myself. The aim of my quest was simple. I sought to find the truth.

In early 2003 documentary-maker Bruce Burgess contacted me with a view to working on a film about the bloodline of Jesus and Mary Magdalene. I had known Bruce and shared ideas with him over a number of years. He was aware of my interest in Rennes-le-Château and the Priory of Sion and because he sought to unravel the mystery with an open mind I agreed to join the production as lead researcher.

Unknown to Bruce, I had encountered the Priory of Sion at Watkins Books in the 1990s and had access to one of its members. As the documentary (titled *Bloodline – the Movie*) progressed it was clear that Bruce and his co-producer, René Barnett, intended to undertake an investigation of the mystery without bias or agenda and so I chose to contact Sion to see if they were willing to become involved in the project.

At the time Dan Brown's *The Da Vinci Code* had attained such a high profile by mentioning the bloodline and the Priory of Sion that it had started a flood of other books and documentaries exploring these ideas. None of these included any new information from Sion itself and many failed even to acknowledge its existence.

By involving the Priory of Sion in the documentary I had hoped to give it a platform to set the record straight. What I was unprepared for was the sheer mass of information they were willing to impart. So far I have received over 300 emails, artworks, designs, documents and a wealth of other information that has previously never seen the light of day. Together with producer Bruce Burgess I met a representative of the Priory of Sion on several occasions and recorded a three-hour interview, some of which appears in the film.

In May 2008 *Bloodline – the Movie* was premiered at the East Village cinema in New York and received a standing ovation from a packed audience. Due to the scope and depth of the information that I had been receiving it had become clear very early on in the project that it was far more than could possibly be included in a documentary. With this in mind I began to organize the material, along with my own eighteen years' worth of research, into the book you are now reading.

In this book I have focussed on the information received from the Priory of Sion itself and attempted to create a coherent picture of who they are, what they claim to be, and more importantly what they claim to possess. A number of chapters were passed to their representative in this matter, Nic Haywood, for his comments. At no time did he ask that I remove or alter any of the content; on the contrary he accepted the text as written and where possible generously clarified or embellished the information that I presented.

After looking at the Priory of Sion as an entity, the book goes on to examine the information that they have provided, which illuminates a vast and diverse range of esoteric areas, from the strange story of Rennes-le-Château to the great and profound mysteries of Christianity, alchemy and the apocalypse. These revelations take the reader into 'the underground stream', a symbolic name for the current of esoteric and heretical information protected and passed down through history by secret societies, noble families – and even the clergy. The underground stream speaks of a secret history, often bound up in symbolism, encoded in art, encrypted in documents or expressed through rituals. But occasionally it surfaces and we catch a glimpse of the arcane mysteries that lie beneath. There are signs and symbols in plain view that stare out of stained glass windows and church statues.

Like Dante's Virgil, the Priory of Sion is our guide through this journey. The members of this secret society claim to have protected and promulgated the secrets of the underground stream throughout history. We must study them closely for they are not only the keepers of these esoteric traditions but they embody the ideals therein. Over time it had become clear that my initial distrust of Pierre Plantard and the Priory of Sion was unfounded.

There is much more to be done in terms of exploring all that has been revealed to me on this journey. Some areas I hope to revisit one day, the rest I leave up to you, the reader.

Fittingly, let us begin this journey with my translation of the abbreviation on that Christmas card. L.V.A.A.T. stands for *Lux Veritatis Alet Altare Templi* – 'May the Light of Truth Sustain the Temple Altar'.

It is time to shed some light on the truth.

Rob Howells, December 2010

PART 1

THE PRIORY
OF SION

CHAPTER 1

THE PRIORY
OF SION

*Behold, I lay in Zion for a foundation a stone, a tried stone,
a precious corner stone, a sure foundation.*

Isaiah 28.16 (KJV)

CONTACT

While working on the documentary *Bloodline – the Movie* I made contact
with the Priory of Sion via an old associate, Nic Haywood. I had
first encountered Nic many years previously when I was working at Watkins
Bookshop in London. At the time I was steeped in secret societies and the
mystery of Rennes-le-Château. It was revealed to me that Nic was a member of
the Priory of Sion via a third party whom he had confided in. I was of course
interested to know more but my only contact with Nic was via telephone in a
purely professional capacity, so at the time it was inappropriate to raise the issue
of his alleged membership.

It was many years later, after I had left the bookshop, that Bruce Burgess
approached me to work on a documentary about the bloodline of Jesus and
how it was linked to Rennes-le-Château. Having amassed around fifteen years of
research and a good-sized library on the subject, I decided to donate my research
to Bruce's project. My intention was to finish the quest I had begun in youth.

Once I had established how serious Bruce and co-producer René Barnett were,
and that their openness and independence would allow the film to have a depth and
direction that other documentaries had failed to achieve, I decided to contact Nic.

Knowing that my understanding of the Rennes-le-Château mystery matched
some of Nic's interests, I wrote him a detailed letter of my intentions and the

nature of the project. He replied in kind and we exchanged emails, establishing a way of collaborating that would continue throughout the project and beyond to this book.

Nic agreed to help where possible but initially he chose to remain anonymous and I acted as mediator between Nic on the one hand and Bruce and René on the other. A number of emails were exchanged and Nic agreed to help with the project and to be interviewed. An initial meeting was held in a hotel and this cemented his involvement.

The Priory of Sion features in Dan Brown's bestseller *The Da Vinci Code* and a number of other documentaries on the subject of the bloodline. These were generally shallow, ill-informed and biased against or dismissive of the Priory of Sion. They brought nothing new to the debate. Nic's cooperation with our project was an opportunity for Sion to set the record straight. As Nic himself put it:

> 'In my 35 years of service I have yet to find a more amiable team
> of "observers". My senses tell me that, having taken the first step,
> this is going to result in a piece that will be memorable. To quote
> your own words: "groundbreaking." And it will be for *all* the right
> reasons!'

(Note: Unless otherwise stated all further quotes from the Priory of Sion were provided via Nic Haywood either by email or interview. Some minor editorial and typographical changes have been made but otherwise I cite Nic's words as I received them.)

Nic acted as an emissary for the Priory of Sion. He said he had been 'aligned' to them for over 20 years. Sion's members are not permitted to reveal themselves publicly as members so during the interview Nic was guarded about his actual membership. This ruling is still in place today.

Much of what has passed between us has been via email, and at time of writing I have received over 200 emails from Nic. In detail and quantity, the information they have provided was far in excess of what could be used in the *Bloodline* film, and in some cases even beyond the scope of this book. Nic's emails were often dense, complex and obtuse and no doubt we stampeded over many a nuance in our initial eagerness to find 'proof'.

The producers and I also met Nic in person on three occasions, one of which we filmed for the documentary. I have met him a number of times subsequently and have maintained communication throughout the writing of this book.

Before looking at the Priory of Sion in more detail, here is an excerpt from the Priory of Sion interview in *Bloodline – The Movie* between Nic, Bruce Burgess and myself:

Bruce 'Why are you speaking to us?'

Nic 'We delight in the right people coming along.'

Bruce 'What is the Priory of Sion about?'

Nic 'To protect and promulgate ancient truths, ancient mysteries. And to protect more than one nameable secret.'

Bruce 'What is the goal of Sion?'

Nic 'Sion's goal is of world unity, evolution of man to the next rightful stage.'

Bruce 'Why a secret society?'

Nic 'We remain in shadows for a better view of the light. Sion surfaces in a manner that allows it to be seen, leaves imprints, at times in history. It is a pre-Christian ideal, concept, many shapes and forms adapt to the changing world, it aids the changing.'

It is ultimately for the reader to take or leave the material that we received from Nic as it is presented in this book. As we are dealing with a representative of the Priory of Sion not everything he says can be taken at face value. Very little can be verified or, in some cases, trusted. Although I believe Nic to be a member of the order of Sion he, like anyone else, was capable of forming his own opinions and slant on the subjects under discussion. I raised this issue of trustworthiness from the outset and expressed it to Nic via email. His response:

'My views *or* Sion's views? They are not always one and the same and the same may be said of all within the P.S. Individually, we may hold personal views that are at variance with "the official". This is a commonplace source of great exacerbation and much tension, but it's the same with *all* peoples who "stand together", is it not? Viewpoints are not always unanimously shared.'

From the outset Nic made clear when his own views were presented and when we were receiving the 'official line' from Sion; any blurring of the two that occurs here is purely the fault of the author.

There was also the risk of Sion using us to fulfil an agenda that remained hidden from us – some act of propaganda in which we were unwitting pawns.

> 'You have been led from the day you set foot on this task to a
> more tangible aspect of that same truth (as the book *Holy Blood,*
> *Holy Grail*). The aim of the current release, this is the next piece,
> unique to us at this time, a proportional release.'

The Holy Blood and the Holy Grail (published in the US as *Holy Blood, Holy Grail*) was the first book in English to break the story of the Priory of Sion and we will return to this later. But for now it may be asked why I put so much faith in Nic as a representative of Sion.

At our initial meeting, Nic reminded me of the classic Rosicrucian figure, wise and deeply knowledgeable in arcane matters. The Rosicrucians, or Brothers of the Rosy Cross, were originally adepts of the Western esoteric tradition, mystics from a bygone age. It later emerged that the Rosicrucians formed the spiritual arm of the Priory of Sion so it came as no surprise to learn that Nic was aligned to this part of the order. (Readers must take this on trust: in order to respect the oath Nic has taken I do not wish to allude to how I know this.)

Further indications that Nic might have Rosicrucian links were his strong and profound interest in fire, which was a central concern of the Rosicrucians, many of whom were alchemists. For example, the Bacstrom Rosicrucian Document in Glasgow University Library states that when challenged to prove their membership, Rosicrucians should explain their understanding of 'fire':

> 'Should I travel either by sea or by land and meet with any person
> that may call himself a Brother of the Rosy Cross, I will try him
> whether he can give me a proper explanation of the universal fire
> of Nature.'

I have a copy of Nic's personal essay on the universal nature of fire and it is the most profound I have ever read on the subject.

Other Rosicrucian aspects of Nic include the adopting of alternative names, the lack of interest in wealth or publicity, the attempt to teach, and certainly his alchemical interests. Nic had supplied us with photographs of his alchemical laboratory and he remains an ardent collector of and expert in rare alchemical manuscripts. While the evidence remains circumstantial, all these features strongly suggest that Nic is a present-day Rosicrucian. But it is his knowledge, above all else, that was, and is, my reason for trusting him:

'I was already familiar with the affairs at Rennes-le-Château and I was a known traveller in and teacher of the occult realm.'

'Naturally, my concerns are a little more philanthropic [than Sion's], but it was clear that we shared a common goal, as it were.'

Nic has admitted to being a high-ranking Freemason and an alchemist and I can verify him to be both of these. He is also polite, approachable and easily one of the most knowledgeable people I have met in this area (and as the former manager of Watkins esoteric bookshop I have met hundreds). He would certainly pass as an 'adept' if such people were still recognized in the West.

Nic gave us a vast amount of time and information, yet never once asked for money or credit. As far as publicity was concerned, it was I and the documentary producers who did all the requesting, so that it would not appear to be something that Nic actively sought. My conclusion is that Nic's motive was genuinely to teach.

Of course, the rule of secrecy among members that I mentioned above means that even Nic's membership of a 'Priory of Sion' cannot be proven, but ultimately, given his knowledge, I think we can take this on trust. The emails he sent me were not always the work of a single person; clearly other members had a hand in these, and influenced what came to me. I expect that the usual accusations will be levelled at Nic, as happens to anyone at odds with the accepted doctrines of history and religion. But the scope of his knowledge is rare and deeply insightful in these areas. And besides, the message is more important than the messenger.

So what of the message?

WHAT IS THE PRIORY OF SION?

After making contact with Nic Haywood and having established a certain amount of trust, a free flow of information began. The initial questions we had revolved around the nature and intentions of the Priory of Sion.

Simply put, the Priory of Sion is a both an organization and an ideal. It claims to manifest as a real order operating in the world at certain times either to release information or to act as a focus to those who follow and protect its ideals.

The esoteric branch of the Priory of Sion appears to be the current name for a group of adepts of the Western esoteric tradition. Throughout history those who have achieved enlightenment or higher spiritual knowledge (gnosis) are bound by a sense of service to teach and enlighten others. They include artists, alchemists and the old aristocratic families. As Nic said:

> 'Please bear in mind that the Prieuré de [Priory of] Sion is
> a collective of alchemists. That is to say, the core [members]
> are adepts of the Hermetic science and *all* have perfected the
> [Philosopher's] Stone at some time or another, (several more
> than once). It would be naive to assert that such a cohort would
> actively court publicity unless it was for the common good!'

It was reiterated on a number of occasions that Sion has a strong esoteric element informed by alchemists among its members.

According to the authors of *The Holy Blood and the Holy Grail*, the name Priory of Sion stemmed from the order's inception in the Holy Land at the time of the Crusades. Jerusalem was founded on a hill named Mount Zion or Sion, which is home to many of its holiest sites. Zion/Sion came to be used as a synonym for the city itself and indeed the entire Holy Land. Later investigators claimed that the name was derived from a hill called Sion near where Pierre Plantard lived as a child. Plantard claimed to be the Grand Master of Sion during the 1970s and provided the information for *The Holy Blood and the Holy Grail* in much the same way as Nic spoke to us.

I think the truth lies somewhere in time and space between the two, but it serves a dual purpose all the same as an ideal and a physical location.

> 'M. Plantard de St Clair, and others, have alluded to the meaning
> of Sion: "The intersection of a branch.... The point of origin."'

The aims of Sion are becoming clearer. According to Nic Haywood,

> 'Constant manipulation of the collective via the arts, makes for
> an orchestrated evolution; culturally, spiritually and, by definition
> politically. That is the underlying reason why, when asked about
> any agenda, the Prieuré will always affirm that "things are going
> according to plan".'

Simply put, Sion manipulates society to achieve steps in evolution. How this is organized is less clear. Here is Nic's initial response via interview:

'The current situation is that religion and spirituality are affected by the Priory of Sion through subtle influence. They take a steering role, using slow filtration through art, media and the written word.'

'The Priory of Sion gave the role to themselves as far back as the nine knights from Calabria. The people in Calabria were part-way down the line with information from the Middle East and Africa, knowledge that had been kept safe.'

The 'nine knights from Calabria' is a reference to the founders of the order of Knights Templar during the Crusades. The links between this order and the Priory of Sion are explored in the next chapter. A later email provided a more esoteric angle on the subject:

'Such political application of spiritually engendered philosophy operates according to the axiom of the Golden Section, the Golden Rule: the lesser is to the greater as the greater is to the whole. ... In fact several Priory documents circa 1977–8 were clear and unambiguous attempts to reconcile the fundamentals of the Golden Rule with a far more esoteric, sacred, geometry. One in particular lay emphasis upon the inherent mathematics of Poussin's Arcadian canvas and, with a degree of success, connected it with the ritual geometry employed by John Dee.'

This was made apparent in a document sent to us by Sion that included the work of Patricia Villiers-Stuart, a student of sacred geometry who had authored a pamphlet called *The Secret of the Templars*. This document contained an interpretation of the geometry at play in Nicolas Poussin's *Et in Arcadia Ego* (also called *The Shepherds of Arcadia*, 1637–8), which matches the designs of the celebrated Elizabethan astrologer, alchemist and sage Dr John Dee (1527–1608). (For more information on this topic see Appendix 1.)

'It's just as well that some individuals comprehend these arcane secrets, this hidden science, and the majority do not. It has always been this way, but we are already in an embryonic stage where such matters are becoming increasingly a matter-of-fact reality.'

'Why else do you suppose that everyone remotely connected with Sion has been prepared to endure public mockery, to risk ridicule, exposure and more? All in the pursuit of planting the

> seed; the seed of a hardy vine that regrafts and resurfaces time
> and again. It blossoms only when mankind is in a state of spiritual
> and conscious despair. Despair and need are eternal bedfellows,
> are they not? Mankind's despair is the rich, black, saturated and
> corrupted soil in which the vine of spirituality and hope can take
> root. "Need" is the element essential to this hybrid's survival, its
> guarantee of renewal.'

This response contains a strong alchemical allusion. The word alchemy derives from the Arabic *al-Kimia,* which comes from the original name of ancient Egypt, taken from the country's rich black soil. However, there is another allusion here to the bloodline of Jesus, depicted as the 'vine' growing from the black soil. In the gospel of John, Jesus famously describes himself as the 'True Vine' (John 15.1). I quickly realized that we must learn to read Nic's communications on more than one level, as there is often a hidden meaning to be derived from his answers.

Nic's statement also contains a social observation, in that historic events of great destructive magnitude – such as world wars – engender a spiritual vacuum in which cults and new religious movements emerge in response to a loss of faith in established religions. This is seen by Sion as an opportunity to infiltrate and influence culture in order to bring about a positive change in society. It begins with the adepts of the order targeting specific influential individuals. Historically, many adepts became part of royal households that provided patronage in return for the use of the adepts' knowledge. The Rosicrucians, for example, were well known for practising an advanced form of healing and for having cured Queen Elizabeth of smallpox and the Earl of Norfolk of leprosy.

> 'The other cause that Sion was disseminating was that of alchemy,
> a process of transformation that would potentially effect all levels
> of being. The whole technique of altering and elevating culture
> by such arcane filtration – alchemically – the tenet stretches
> far back into ancient Egypt. One can easily discern its traces in
> Christ's parables, miracles and in the manner of the ministry of his
> disciples.'

The overall message is that Sion has a secret knowledge that has remained constant throughout history and has been passed down through the ages to guide and direct humanity. It is no single secret but a body of esoteric knowledge:

'It might be a sound starting point were I to confirm something which I conclude you already suspect. That the *Antiquus Ordo Mysticusque Prioratus Sionis* [Ancient and Mystic Order of the Priory of Sion] is more about an Ideal than any one specific secret.'

To be 'more about an Ideal' may seem to imply that Sion is a loose and unstructured organization that coalesces when necessary into three distinct branches; the spiritual, physical and alchemical. Contrary to what others have assumed, the order has no degrees like Freemasonry. According to Nic Haywood, there exists a small hierarchy of 22 core members headed by a 'helmsman'. Beneath these are three strands and then many satellite groups.

Historically, as mentioned previously, the spiritual arm has been represented by Rosicrucian groups. I am also aware that Sion has used the term 'university' to describe their order, which is reminiscent of the 'Rosicrucian College' which the esoteric author A E Waite (1857–1942) claimed to have existed at the time of the pharaohs of ancient Egypt.

According to Nic Haywood, Sion also makes use of individuals

'who, by dint of social status, credibility, are well-placed to serve the promulgation of its message. Likewise, those who are alchemical adepts are favoured in its ranks... as to alchemical discussions. This is at the core of the Priory and is, therefore, difficult to circumvent entirely.'

I will cover Sion's links to alchemy at length in Chapter 17, but for now I can confirm that I have known for some time that Sion had alchemists among its members. The text entitled *Le Serpent Rouge*, discussed in Chapter 10, attests to the order's alchemical slant.

'Yes. [Regarding] the alchemical nature of the Prieuré de Sion. We are here, naturally, widening/amplifying the *Materia Prima* to concern ourselves with a much larger "stone" indeed.'

'Such work is of little use unless the individual can ultimately set his sights on assisting in the worldly journey of his fellow man; facilitating changes and shifts in the collective consciousness. It is to this underground stream that such energies are directed. A vision better achieved in unison, en masse, as a collective Chariot.'

The *Materia Prima* is the base matter for alchemical transformation, either lead or, on a more profound spiritual level, the adept's soul. The 'stone' is the 'Philosopher's Stone', the supreme goal of the alchemical process toward perfection. The 'Chariot' is a reference to the Tarot card of that name. It often shows a charioteer driving two horses, one black and one white. This has been interpreted as a man unifying the opposing forces of duality and harnessing them in order to progress toward success. To do this on a grand scale requires that like-minded people band together to influence society. They have done so throughout history under a number of different names, but always with the same ideal. This formed what is termed the 'underground stream', as I mentioned in the Introduction.

The symbol of the underground stream is explored at length in later chapters. It appears, for example, in many aspects of the Rennes-le-Château mystery and is linked to the theme of Arcadia, a perfected state. Depictions of Arcadia, such as those of Poussin and others, often include a tomb or place where water surfaces from an underground source.

To bring the underground stream to the surface is to reveal something of it to the general public. Central to how Sion operates is the notion of releasing information slowly so as not to have adverse effects on society:

> 'We are concerned with a shifting of world vision, people's attitudes. What if alternative history, a release that would be shocking whole, is let out piecemeal?'

There are ideas — such as the existence of the bloodline of Jesus and Mary Magdalene — that are not new but could only be seeped into culture when society was ready to accept them. A number of the European royal families have claimed that their ancestry went back to Jesus and beyond for hundreds of years, but it was not until the publication of *The Holy Blood and the Holy Grail* in 1982 that the idea found a wider audience. Had the book been published just twenty years earlier I think a lot of bookshops would have been burned in the same way that Beatles albums were burned when John Lennon compared the group's popularity to that of God. In the West we are suddenly tolerant of what was once considered heresy — although, hypocritically, we now frown upon those who are not.

The issue remains that while there is evidence for many of the historic claims of the goals of Sion, there is little proof of the order itself existing prior to the 20th century. The idea that an organization such as the Priory of Sion can work in the shadows of history without coming to the attention of the public may seem unlikely, and there is a general consensus that it would have been widely known about long before it first chose to go public in 1956. But Sion exists within the milieu of secret societies and it is important for us to look toward these for further insight into how the Priory remains in the shadows. Secondly, there is such a crossover of ties, rituals and membership among secret societies that it is possible to learn a great deal about Sion from the orders that it informs or emulates.

With this in mind we will now look at the history of the Priory of Sion and the secret societies that surround it.

CHAPTER 2

A HIDDEN HISTORY

SECRET SOCIETIES

The existence of the Priory of Sion first became public knowledge in the 1950s with the discovery of its journal *Vaincre* in a Freemasonic context, namely the Grand Lodge Alpina in Switzerland, one of the main global Masonic organizations. This fact alone shows that the Priory of Sion does not exist in a vacuum: secret societies have existed and cross-fertilized on every continent throughout much of history. From the followers of Pythagoras in Greece circa 500 BCE, through the medieval Assassins in the Middle East, the Thuggees in 17th-century India, the Carbonari in 19th-century Italy, and the ongoing forms of Rosicrucianism and Freemasonry, secret societies have always thrived in one form or another. Some fail in their purpose and disappear, others fragment into new societies or reinvent themselves, and a few have continued from antiquity to the present day.

Today there exist thousands of esoteric societies, secret and otherwise, scattered across the world. Some, like Freemasonry, are well known but most go unheard of and as such are truly secret. Of course, anyone can create a secret society; all it takes is a few friends and the pretence of possessing or doing something secret. For these groups the 'secrets' have no real value and must be kept secret or members would cease to pay fees and their self-important hierarchies would collapse.

The secret societies that endure the longest tend to have unique information, a core teaching, or a belief system into which they can enrol initiates and which they can pass down through generations. These are often created to protect information or beliefs that would not be tolerated in their contemporary religious or political climate. They are preserved in ritual and teachings, often in symbolic form, and passed down through family members or initiates.

Sion is in a good position to work in this manner as it claims many aristocratic families among its members.

A second form of transmission occurs when the ideals and beliefs of an old society, and sometimes something of the source material, are rediscovered and resurrected to recreate a new society. Researching these resurrected groups can be difficult as many have names adopted from earlier groups, such as the numerous Rosicrucian or pseudo-Templar orders at large today. Of those that claim direct descent from their predecessors, some are actual recipients of the original materials, knowledge or spirit of the society's previous incarnation. Others simply wish to emulate past glories or use an ancient precursor to bolster their credibility.

The notion of secret societies naturally engenders a feeling of mistrust in all of us. There may seem to be something unhealthy about keeping secrets, but it is a trait all humans have. By withholding information, such societies maintain a certain power and mystique which can be used as a means of control in the same way that the Roman Catholic Church for so long resisted the publishing and dissemination of the Bible in any language other than Latin.

There is also the risk that such groups can act as cover for anything from international espionage to political revolution or serious crime. The problem is that new members often cannot know what they are getting into until they have progressed through the ranks. Even in Freemasonry, many members in the lower degrees never truly grasp what they have joined. As one anonymous Third-Degree Freemason put it to me: 'I don't really know what it's all about, something to do with Ancient Egypt, I think.'

Freemasons in Britain can be considered as falling into two groups: those who see it as part of the Western esoteric tradition and those who treat it as a men's lunch club. Sadly the recruitment of the latter, probably to fill the coffers, has far outweighed that of the former in recent years. Many members are content to treat the rituals as a meaningless tradition, and in their ignorance they play hopscotch on the Kabbalistic tree of life. However, there remains a body of members who research arcane matters and treat Freemasonry's rituals, those strange mystery plays, with due respect.

RITUAL AND INITIATION

We all develop and evolve throughout our lives. Our experiences change our perceptions and how we relate to the world, they change how we think and behave. But life is a slow teacher and at various points civilizations have sought to develop tools to accelerate the process. These can be encoded in the form of rituals. The initiations and rituals of all secret societies are an important means of both transmitting information and imprinting ideals on an individual.

An initiation can be used to teach or impress upon the candidate something at every level of being. Through mental contemplation, physical enactment and emotional impact a true initiation exerts upon the candidate an experiential level of teaching. It is a direct form of receiving wisdom that carries a strong psychological impact.

Rituals are central to many secret societies. Handled correctly, they can be very powerful tools for human growth. Such tools might be considered of immense value to the general public were they to be made known, but there are a number of factors that argue against this.

The first is that rituals work better if the candidate is unaware of what they are about to experience. By surrendering the known we are open to receive and learn. This can be challenging, as all personal change takes place at an emotional level. All learning is loss (of old perceptions, emotions and mindsets), so advanced warning would allow the mind to prepare mental and emotional barriers to accepting challenging insights.

The second is that in the wrong hands the power of rituals can be perverted to serve a less altruistic cause. There was once a member of the Order of the Golden Dawn who took Aleister Crowley's dictum, 'Do what thou wilt' – meaning act in accordance with your own true will – and created a group to do *his* will and not their own. It worked for him until the power sent him insane, but for his followers this was, and continues to be, a spiritual dead end.

A third issue is that the rituals may contain teachings that are counter to the existing power structures in society. Historically the penalty for upholding or transmitting heretical doctrines (in either the political or religious sense) has been imprisonment or death.

For these reasons the tools of secret societies are often shrouded in the symbolic experience of ritual and, in theory, are only transmitted when the candidate has proven to be ready to receive the experience they impart.

That is not to say that *some* of the wisdom or teachings of rituals cannot be disseminated. How they are made public is the key to managing the impact they will have, if that is an issue. Should the threat of censorship be an issue there are a number of ways of releasing information via other means, such as symbolically through art and literature. Later we will discover that the Priory of Sion has done just that.

Many rituals in Western magic and occultism have the same roots, often being variations on earlier workings. These can be found in many different secret societies and show a level of cross-fertilization of ideas and beliefs that has come about through either shared membership or direct influence. For example, some of the symbols that appear in the Priory of Sion documents can be found in Freemasonry, Rosicrucianism, Templarism and even Catholicism. The question is: who is influencing whom?

INSIGNIA

When I first met with Nic Haywood I saw that he had a ring and a small badge that looked Masonic in origin. I mentioned this to him later. His response:

> 'I was in fact wearing a small and somewhat understated Prieuré
> device during our interview of yesterday. A small double triangle –
> a diamond-shaped device surrounding a balance or pair of scales
> the counterpoise of which is an upright flaming sword pushing
> upward through a pentagon of five small pentagrams. The whole
> gives the immediate impression of a fleur-de-lys either side of
> which are the letters: 'P' and 'Z' (the alternative spelling of Sion –
> Zion). There are quite a few pieces of insignia, all of which bear
> designs and devices which are all-too-familiar in respect of the
> affairs at Rennes-le-Château.'

Nic also supplied me with a photograph of a Sion 'Jewel': a two-headed leaden phoenix carrying a solid gold sword and surmounted with a gold crown. The design includes the double-headed eagle, which appears in Freemasonry and Rosicrucian circles. It can also be found in alchemy, one of the foundations of esoteric thought and secret societies in the West.

In Freemasonry regalia are often used for ritual purposes but Sion itself avoids many of these trappings. The differences between Freemasonry and Sion were explained to me in conversation:

'Sion does not have robes and rings, established along Masonic
lines. It doesn't have the attendant regalia, no Masonic boards,
there are some regalia, [but members would wear them when]
they would gather to make decisions and to vote, not to perform
rituals. Now it is a modern organisation, votes etc are now done
by email.'

We can see from both the rituals and regalia in circulation that there is a lot
of hard evidence for the transmission of ideas between secret societies. This
becomes more apparent as we attempt to establish whether the Priory of Sion
existed prior to the 20th century.

THE CONTEXT FOR THE PRIORY OF SION

On the matter of historic proof the Priory has prevented any members from
revealing evidence for a sustained existence from the time of their origins
to present. This is not to say that one should blindly either accept or reject
the Priory as an ancient, mystical order; it just means that the jury is still
out until more information is revealed. I present below three of the Priory's
statements regarding its history and influence from which you can draw your
own conclusions:

'The Prieuré de Sion has a long, and murky, past. Given that it was
constituted from an Ideal, it is only fitting that one understand
that a small group of monks, whose anonymity was assured
amidst the vast ranks of the Knights of the Temple, continued
to operate as they did. Naturally, it was their intention to remain
oblique and many would be forgiven for assuming them to be
what are these days referred to as the Illuminati. A select group
of learned incarnates whose concern is the advancement of
mankind. A Hermetic conclave whose task has been, is and always
will be the transmutation of the Ideal into the Real; the spiritual
into the corporeal. To enrich the very existence of man; set his
aspirations and advance the knowledge of *his* world and *his* part
in it. To that end one might conclude it a thankless task, but the
results are reward enough.'

The idea of the Priory as a 'small group of monks' from the time of Templars seems at odds with an earlier statement on Sion's pre-Christian origins going back as far as ancient Egypt. I think the confusion stems from the ideals of the order being in existence long before the formally named organization was put into place. It is a situation reminiscent of Freemasonry also recognizing its roots in the rituals of ancient Egypt. The mention of the Illuminati is more a reference to the existence of enlightened adepts (which is the meaning of *illuminati*) than the actual secret society of that name founded by Adam Weishaupt in the 18th century.

'You will recall that the first apparent socio-spiritual and cultural shift – which resulted in the construction of the magnificent Gothic cathedrals with its attendant knowledge of the sciences: optics, pigments, metallurgy and mathesis – came about (Classical heritage apart) through direct contact with the Arabic world engendered during the initial Crusades. However, those openly responsible for facilitating the synthesis of East-West culture played erroneously into the power-hungry hands of the ever-greedy Catholic Church and were ultimately betrayed. The small core group were, naturally, unscathed. What use would they, could they be to mankind were they so readily identifiable?'

'Other cultural & spiritual shifts such as the Renaissance, the Age of Enlightenment, etc. have equally been orchestrated and rely upon the free flow of socio-spiritual ideals and ideas and the freedom of expression, no more so than from East to West and vice-versa. In that respect the West – Europe in particular – is unique because it has acted as the crucible.'

The Templars will be covered below but the point of importance here is the sharing of ideas between Eastern and Western esoteric philosophies.

The esoteric aspects of Sion have a verifiable line of succession, under various names and mantles, predating the Crusades. It would seem that these aspects remain dormant until resurrected at certain times in history as events unfolded.

LINKS TO OTHER SECRET SOCIETIES

The crossover between secret societies is evidenced throughout history, with many individuals joining more than one secret society. By the beginning of the 20th century cross-membership was known to exist among the Freemasons, the Rosicrucians, neo-Templar orders, occult orders such as the Ordo Templi Orientis and the Golden Dawn, and even orthodox religious groups and the priesthood. The occultist Aleister Crowley (1875–1947) once claimed to have been initiated into so many groups that if he wore all his regalia at once he would fall over.

Even today a number of the Priory of Sion's members are also members of other secret societies. They have so much in common with the Freemasons in terms of symbolism and membership that I raised the issue with Nic Haywood, who gave me this response:

> 'You will have gathered, by now, that Sion is not a Masonic institu-
> tion, but that it operates after a similar fashion. It is not necessary
> to be a Mason to join the Priory of Sion.'

This implies that at least some members of Sion are Freemasons. I am also aware of other groups that share members with Sion, although the groups may not be aware of this fact because members are sometimes under oath, like those of Sion, to keep it a secret. Sion has made it clear that partnering or collusion is a matter of record:

> 'The *Priory* makes accords and alliances with other groups and
> societies *only when events, (or their lack), make it expedient to do so.*
> Such amalgams are, with a few exceptions, *temporary; transitory
> unions which serve a common aim.*'

A more direct form of influence takes place when a secret society creates or works through other groups or orders. This is how Sion accounts for its lack of appearance in the historic records of secret societies. Sion has been known by a number of different names and worked through other organizations to meet its aims at various points in history:

> 'Perhaps it is for this reason that a United Europe has often been
> associated with the Prieuré de Sion … the group once known by
> such names as Hieron Val d'Or, Compagnie du Saint Sacrament,
> Rose-Croix, Prieuré de Sion, etc. formally lodged its existence
> in 1956 in France. It was in a "safe" post-war Europe and by this
> time [the group's] tentacles extended into every field of human
> existence. A "United States of Europe" was most definitely on the
> agenda of the day!'

Here we arrive at the proliferation of secret societies whose names the Priory of Sion has used as a cover. Nic Haywood mentioned others over time: Ordre Orval du Chevalier; Zion (twice); and the Salon de la Rose-Croix. These offer great vistas of potential research in their own right and I have made some comments on this later in the chapter (*see* page 31).

> '[The Priory of Sion] is / has been linked with other societies and organizations for purposes already defined and, upon occasions, it has acted as a mechanism for "breaking" such institutions that would impede this common goal.'
>
> 'For reasons, already outlined, the Prieuré de Sion has [held] / holds some organizations and institutions to account by virtue of original documents and materials held for such purposes... In this respect, the Prieuré de Sion is considered, by some, to be the *cause célèbre par excellence*. It gets its power, not only from the wealthy families and individuals who by tradition or dint of agreement act as generous patrons, but also from the essential pressure that it tries to maintain on those groups who obtain their momentum from a divided world picture.'
>
> 'As such, Sion's spiritual roots are at the heart of Man!'

Partnering or creating other secret societies would have provided cover and a means of dissemination for Sion without putting its core members at risk. It would also have served to keep Sion in the shadows throughout history.

In a clear statement, Sion confirmed that the message it sought to communicate was passed down through the ages using a variety of names as a cover until the late 20th century:

> 'It is true that it carried, and was carried, throughout times past under a variety of names and only during the *fin de siècle* [the later 19th century] did it rest back with a name very similar to that which it obtained at its birth.'

The revelation that Sion did indeed use different names explains the difficulty in finding proof for its existence in antiquity. The idea that it originated with the name the Priory of Sion is also important, because the search for this early group becomes a key to the origins of Sion as a physical secret society.

'It all goes back to the nine knights of Calabria. The Rose-Croix [Rosicrucians], Priory of Sion, the Freemasons, [Jean-Jacques] Olier and the Saint-Sulpice groups – the influence of the Templars can be seen as the source or a major influence on many of these.'

We will return to Olier and Saint-Sulpice in a later chapter. The importance of this statement is that historically it places the 'nine knights of Calabria' – the first Knights Templar – as the starting point for our enquiries.

THE KNIGHTS TEMPLAR

Sion's links to the Knights Templar have often been stated. However, history has subjected the Templars to so much speculation and romanticism that it is difficult to view them objectively. Since their demise in 14th-century France they have become fodder for conspiracy theorists of all periods. This is caused in part by the influence of the Templars, which can be seen in many European secret societies: for example, all Masonic temples are constructed to represent the original Temple of Solomon, the physical and spiritual home of the Crusades. Aspects of the Templar legacy can also be found in Catholic architecture, for example in the design of the church of Saint-Sulpice in Paris and also the church at Rennes-le-Château, which we will explore in depth later.

The military order of the Poor Knights of Christ and the Temple of Solomon, to give the Templars their full title, was created to protect Christian pilgrims heading for the holy city of Jerusalem. They were founded c1118 by Hugues de Payens and eight other French knights, who embarked for the Holy Land from Calabria in southern Italy. The Templars took upon themselves vows of poverty and chastity and offered to protect pilgrims on the road to Jerusalem, which had been captured by Christian forces in the First Crusade (1096–9) and was now the capital of a Crusader state. The king of Jerusalem, Baldwin II, granted Hugues de Payens the former Al-Aqsa mosque on the Temple Mount as head-quarters for the knights. Converted by the Crusaders into a palace and a church, the mosque was believed to be the site of the ancient Temple of Solomon, hence the Templars' name.

Bernard of Clairvaux subsequently formulated a 'Rule of the Templars' based on the monastic rule of St Benedict and instructing them how to live and behave. The Templars adopted this in 1128 and were recognized by the

Pope as an official monastic order around the same time. However, it is unlikely that they adhered greatly to the Rule beyond the early days of the order. Its strictures included a ban on chess – curious considering that the chessboard design featured so heavily in the groups that followed the Templars – but they were permitted to play hopscotch. The sight of a knight playing hopscotch on the streets of Jerusalem seems greatly at odds with the image of the heroic warrior held in such high esteem today.

In the early days, some knights travelled across Europe in an attempt to secure more funds for the order, spreading tales of heroic deeds and adventures. The romance of the Templars took hold and suddenly many wealthy nobles were heading east, eager to join the Crusades. The Templars gathered donations of wealth, and more importantly land, across Europe.

Some of Europe's finest warriors and leaders joined, and during the Knights of the Temple amassed armies from European prisons and the like to join the Crusades.

The Templars were at the core of the Christian forces during the principal Crusades of the twelfth and thirteenth centuries. They scored some great victories and also some memorable disasters, such as the Siege of Ascalon in 1153, as recorded by William of Tyre. According to William, at the end of this siege the Muslim armies opened the city gates and the Templars, wanting the spoils for themselves, blockaded the entrance to prevent other armies following them as they charged into the city. The Muslim troops seized the opportunity and closed the gates behind the small Templar army and massacred them. Assuming William of Tyre's account is basically accurate (he was no fan of the Templars), such a disaster illustrates the greed and pride to which the Templars had succumbed.

Although the Templars began as humble Christian warrior monks, by the time of their demise they were an immensely wealthy order. In addition, it seemed that members dabbled in all manner of arcane practices. They were charged with heresy for allegedly spitting on the cross and worshipping a head they called 'Baphomet'. While it has to be considered that confessions were extracted under torture, they had certainly come a long way from the 'poor knights' that first arrived in Jerusalem.

Legends are rife about how the Templars excavated the Temple Mount and discovered all manner of relics from biblical times. A number of theories have arisen to explain what the Templars actually discovered. Even among their own accounts they claimed on more than one occasion to have discovered the True

Cross of the Crucifixion. The Copper Scroll from the Dead Sea Scrolls is an inventory of treasures and deposits hidden around the Holy Land in Roman times and attests to the act of burying and hiding deposits of valuable material to prevent it from being looted by invading armies. The Templars may have uncovered a record of this kind, or perhaps they found an actual repository of information. One theory is that they discovered documents that had survived since the time of Jesus and gave an alternative view of Christianity. In the light of finds such as the Gnostic texts of the Nag Hammadi Library, discovered in Egypt in the 1940s (*see* page 217), this is entirely possible.

However, a more likely method of discovering different perspectives on biblical times would come via the Templars' contact with the Assassins and with Islamic mystery schools. They had met with the Assassins on a number of occasions and through truce and battle it was likely that they gained a deep knowledge of some of their beliefs and rituals. Over the course of their occupation, the Templars seem to have grown less arrogant toward their Muslim enemies and eventually acquired a level of tolerance and even respect. By the 13th century the Templars had been in the Holy Land so long that many members, including some heads of the order, were born there. Most were entirely fluent in Arabic and could not help but absorb aspects of the rich culture around them.

Sion would have us believe that the actual exchange of knowledge was recorded at the highest level:

> 'Western chroniclers have always maintained that Richard [the Lionheart] and Saladin never met, but we would demonstrate otherwise. And that an agreement, an accord, was struck between them'.

> 'On the initial Crusade, when the knights had first entered the city of Jerusalem *en masse*, they had slaughtered the "infidel": man, woman and child. But … when the city fell back into Muslim hands [in 1187], Saladin gave the order that no Christians were to be harmed. In fact, a decidedly respectful "ritual cleansing" was undertaken wherein the streets, houses and places of worship were washed with an infusion of holy water and rose petals. Likewise, the thoroughfares were strewn with them.'

> 'Bearing in mind that the great Gothic cathedrals of medieval Europe had been constructed using sciences, skills and arts learned from the "infidel" [and] financed, in general, by the Order of the

Temple, we should conclude that this accord, this spiritual–cultural confluence, ran far, far deeper.'

Toward the end of the Crusades there was an opportunity to join the Eastern and Western churches and also to find common ground and a common place of worship for all the religions that understood the importance of Jerusalem. Unfortunately peace did not last and eventually the entire Holy Land was reclaimed by the Muslims. The Templars were forced to retreat back to Europe and abandoned their last eastern stronghold, the island of Arwad off Lebanon, in 1303.

By the end of the Crusades the Templar order had grown dramatically in size, knowledge, wealth and power. What the Templars and other groups had learned in the East had already influenced Western thought. The construction of soaring Gothic cathedrals with their beautiful stained glass windows owes much to Arabic thought and architecture. It is said that the blue used to colour the glass has never been bettered, the builders and glaziers using skills transmitted from Arabic artificers. Among the glories of these great cathedrals, which took decades to complete, are their great 'rose' windows. The rose is sacred in the East and alludes to the sacred feminine and its use especially in cathedral east windows is apt: as the direction of Jerusalem and the rising sun, the east symbolizes Christ's birth (from the Virgin Mary) and his resurrection.

The flow of information into Europe also included advances in science, maths, medicine, art, architecture and new religious thought. Not until the fall of Constantinople in 1453 would such a mass of important information, much of it from the ancient Classical world, be released into Western Europe.

Since their foundation the Templars had spread out across Europe but the largest concentration took residence in the Languedoc in the southwest of France. Here too, the Templars found themselves surrounded by heresy and original thought, for around this time the Gnostic dualist faith of the Bogomils had also taken hold in the region. The followers of this religion were called Cathars (Purified Ones), Perfecti or Albigensians (from their stronghold in Albi), and believed themselves to be in possession of the purest form of Christianity. Among Cathar tenets was the belief that Jesus and Mary Magdalene were married.

The stories of the Templars' heroic deeds became intermingled with the Cathar heresies, with the popular Arthurian Grail romances allowing such traditions to continue in the face of a growing suspicion and hostility from the mainstream Church.

Eventually the Cathars were destroyed in the Albigensian Crusade of 1209–29, the last pockets being crushed by 1244. Their destruction foreshadowed the fate of many other heretics in the Inquisition that would sweep Western Europe in the years that followed, as Rome began to enforce its doctrine in earnest. The Templars, who officially adhered to the mainstream Church, seem to have been surprisingly ambivalent about the Cathars' destruction and there are accounts of Templars fighting both alongside and against the Cathars.

SUPPRESSION

By 1307 the Templars must have been aware of what was coming. No longer focussed on the Levant, they were a powerful organization that owned vast swathes of land, especially in France, and had become the repository of much wealth. They acted as bankers and cashed promissory notes in lieu of gold, inadvertently inventing the cheque. King Philip IV had inherited an impoverished kingdom and owed the Templars a lot of money. In 1307 Philip issued a warrant for Templars in France to be arrested and interrogated about allegations of heresy, and attempted to get neighbouring countries to do the same. With the backing of a reluctantly compliant Pope Clement V, hundreds of knights were rounded up on Friday, October 13, of that year. Under terrible torture, many senior-ranking knights confessed to heresy.

Beyond the borders of France the Templars were less violently persecuted. In England, for example, the charge of heresy failed to stick. Nevertheless, in 1312 Philip IV compelled the Pope to dissolve the order. Across Europe there was an attempt to seize the wealth of the Templars, but on papal orders their lands were given over to another famous crusading order, the Knights Hospitaller (the Order of the Hospital of St John of Jerusalem). Some of this former Templar land was in the Languedoc, specifically near the town of Rennes-le-Château. The Hospitallers later became the Knights of Malta and still exist today, headquartered in the Vatican.

TEMPLAR 'HERESIES'

Philip IV's incarceration of the Templars was legendary for its brutality and the tortures that many knights endured must render all Templar 'confessions' as suspicious. There is one account of a Templar arriving at court in Paris holding a small bag containing the charred bones of his foot that had been forced into hot coals until the flesh was entirely lost to the fire.

However, certain threads running through the confessions may have some basis in fact. One charge against the Templars is connected to their mutual exchange of knowledge with the Assassins, as mentioned earlier. The Templars were accused of worshipping a mysterious head called Baphomet. This head was said to speak, imparting information as an oracle. Accounts of similar heads can be found in medieval grimoires (magical texts) such as the *Picatrix*, itself originally written in Arabic around the 11th century, and the Baphomet also resembles the 'Golden Head' of later alchemical texts (*see* page 259).

The mystery of the Baphomet deepened when I met, by chance, an Arabic scholar who had studied the rituals of the medieval Assassins. He revealed to me that in one of their higher degrees, the candidate would be led into a room where an apparently severed head resting on the floor would speak to the candidate, telling him important knowledge. This dramatic effect was achieved by burying the speaker up to his neck in the ground. (Unfortunately for him, the Assassin masters of the ceremony would then decapitate him so that they could later show the head to the candidate to prove that it was indeed severed.)

The Templars were found guilty in the French courts but relatively few faced trial and execution for heresy, notably the order's last Grand Master, Jacques de Molay, who died at the stake in 1314 cursing the king and the Pope – both of whom died later that same year. Some less senior knights were pardoned and joined the Hospitallers. But many others, along with much of their wealth and the entire Templar fleet, simply disappeared from France and into the mists of history. The order was formally dissolved by Clement V in 1312, but claims have been made for its uninterrupted existence and there are currently a number of Templar organizations worldwide that assert their direct descent from the original order.

In 2001 a Vatican archivist, Barbara Frale, came upon the so-called *Chinon Parchment* in the Vatican Secret Archive. Lost for 700 years, this document is a letter written in 1308 by Pope Clement V revealing that although he had colluded with the French king in the suppression of the Templars he was unwilling to condemn them, explicitly absolving the order as a whole of heresy.

I am always suspicious when any important historical document suddenly 'reappears' after a long absence. I contacted Barbara Frale for clarification as to how such a key papal document could have been 'lost' for so long. She replied that the parchment had been in the archive for 700 years but at some point had been under an 'erroneous classification. Nobody had studied it before'.

At the conclusion of the Chinon Parchment the Pope instructs the Templars that they will be allowed to continue but must change their name. It is not clear whether a group of Templars immediately assumed the name the Priory of Sion, which strikingly echoes the order's first monastic headquarters in the reputed 'Temple of Jerusalem'. But given the transmission of Templar knowledge down the centuries to the present day it is naive to think that the Templars completely disbanded. It seems that over the coming centuries they continued to exist under many different names and guises.

In the four-year gap between the letter and the dissolution of the order in 1312, many Templars would surely have been wise enough to heed the Pope's call for them to assume a new collective identity and 'vanish'. There is little firm evidence for this, but after the events of 1307 it would have been an obvious course of action for French Templars in particular.

For all their occult links and possible treasures, I consider the most important aspect of the Templars is that they were rumoured to have maintained a temple on the Temple Mount in Jerusalem that had three altars, one for Muslims, one for Christians and one for Jews. If this is true, people of all three faiths would have prayed in harmony alongside one another on the Temple Mount, which is sacred to Judaism, Christianity and Islam. In nearly a thousand years it has not been possible to replicate this in Jerusalem.

Any direct relationship between the Priory of Sion and the Templars remains unproven but the Priory's knowledge of the events that transpired at the time of the Templars gives credit to their claims.

Let us now consider Sion in relation to later groups, beginning with the Rosicrucians.

SION AND THE ORDER OF THE ROSY CROSS

An esoteric secret society of obscure origins, Rosicrucianism, or the Order of the Rosy (or Rose) Cross, is the most closely aligned to what we think of as the Priory of Sion. Sion itself claims that Rosicrucian orders (*Rose Croix* in French) are its spiritual arm and a key means by which it can influence society. They assert that Sion is the small group that oversees and controls a particular French Rosicrucian order called *Veritas* (Truth) and its subgroups or 'chapters'. They would also use it to recruit members of Sion.

The scope of Sion's reach was explained when I enquired why it was only officially registered as an organization by that name in the 1950s. Through

Nic Haywood, Sion had this to say on the matter:

> 'Just as Freemasonry is divided into various camps (lodges) and
> has a number of branches ('sides'), Sion is ... itself divided into
> lodges assigned specific social and moral roles and tasks, etc. ...
> The official registration of Sion occurred under new laws in a
> post-war France in a vulnerable and somewhat decimated Europe.
> However, as was stated in initial communications, the order
> reassumed the mantle by which it had undertaken transactions,
> both fiscal and temporal, during the 11th to 16th centuries, albeit
> a variation on the name, in keeping with a modernist Europe.'

> 'Prior to 1925, and in the 19th century, the order of Sion
> had not made itself public other than by the use of its spiritual/
> esoteric body: the Ordre Rose+Croix Veritas. This is the "trunk"
> of what is now known as Priory of Sion, and it is the same
> "society" which held the Salon de la Rose-Croix in Paris in the
> late 19th century [headed by] Joséphin Péladan.'

Further evidence for the link between the two orders can be seen in the use of
an old alchemical phrase. Documents I received from Sion were headed with a
fleur-de-lys with the initials L.V.A.A.T. underneath. This abbreviation, which
I mentioned in the Introduction, sometimes appears on Sion documents and
stands for the Latin *Lux Veritatis Alit* [or *Alet*] *Altare Templi* – 'May the Light of
Truth Sustain the Temple Altar'. L.V.A.A.T. is the old motto of a Templum
Rosae Crucis (Temple of the Rosy Cross) and is written around the inside of
a Rose-Cross badge of office.

Unfortunately the origins of the Rosicrucians are almost as difficult to
substantiate as those of the Priory of Sion itself. They can publicly be traced
to a few anonymous tracts that surfaced in the 17th and 18th centuries, and
some researchers, such as Masonic historian A E Waite, claimed that a form of
Rosicrucian Academy existed in ancient Egypt. Like Sion, their structure and
membership was a cause of much speculation, although now it is possible to
investigate these with a far greater understanding.

The Rosicrucian publications that appeared in the early 17th century were
the *Fama Fraternitatis Rosae Crucis* (*Report of the Fraternity of the Rosy Cross*, 1614)
and *Confessio Fraternitatis* (*The Confession of the Laudable Fraternity of the Most
Honorable Order of the Rosy Cross*, 1615), and describe the Rosicrucian movement
in allegorical form relating to the transmission of secrets that have their roots

in [Middle] Eastern esoteric movements. A third text, *The Chemical Wedding of Christian Rosenkreuz* (1616) is an alchemical allegory describing a succession of rites. As Nic Haywood put it:

> 'The very name "Rosicrucian" derives, in part, from ancient Sufi tradition and adept practices. It was after the fashion in which the Sufi, and hermetic tradition so named its illustrious and spiritually-esteemed adepts: *'The Rose'*, etc.'
>
> 'Its connection with the Crusades is crucial ... and far less known.'

Here again we see echoes of the Templars and their fusion of the spiritual, cultural and scientific elements of West and East.

Europe was enthralled by the appearance of the Rosicrucian documents. They were a call to arms for the free-thinkers of their era, but they contained no obvious means of contacting the order. As they circulated among the intelligentsia they were thought by many to be the work of a single individual but this would not account for the impression they left on society.

The anonymous appearance of these publications is reminiscent of the Priory of Sion's *Dossiers Secrets* and *Le Serpent Rouge* texts coming to light in the 1960s (*see* Chapter 10).

As mentioned earlier, my principal Sion contact, Nic Haywood, exhibits many of the traits one would expect of a Rosicrucian adept, such as a deep interest in the nature of fire (*see* page 293).

The authentic Rosicrucian lineage disappeared at the end of the 19th century with Joséphin Péladan's Salon de la Rose-Croix in Paris; and it was in Paris that the Priory of Sion emerged in the 20th century. Therefore it would seem not too big a leap to consider that the two might be related. This, perhaps, is why historians have such trouble tracing the Priory of Sion back through history: for most of the time they might simply be hidden from plain view.

Nic reminded me of something about the Rosicrucians that would fit well with any understanding of Sion through the ages:

> 'The order shall wear the robes and masque accordant to the day and to its survival, but shall be known to the initiates always by her true name...'

Fama [*Fraternitatis*] appeared in 1614 and it is in the 17th century that we see the first possible links between the Priory of Sion and the mystery of Rennes-le-

Château. The revised structure and concept of Sion was drawn up by Michel Le Gras, a resident of the locality and the son of Louise de Marillac, to whom we will return later (*see* page 51). Le Gras secured essential documents, deeds and other papers of great import to Sion likely to have been passed down through families related to the Templars. His children married into the prominent local families of Hillier and Hautpoul, placing the information firmly in the vicinity of Rennes-le-Château, which takes its name from the Château Hautpoul.

As evidenced by the 1616 *Chemical Wedding* tract, the Rosicrucians were closely linked with alchemy. In Vienna, for example, they constructed a fabled alchemical laboratory that was mentioned in communications between members of the order.

The Rosicrucians' adherence to the alchemical path and their subsequent creation of many complex alchemical designs also made them a magnet for alchemists and occultists of the time. Rosicrucian members scattered across Europe and became know as healers, alchemists and chemists. They included such luminaries as the fabled immortal Count of St. Germain among their ranks and are thought by some to have used tantra and sexual magic as part of their rituals (see for example *The Rosicrucians* by Christopher McIntosh).

This infatuation with alchemy continued through to the 19th-century Rosicrucian orders such as the Salon de la Rose-Croix and continues today as a core part of the Priory of Sion. (Alchemy is covered in more depth in Chapter 16.)

The head of Salon de la Rose-Croix was Joséphin Péladan (1859–1918), a novelist and occult expert inspired by Eliphas Lévi. Péladan believed that the Catholic Church was a repository of knowledge that it had itself forgotten, and he was particularly interested in John's gospel. There is in Rosicrucianism a belief that a 'true' form of Christianity survived outside the orthodox teachings of the Catholic Church. Threads of this can be seen in the heretical beliefs of the Cathars and the reformist Catholicism of St Vincent de Paul and Jean-Jacques Olier, examined in later chapters.

The Rosicrucians had a major impact on Freemasonry via the introduction of the Rose+Croix 'higher' or 'Ecossais' (Scottish) degrees into the Ancient and Accepted Scottish Rite of Freemasonry. It is the links between the Priory of Sion and Freemasonry to which we shall now turn.

SION AND FREEMASONRY

By now the strands of Sion's influence are becoming clear. The body of knowledge gathered by the Templars was in part passed on via Sion to be used by the Rosicrucians. The custodians of the secrets were the old European aristo-cratic families. Once the secrets had passed back into secret societies they were encrypted in symbols and rituals that eventually passed from those societies into Freemasonry. The nature of these secrets was offensive enough to the Catholic Church for it to pass an edict banning Catholics from becoming Freemasons.

Even Masonic researchers struggle with the notion that Freemasons are descended from the Templars. Historically it is difficult to find direct links, but throughout the body of Masonic rituals are clear references to and re-enact-ments of Templar history and lore, such as the central symbolism of the Temple of Solomon. Unfortunately the Masons seem to have forgotten this. It seems that only 'fringe' researchers have tried to approach the esoteric side of Masonry and uncover the meaning of the rituals, even though it is clear that a great body of knowledge is available to initiates that the society itself fails to communicate. For this reason the Freemasons often seem like a mere hazy shadow of the Templar tradition. In England, for example, where the modern forms of Freemasonry were made public in the 18th century, the majority of the brethren would appear to join principally for social reasons, preferring the knife and fork over the square and compass. However, I do not doubt that there are a core number of Masons who still subscribe to the mysteries, as evidenced in recent years by the creation of the Canonbury Institute in London, an attempt to consider the more esoteric aspirations of the lodge.

The Freemasonry of the United Grand Lodge of England (UGLE) is based on old morality plays, its rituals originally being allegorical enactments aimed at promoting the better qualities of its members. It was not originally a Hermetic or occult order and early British Masonic writings tend to support this by displaying no occult knowledge.

It was later, with the adoption of the higher Rosicrucian degrees in the early 19th century, that occult philosophy was introduced. The Grand Lodge would prefer to downplay the occult leanings of the Masonic traditions but there is evidence from occult groups such as the Order of the Golden Dawn adopting many of the trappings – regalia, titles and temple designs and so on – from the Royal Arch Degree of Freemasonry (see R A Gilbert's lecture, 'Freemasonry and Esoteric Movements', available from the Canonbury Institute).

It surprises me how much esoteric material exists in the workings of Freemasonry. The Grand Lodge seems to be embarrassed by this and I recall asking a guide during a tour of the UGLE in Great Queen Street, in London's Covent Garden, why the lodge's temple contained vast depictions of all the astrological figures. The guide's response was that they were 'purely decorative'.

While the UGLE has became less and less esoteric in the past century, European Freemasonry, under the control of Grand Lodge Alpina in Switzerland, continued down its esoteric path and had no such qualms promoting the Hermetic message. Freemasonry in central European countries was very much the domain of the aristocracy and was infused with the Western occult traditions of which they were the keepers. Freemasonry sat well with these traditions, as it possessed much of the structure and occult leanings of a ritual magic order.

While there are many good, decent and serious Masons, there have unfortunately also been plenty of abuses, for example in the realm of politics. The US election of 1832 was a case in point, as reported in *The Men's House: Masonic Papers and Addresses* (1924), an American Masonic publication:

> 'Masonry was made an issue in a political campaign, the result of which was the defeat of Henry Clay because he was a Mason – and incidentally the election of Jackson, another Mason!'

It is difficult to see democracy in an election where both candidates are members of the same secret society. The political influence of secret societies will always come as a shock to the traditional historian, but the simple statement above not only undermines any notion of democracy but also illustrates that there are aspects of politics that are entirely obscured by secret societies.

Conversely, a number of organizations have attempted to influence or even subvert Freemasonry over the centuries. In *Proofs of a Conspiracy* (1798), the distinguished Scottish scientist and philosopher John Robison accused the Illuminati of having sought to recruit Masons to help instigate the French Revolution; and in the 1980s Freemasons were claimed to be in the top five groups targeted by Russian spies infiltrating British society (see Stephen Knight's *The Brotherhood*).

Nic Haywood confirmed the powerful influence and esoteric lore that remain within Freemasonry, even if the majority of members deny that the society has any such elements:

'It is well to remember that Freemasonry, however questionable
the cause, is an international brotherhood to which a great deal of
power and influence obtains.'

'Whether the underlying myth(s), upon which much [Masonic]
ritual is set, is taken as genuine matters little. However, the
attending legend vis-à-vis Solomon's Temple etc., and the notion
of [those in] the higher Ecossais [degrees of Freemasonry] being
custodians or guardians of an incredible secret is a correct one!'

The Priory of Sion provided me with a design that confirmed their direct
influence on Freemasonry. It is the frontispiece to a book (*see* page 38). As
Nic Haywood says,

'The frontispiece is interesting inasmuch as it affirms links with the
overseeing Chapter of the UGLE, GLAS, and others.'

'There exists no printed literature in respect of this body of
overseers, and it has never been so. The motif of the Secret Monitors
is all that any might hope to encounter short of induction.'

The abbreviations used above, UGLE (United Grand Lodge of England) and
GLAS (Grand Lodge Alpina, Switzerland), are the largest and most influential
Masonic factions in the world.

The frontispiece provided by Sion closely resembles the logo for the Order
of the Secret Monitor, a well-established Masonic lodge under UGLE. There
are variations to the design but they are clearly indicating a link between the
two orders. Like the Rosicrucians, the OSM have been known to claim that
their order can be traced back to ancient Egypt.

MASONS AND TEMPLARS

The influences on Freemasonry have generated a lot of confusion over the years.
Officially it did not even 'exist' until the 17th century, but the Rosslyn Chapel,
built c 1456 near Edinburgh, Scotland, has elements of both Masonic and Gothic
symbolism. The creation of this remarkable building began over a century after
the Templars had officially ceased to exist and two centuries before the accepted
date for the first Freemasons, and it provides a good argument for an attempt
at continuity, bringing together two organizations, Templars and Masons, at a
time when neither supposedly existed. According to Sion,

Sion 'frontispiece'. The design is linked to the badge of the Masonic Order of the Secret Monitor.

'Modern Freemasonry is a speculative system derived from the medieval craft guilds, who protected their work in symbolic, sacred architecture, by a code of passwords, signs, grips and rituals. These operative masons, as they are known, enshrined much of their lore in geomantic proportion and the alchemical symbolism of Gothic architecture. In reality it had its true roots in the Sufi order known as 'the Builders', founded by Dhu'l-Nun in the tenth century.'

The Dhu'l-Nun were said to be steeped in alchemy and sacred geometry and influenced the origins of Freemasonry, as described by Sion:

'It [Dhu'l-Nun] began as a Sufi alchemical society, which first reached England during the reign of King Athelstan (924–939), and was introduced into Scotland disguised as a craft guild at the beginning of the 14th century by the Knights Templar. Its 'reformation' in early 18th-century London by a group of Protestant sages who mistook its Arabic terms for Hebrew, has obscured so much of its earlier tradition. It is for this reason, and no other, that the ASR [Ancient Scottish Rite] is the true and legitimate Freemasonry. This is the real reason why it had to be "accepted" or recognized by the UGLE.'

The disguised 'craft guild' is what developed into Ancient Scottish Rite Freemasonry, with the influence of the French aristocracy, while the early 18th-century 'reformation' refers to the creation of the UGLE. Robison's *Proofs of a Conspiracy* (*see* page 36) gives an account of how he came across documentation in Grand Lodge Alpina on the existence of Adam Weishaupt's secret society, the Illuminati. By coincidence, the Priory of Sion first came to wider attention in the 1950s with the discovery of its journal *Vaincre* in the same Grand Lodge Alpina. Here again we see the pattern of crossover in membership between secret societies.

The proliferation of secret societies in Europe peaked with an 'occult revolution' just before the turn of the 20th century, when all forms of occultism and spiritualism were becoming both fashionable and better researched. In France, Freemasonry was influenced by the Martinists, a mystical Christian order under the direction of Papus (Gérard Encausse, 1865–1916), a leading French occultist who published his own Tarot deck and many esoteric works. The Martinists, whose leading members included Joséphin Péladan, resurrected old Masonic rites. I mention the Martinists here because a confirmed Martinist once referred to Sion members as 'brothers'.

POLITICS AND CONFLICT:
SECRET SOCIETIES TODAY

Although much of the information on secret societies is historical, their presence and influence is still very much in effect today. Sadly, the original core purpose of their existence seems to have become overshadowed by politics and in-fighting, though it is understandable how this may have come about.

The current state of the modern Templar order is one of disarray. In recent years the order has split geographically, with the UK separating from the worldwide order, which continues to be directed by the Portuguese Grand Master. The formerly separate Scottish and English lodges have united under a single banner but I fear that in doing so they have lost more than they have gained. There are conflicting views from both sides as to why this has happened, with the British contingency claiming that the reason for their breakaway was due to succession: the Grand Master's successor should have been decided by vote but instead he passed the title to his son.

A representative from Portugal also threatened to disband the English faction of the order for accepting too many Freemasons into its ranks.

Unfortunately strife and upheaval seem to be the norm among secret societies. Sion has its own seemingly irreconcilable factions and will also inevitably fall into disarray from time to time. Its current aim of 'seeding' information into society is not welcome in all quarters. As the release of information is intended to create a shift in perception, this would inevitably cause the demise of some existing social structures, most notably the Catholic Church. A number of Sion's members, referred to as the 'Italian contingent' for their Catholic leanings, are attempting to slow the pace of release. This has led to internal struggle within the organization. The 'Italian contingent' includes dual members of the Knights of Malta, a popular order in the US that has included many senior members of the CIA. In their present incarnation the Knights of Malta have their headquarters in the Vatican.

During an interview with Nic Haywood, I directly raised the question of whether the Vatican is an adversary of Sion. Nic's response:

> 'They have always been at war with Rome. There was a reason why Rome made an offer to the Knights of Malta [after the dissolution of the Templars in 1312]. They ended up with a lot of Templar goods they shouldn't have had. It is the biggest game of chess, fighting for the souls of individuals, the future of mankind.'

I knew that Sion claimed to have members in other secret societies and in the Vatican, and I asked if the latter had remained anonymous.

'Rome knows, some people you cannot remove, you can appear to uphold Rome but be a member of Sion. There is someone in the headquarters in the Knights of Malta that might speak to you.'

Unfortunately this interview has yet to take place but the battle lines are drawn.

During my time working with Sion on the *Bloodline* documentary I realized that all was not well within the organization. Offers of material, documents, access to libraries were often thwarted by other members. Emails were being hacked and phone taps were traced on a number of phones in use by the *Bloodline* documentary team. Apparently my enquiries and the candidness of those I spoke to were fuelling an already heated debate within the society.

As research progressed, the interference escalated to a stalemate at various points. Speaking to Nic I got the impression that the revelation of information was adding to a rift within Sion. Gino Sandri, an unofficial Priory of Sion spokesman, referred to it as a 'war' but Nic explained that this is probably too strong a word. The organization's core and purpose remain intact and the release of information to the public is still on the agenda. The disagreement lies in the 'when'. The timing of release is very important:

'I thank you for your apologies re any "discord" that might have been created by your requests. However, there are certain individuals who believe that: "the time is not right" for certain matters.'

'Whilst ... this is (in part) true, it is time that certain additional pieces of this affair be put in the global domain.'

'Some are under great pressure not to co-operate and, not for the first time, we have fallen into two distinctly opposing camps.'

From a meeting with Nic I learned that family feuds and in-fighting, rooted in old rivalries and rifts, sometimes surface in the gaps between periods of release. I got a sense that when information is released it is sometimes misinterpreted by authors and researchers and simply adds to confusion around the issues.

CONCLUSION

Returning to the existence of Sion prior to its appearance in the late 20th century, we are left with a choice of two conclusions. One is that Sion is a real order that has a long tradition going back to the Templars and incorporating the Rosicrucians and other secret societies as its public façade, with knowledge and beliefs rooted in antiquity. The second option is that the Priory of Sion was created as a means to release information from other sources, such as Freemasonry and Rosicrucians, by acting as a kind of 'franchise'.

Sion, of course, claims the former – that it has a long and illustrious history under the guise of various other organizations. They would have us believe that it is a misconception to see Sion as a modern fabrication, fashioned upon earlier organizations and adopting notable historic figureheads as 'Grand Masters'.

Many readers may see Sion at best as the crafting of a 'new mythology' which, like all myths that endure, is not without some archetypal truth that resonates through modern society.

During the filmed interview for *Bloodline* Bruce Burgess asked Nic if the Priory of Sion could prove its history. The answer was simple: 'Yes, if it shows its hand.' I probed further. The 'hand' that Sion holds is presumably an important secret. Does Sion exist because of this secret?

> 'Sion is not the secret. It protects the secret. It doesn't need to
> prove it exists....There will come a time when it is all too clear. It
> is a real order, with a history to pre-Christian times. [Sion is] not
> an invention of the 1950s.'

Obviously we would need firm proof before coming to any final conclusions about Sion's origins. But for me, the quality of information was always the most important aspect of what we received. In light of this, we have to acknowledge that the Priory of Sion has a historic pedigree at least in the sense that its members are party to information that has its origins in the Rosicrucian and alchemical movements. These in turn that take us back to the ancient civilizations of Greece, Egypt and Sumeria, as well as medieval Arabic influences via the Templars.

But what do we know of Sion's members, those illustrious adepts who have attempted to serve humanity as keepers of the light of truth? Sion claims many key historical figures among its ranks, and we must look to them to guide us further. A secret society is nothing without members.

CHAPTER 3

ALUMNI

All artists see with the heart, a higher spirituality.

Anonymous Priory of Sion member

THE GRAND MASTERS

The ideal to which Sion aspires – that of influencing society through culture – requires that throughout history it has at its disposal many creative individuals. As Nic Haywood put it,

> 'It draws its members from literature, the arts, ecclesiastical [circles]. They are spiritually orientated, philosophical. They are approached to join.'

The Priory of Sion actively recruits 'sensitives' – artists, those who already communicate the immutable truth, as well as alchemists and 'bloodline' families. The bloodline families are those who are believed to be direct descendants of Jesus and Mary Magdalene or in some cases the disciples of Jesus. These tend to be European aristocracy. The work of artists is said to vibrate at a higher level that can be recognized by adepts. Certain symbols also signpost esoteric meaning within works of art, such as the reversed letter 'N', as seen in the signature of Emile Signol (1804–92), whose works adorn Saint-Sulpice church in Paris.

There is a saying that if you ask for a teacher one will appear. The teacher/pupil relationship is central to the transmission of information through generations, whether it is via a secret society or in the private confines of an alchemist's laboratory. This transmission goes from person to person and in this way the knowledge is protected from the curse of forgetting.

Sion has always maintained that it has managed to influence society through the ages. But how could it have done so without having educated key individuals in its cause?

In the 1950s Sion deposited a collection of documents called the *Dossiers Secrets* (secret dossiers) in the Bibliothèque Nationale, the French National Library. Among this collection was a list of Grand Masters of the order reaching back to the Crusades. The subject of much interest and speculation, it reads as a 'wish list' of prominent members for any secret society claiming historic credibility. It is now agreed, both within and outside Sion, that this list is not accurate and may have been used to attract like-minded individuals or members who have lost contact with the order. However, the list of Grand Masters includes alchemists, artists and members of bloodline families and as such certainly goes some way to illustrate the ideals of Sion. Here is the list of Grand Masters, with their periods of office, as given in a copy of the *Dossiers Secrets* sent to me by Nic:

1. Jean de Gisors (1188–1220)
2. Marie de Saint-Clair (1220–66)
3. Guillaume de Gisors (1266–1307)
4. Edouard de Bar (1307–36)
5. Jeanne de Bar (1336–51)
6. Jean de Saint-Clair (1351–66)
7. Blanche d'Evreux (1366–98)
8. Nicolas Flamel (1398–1418)
9. René d'Anjou (1418–80)
10. Yolande de Bar (1480–83)
11. Alessandro di Mariano Filipepi (Sandro Botticelli, 1483–1510)
12. Leonardo da Vinci (1510–19)
13. Connétable de Bourbon (Charles, Duke of Bourbon, 1519–27)
14. Ferdinand de Gonzague (Ferdinando or Ferrante Gonzaga, 1527–75)
15. Louis de Nevers (1575–95)
16. Robert Fludd (1595–1637)
17. Johann Valentin Andrea (1637–54)
18. Robert Boyle (1654–91)
19. Isaac Newton (1691–1727)
20. Charles Radclyffe (1727–46)
21. Prince Charles Alexander of Lorraine (1746–80)
22. Archduke Maximilian Franz of Austria (1780–1801)
23. Charles Nodier (1801–44)
24. Victor Hugo (1844–85)

25. Claude Debussy (1885–1918)
26. Jean Cocteau (1918–63)

At one point I was given the impression that at least part of the Grand Master list was accurate and that Leonardo da Vinci and Fludd had indeed been Grand Masters. It seems that Sion maintains a loose willingness to uphold the credibility of this list.

I asked Nic why there is a fluctuation in the list between Grand Masters drawn from aristocratic families and those who were men of the arts. He explained that the old noble families were the custodians of 'the secret' – the mystery that lies at the heart of Sion – and many of these families had commissioned artists to promote their concerns. The artists, he said, took an interest because it is fundamentally a 'philosophical secret'.

There are many works available on each of the individuals in the Grand Master list and many researchers have scrutinized their works for clues to their links with the Priory of Sion, so I shall avoid repeating that in detail. And for reasons that will soon become clear, I shall not linger on this list save for a few examples of interest.

Leonardo da Vinci (1452–1519) and Dutch fellow artist Hieronymus Bosch (1450–1516) are known to have met on occasion in Florence. It would have made for an interesting exchange of ideas and philosophies. The work of Bosch contains many heretical and Cathar themes and at least one author, Lynda Harris (in *The Secret Heresy of Hieronymus Bosch*) makes a very good case that in origin his family were Cathar refugees from southwestern France. The Cathar belief that Jesus and Mary Magdalene were married is in keeping with the beliefs of Sion and will be covered later.

Of the old families represented in the Grand Master list I have encountered that of de Bar, who are still in existence, so at least a few of these families have survived. Since this list came to light there has been the emergence of a trend to create and sell titles of nobility. Even in this age of equality it seems that many still desire to appear of noble origin.

There is also a strong possibility that the original Grand Master list is intended less as a historically accurate record and more of a signpost, highlighting the creators of work that contains keys to the secret. The *Dossiers Secrets* are telling us that these men are worth further consideration and investigation, that their work will contain something of the 'underground stream' of hidden knowledge that is being passed down to us through history. These figures certainly courted heresies and secret wisdom, or had alchemical leanings – all of which Sion promotes.

There is another interesting link. Some of those on the original published list, including Robert Fludd, Johann Valentin Andrea, Robert Boyle, Isaac Newton and Charles Radclyffe, had all either influenced or directly contributed to what became the Byrom Collection papers. These later appeared in *The Queen's Chameleon*, a biography of poet John Byrom (1692–1763) by Joy Hancox. Hancox had discovered an entire archive of designs and writings from this period, as well as a list of their names. As this list was not discovered until the 1980s, the compiler of the *Dossiers Secrets* , which was published in the 1950s, could not have known of its existence.

Hancox's discoveries showed that this group were in contact with one another. Of particular interest is the fact that two diagrams from two different personal collections of these men have identical mistakes. This is evidence of important symbols being copied and circulated among an intellectual élite with esoteric knowledge and interests. It is likely that they were Rosicrucians, and because Rosicrucianism is effectively a branch of the Priory of Sion (see preceding chapter) this may well explain the appearance of these men on the original Grand Master list published in the *Dossiers Secrets*.

The *Dossiers Secrets* list (which was reproduced in *The Holy Blood and the Holy Grail*) was superseded by a more accurate version published in the September 1989 edition of *Vaincre*, Sion's newsletter. This is thought to be closer to a correct list, but is also known to contain errors:

1. Jean-Tim Negri d'Ables (1681–1703)
2. François d'Hautpoul (1703–26)
3. André-Hercule de Rosset (1726–66)
4. Prince Charles Alexander of Lorraine (1766–80)
5. Archduke Maximilian Franz of Austria (1780–1801)
6. Charles Nodier (1801–44)
7. Victor Hugo (1844–85)
8. Claude Debussy (1885–1918)
9. Jean Cocteau (1918–63)
10. François Balphangon (1963–9)
11. John Drick (1969–81)
12. Pierre Plantard de Saint-Clair (1981)
13. Philippe de Chérisey (1984–5)
14. Patrice Pelat (1985–9)

15. Pierre Plantard de Saint-Clair (1989)
16. Thomas Plantard de Saint-Clair (1989)

Clearly, some of the more glamorous names from the original list, such as Leonardo da Vinci, have been excluded, although this does not preclude them from having been members. However, this list is not without a few famed and noble persons. Prince Charles Alexander of Lorraine and Archduke Maximilian Franz of Austria were both heads of the Teutonic Knights, the third of the great military orders created during the Crusades. De Rosset was a member of the de Fleury family who owned many lands around Rennes-le-Château, and whose family will loom large in other parts of our story. Both are also true of the Negri d'Ables family, who were also deeply embedded in the Rennes-le-Château affair, which will be discussed in greater detail later.

According to Nic Haywood, the succession of Thomas Plantard, the current Grand Master, in 1989 is the subject of 'an ongoing dispute' and 'schism' that to date 'remains unresolved'. Thomas himself refuses to enter into a dialogue on the matter.

Finally, Nic confirmed that the 1989 list was as close to accurate as we would get, although it was still not perfect. Even setting aside the disputed rights of Thomas Plantard, said Nic, 'two names are incorrect.' These are Pelat, who should not be on the list, and Pierre Plantard, who did not serve a second term.

Nic then chose to supply me with yet another list of Sion 'brethren' from the specific period of 17th- and 18th-century France, 'from the period of Louis XIV to the Revolution'. They are given with their years of birth and death:

Comte de St Germain (dates uncertain; active mid-18th century)
Sigismund Bacstrom (c 1750–1805)
Comte Louis de Chazal (1717–1856)
Juste-Aurèle Meissonnier (1693–1750)
Charles Perrault (1628–1704)
Claude Perrault (1613–88)
Stanislas-Jean de Boufflers (1738–1815)
Jean-Jacques Olier (1608–57)
[St] Vincent de Paul (1581–60)
St Louise de Marillac (1591–1660)

This list provides a snapshot of how Sion influenced society at the time prior to the French Revolution, with the three aspects of Sion clearly represented: the alchemical (St Germain, Bacstrom, de Chazal); the creative (Meissonnier, the Perrault brothers, de Boufflers); and the spiritual (Olier, St Vincent de Paul, St Louise de Marillac). It confirms our suspicions that the underlying thread of Sion is alchemy, and that the vehicle for communicating its esoteric knowledge and wisdom is Rosicrucianism.

Apart from the Comte de St Germain, who remains a largely enigmatic figure, this group seems to revolve around the church of Saint-Sulpice in Paris, with Olier gravitating toward the centre of this group. Since these individuals have clearly been singled out for our attention, they would benefit from some brief explanation.

Comte de St Germain

The 'immortal' St Germain has been the subject of much speculation over the years. Like many of the individuals on this list it would take a whole book to fully explore his life and actions. For our purpose, I will give just a few points of interest. The most remarkable thing about the elusive St Germain is his alleged longevity – it is claimed by biographers, including Manly P Hall and Elizabeth Cooper-Oakley, that he manifested among the European aristocracy at various points over a period of 200 years. Hall and Cooper-Oakley also believe that he was of East European royal descent. He was said to be an artist working in paint, music and literature, but very little of his work survives. I can recommend for further reading *The Most Holy Trinosophia*; a short, symbolic work that is attributed to him. As Nic put it:

> 'As for St Germain, it is true that in part "the man who does
> not die" is synonymous with "the message that does not – cannot
> – die". However, in the case of St Germain we would seek to
> show him an active Brother of Sion.'

St Germain was also said to have taught alchemy to another member on our list, Sigismund Bacstrom.

Sigismund Bacstrom

Believed to be of Scandinavian origin, Bacstrom was a translator of alchemical manuscripts and a member of the Rosicrucians: the record of his initiation into the order is in the library of Glasgow University, Scotland, along with many of his alchemical manuscripts and writings. Bacstrom was initiated into the Rosicrucians by the Comte Louis de Chazal. Nic Haywood was also keen to make it known that Bacstrom had influenced Francis Barrett, one of the great occult writers of his age. Bacstrom, he said, had provided Barrett with the 'Table of Correspondences' for his work *The Celestial Intelligencer*, published as *The Magus* (London, 1801).

Comte de Chazal

The Comte de Chazal was a Rosicrucian and alchemist who, it has been said, was trained by the Comte de St Germain in Paris in 1740. The dates supplied by Nic of 1717 to 1856 are unlikely to be accurate as this would make his age at death 139. In 1794, he initiated Sigismund Bacstrom into the Rosicrucians on the French island of Mauritius. Both Chazal and Bacstrom claimed to have achieved the 'Great Work' of alchemy and perfected the *Lapis Philosophorum* (Philosopher's Stone). According to Nic,

> 'Chazal did everything in his power to keep Bacstrom on the
> island [of Mauritius] so that they might "make a Golden Head".
> In other words Chazal wanted to show Bacstrom how to
> accomplish the *Magnum Opus* [Great Work].'

In psychological terms, the 'Golden Head' can be seen as the transcending of the egotistic mind into the enlightened, spiritual mind, but it is also possible to interpret this as something akin to the Templar oracle of the severed head mentioned earlier (*see* page 26).

Juste-Aurèle Meissonnier

Meissonnier was an influential French sculptor, painter, master goldsmith, architect and designer of lavish interiors. While based in Paris he was employed by Louis XV as a goldsmith and interior decorator and also worked on the designs of Saint-Sulpice church, thus cementing his links with Jean-Jacques Olier (*see* below).

Charles Perrault

Most famous for his fairy tales, Charles Perrault authored such classics as *Cinderella*, *Mother Goose* and *Sleeping Beauty*, which is considered an alchemical allegory. *Sleeping Beauty* is also mentioned in *Le Serpent Rouge*, a document heavily linked to the Rennes-le-Château mystery that will be examined in depth later (*see* Chapter 10).

Claude Perrault

History has attempted to reverse the roles of the two Perrault brothers, but during his lifetime Claude was more famous than Charles. An architect, anatomist and scientific author of some repute, he was also a member of the French Academy. The architecture of the east wing of the Louvre stands as a solid reminder of his talents.

Stanislas-Jean de Boufflers

The Chevalier de Boufflers studied for the priesthood at Saint-Sulpice but did not take up a position. An author and artist, he was a member of the Knights of Malta and the French Academy. He wrote *Aline, Reine de Golconde* and his complete works are available in French.

Jean-Jacques Olier, St Vincent de Paul and Louise de Marillac

While the others on this list each left their mark on the society of the day, it was the combined efforts of Jean-Jacques Olier, St Vincent de Paul and Louise de Marillac that had the most profound effect on the spiritual direction of France.

Seventeenth-century France was in spiritual decline. The Catholic Church, while gaining political power and wealth, had lost its connection to the laity. Many of the peasants became Protestants (Huguenots), to whom Henry IV had granted freedom of worship. Into this arena came Vincent de Paul, Marillac, Olier and the various movements founded at Saint-Sulpice (*see* below, page 53). Their mission seemed to be to revitalize the Church from within and they achieved a certain amount of success and popularity. The Order of Saint-Sulpice and Vincent de Paul's Order of Lazarists both have links to the Priory of Sion.

Jean-Jacques Olier

A forward-thinking priest, Olier directed his teachings and wealth entirely towards the poor. In 1641 he was given the parish of Saint-Sulpice in Paris. He fought to raise the status of women within the Church and is mentioned by name in the *Le Serpent Rouge*. Olier's influence cannot be underestimated as the seminary he created in 1641 despatched priests to all areas of France and became the model for seminaries in all parts of Catholic Christendom. Nic tells us:

> 'Bearing in mind that Olier's mentor was an adept of the
> alchemical process (having gleaned his "clues" from the distilled

material which had been well guarded by our old friends the Templars), he set about a synthesis which was itself known in ecclesiastical circles as a form of heresy, but which could not be suppressed. St Vincent de Paul was present at Olier's death and witnessed Olier's final realization that Christianity, as an institution, had been founded upon a vast panoply of disseminated untruths.'

Sion believes that the legacy of Louise de Marillac and St Vincent's Daughters of Charity had been based upon the benevolent acts of Mary Magdalene and her mission to disseminate a true Christianity and protect the son of Jesus. Certainly the Daughters of Charity's main concern was the protection of women and orphans. This concern echoes the Masonic cry of 'Who will protect the Widow's son?'

St Vincent de Paul

St Vincent de Paul was arguably the most famous of this group. Canonized for his charitable works he devoted the latter part of his life to helping the poor and the orphaned. At the same time he quietly set about addressing the spiritual poverty that had overcome France by inspiring and reinvigorating those around him within the church. In the latter part of his life he found a kindred spirit in Meissonnier and together they created the Daughters of Charity. This organization, while providing support to the destitute, was also an attempt to make the role of women more prominent within the Church, in order to redress the balance. The Daughters became a highly respected force within the Catholic Church and denote a subtle shift towards an equality of gender.

St Louise de Marillac

Louise de Marillac founded the Sisters of Charity under the direct tutorage of St Vincent de Paul. The Sisters concerned themselves with the housing of widows and orphans and continued the work of Olier and St Vincent de Paul after their deaths. De Marillac's son, Michel Le Gras, is mentioned earlier in relation to resurrecting the Priory of Sion in order to further the work (*see* page 34).

By throwing the spotlight on this specific period of history, Sion has illustrated how its associates came together to capitalize on the general ambivalence of the masses to play an active role in the spiritual wellbeing of the population while subtly influencing the theological direction of the Catholic Church.

These individuals helped to reinstate spirituality as a force in France in a way that also embraced their own ideologies, under the cover of the Church and popular culture.

SAINT-SULPICE

The church and seminary of Saint-Sulpice in Paris has an important role to play in this story. For many centuries it has been the epicentre of heretical thought and esoteric learning in France and an expression of Sion's aims. The library at Saint-Sulpice, where academics gathered to translate rare and ancient religious manuscripts, has educated and inspired the likes of Eliphas Lévi, the celebrated 19th-century occultist. As it was a centre for learning, translations of rare and esoteric documents from across Christendom would have found their way into its library. Anyone with access to enough apocryphal material and writings that present an alternative Christianity, such as Saint-Sulpice holds, could not help but be swayed into diverse forms of Christian thought. Lévi, for example, went on to write *Transcendental Magic* and works on Tarot and Kabbalah. He greatly influenced Aleister Crowley and many of the 20th century's most important magical writers and groups.

Another Priory of Sion member, who wishes to remain anonymous, stated in relation to the mystery of Rennes-le-Château that the priest of that village visited the academic translators of Saint-Sulpice at the time of Joséphin Péladan (1858–1918), who headed the Salon de la Rose-Croix in the late 19th century (*see* page 34).

Other members of the Saint-Sulpice seminary around this time included another French occultist, Papus (1865–1916), whose Tarot designs and writings are still in use today. Papus helped Péladan found the Order of Rose+Croix of the Temple and Grail, one of the many Priory of Sion branches. Péladan's Rose+Croix also has links to the artist Nicolas Poussin, whose work will feature later in this story, in that it was attended by the Comte de la Rochefoucauld (1862–1960). La Rochefoucauld was thought to be in possession of Poussin's early papers, stolen by one of the count's ancestors.

All this adds to the impression that important and diverse ideas and documents were in circulation at this time in Paris. Evidence for secret information still exists in the church of Saint-Sulpice, with Olier himself directing us to its existence. In *Le Serpent Rouge* mention is made of Olier 'putting his hand to his mouth'. The bust of Olier on display in Saint-Sulpice shows no such action, but if you examine the murals in the church a fresco in the Chapel of St John has an additional figure. Looking out from the painting is none other than Olier, with his right hand to his mouth as if to indicate silence. Beneath his left arm is a pile of scrolls. The documents that Olier is holding – the secret that he is indicating with his finger of silence – could well be the source material relating to these esoteric fields.

The library at Saint-Sulpice was said to contain a number of important manuscripts, some of which form part of Sion's archives. In 2005 these manuscripts were removed from the church to prevent them being accessed by myself and the *Bloodline* documentary team. At this stage it became apparent that some members of Sion were less than happy with Nic Haywood's candour and were actively trying to impede our progress. Since that time my investigations have been dogged by material being diverted or removed from circulation. As yet this remains unresolved and Appendix 1 (Documentation) covers some of what I was expecting to find.

Sion maintains that many of the more overtly Christian members of its order were based around Saint-Sulpice, by which are implied Olier, his associates and the later occult and Rosicrucian groups.

Another interesting aspect of Saint-Sulpice is the fact that the Paris Meridian passes through it. The Paris Meridian was used on French maps as the prime meridian (0° longitude) even after the current Greenwich Meridian was internationally agreed in 1884. The meridian is marked in the church by a marble dolmen. Dolmens in all ages and cultures represent the male phallus, particularly those raised after the Egyptian tradition, in which they represent the phallus of the god Osiris, which according to myth was cast into the Nile by Seth, the god of chaos, and lost.

The Paris Meridian continues on down through France and passes within a few miles of Rennes-le-Château, and closer still to the ruined tomb at Pontils, which is said to be the subject of Poussin's famous painting *Et in Arcadia Ego* (*The Shepherds of Arcadia*). Some describe the shepherdess in this painting as the Egyptian goddess Isis, but any feminine archetype is appropriate.

The Paris Meridian is also known as the 'Rose Line', the line of secrets. As used by the Rosicrucians, the rose is a symbol of secrets. It has also been likened through the Phonetic Kabbalah to Rosslyn Chapel and to St Roseline – of which more later (*see* page 250).

CONCLUSION

We have reached the point where both the secret societies and the work of their individual members are beginning to coalesce into a clearer picture of the Priory of Sion. The stage is set for the secrets that Sion sought to protect to come to light. For centuries it built up a body of knowledge and kept this as a private matter, only for the initiated. But then two things happened to help bring this knowledge into the open. The first was the action of a priest in France at the end of the 19th century, and the second was the publicizing of the Priory of Sion itself by Pierre Plantard in the 1970s. Sion had decided to go public.

CHAPTER 4

SURFACING

As history marched on toward the 20th century and the various Rosicrucian orders came to an end, the Priory of Sion found another outlet for an expression of its knowledge. At the turn of the 19th century in Rennes-le-Château, a village in the Languedoc in southern France, a young priest, Bérenger Saunière began renovating his church using a number of ideas and symbols known to us from the rituals of Freemasonry and the Rosicrucians. By encoding these symbols in his church the priest was preserving the information for future generations.

Sion itself lay dormant for the next 50 years, its members scattered by two world wars. Then in the 1950s it was publicly registered in France by Pierre Plantard. Sion had surfaced for another round of dissemination. Previously there was no reason for them to expose themselves by way of public registration. They were a secret society. But two events conspired to cause this shift in how they appeared. The first intention was to summon members and would-be members back to the fold. The second was that they considered the time to be right for their goals to be revealed to the public.

The old families had lost contact and many members had been killed or incarcerated during the Second World War, when France was directly or indirectly under Nazi rule. Also, there was a pervading loss of continuity and a loss of faith within society. The impression given is that Sion was working to a timetable but that events were delayed by the Second World War. Sion says that it was imperative that the existence of the order be known by the mid-1980s as if it was preparing society for the release of information linked to a coming event.

Pierre Plantard had been set a challenge and set about making the Priory of Sion known. His name was added to the list of Grand Masters and he began to circulate material on Sion's behalf. In 1956 the Priory of Sion was registered at St.-Julien-en-Genevois, on the Swiss border in southeastern France (why this particular place was chosen is uncertain) and the statutes of Sion were deposited there by Plantard. These statutes have yet to emerge in an unedited form and we only have references from Nic Haywood to illuminate what they may contain. In their first publicized form the statutes were modified from the originals. These were modern day variants on much older statutes and their purpose remains partly hidden as one passage, Article 'O', has never been made public. This article allows for the rewriting of all other articles in times of oppression or to achieve a specific purpose and as such changes the context of all the articles that follow.

Shortly after the registration of Sion a collection of documents compiled under the banner *Les Dossiers Secrets (Secret Dossiers)* surfaced in the Bibliothèque Nationale de France in Paris. The *Dossiers Secrets* appear to have been a tool to communicate information about Sion to other interested parties via documents and clippings deposited over a period of time. This was Sion's attempt to reorganize after the Second World War – a noticeboard of sorts for those who knew how to read its contents.

We know for example that the Freemasons were actively hunted by the Nazis as they were seen as having the potential to undermine the regime. Many of Sion's members are also Freemasons or members of other secret societies. During the war a number of Sion's members would have been killed, imprisoned or displaced, and many meeting points in Europe would have ceased to exist.

Also, post-war disillusionment was seen as an opportunity to reintroduce some of the more meaningful religious ideals back into society. In such a climate it was felt necessary to reopen lines of communication as quickly as possible.

The *Dossiers* were treated as a 'pigeon hole' where members of the order could leave relevant fragments and notes for each other. It was a gathering of material reflecting Sion and its aims that could easily be identified by those who were in possession of related material. Additional to the *Dossiers* were a number of 'stacks' secreted in other locations that were used to gather information. They were created in the Bibliothèque Nationale and kept hidden by not being listed in the main catalogue. A member of staff known to Sion would retrieve them only by direct request. Even today there exists a contact for Sion in the Bibliothèque Nationale whose name I am not at liberty to divulge.

According to Nic Haywood, the *Dossiers Secrets* no longer serve any real practical purpose beyond signposting, but they are still updated regularly. A matter more of tradition than the once-was necessity. The secret dossiers were not meant for the public and certainly not meant to be taken at face value. They served a different purpose as a means to communicate between different factions but for now it is important to recognize that they contained references directing the reader to Rennes-le-Château. Continuity is central to the survival of secret societies and Sion's post-war signposting actions may well attest to this desire to ensure the re-establishment of a disrupted tradition.

PIERRE PLANTARD

It is mainly on account of Pierre Plantard (1920–2000) that the Priory of Sion has attracted both respect and ridicule in equal measure. I never met or conversed with Plantard and I have no intention of casting aspersions on his name, but I can provide some information and context for those interested in this period of Sion's history.

Plantard, who added the 'de St.-Clair' to his name in later years, claimed to have been initiated into the Priory of Sion in 1943 by Abbé (later Monsignor) François Ducaud-Bourget (1898–1984). Plantard had set up a number of front organizations in the 1930s and 1940s that seem to have had few members and produced very little beyond the occasional newsletter. It has to be noted that during the Nazi occupation these newsletters included anti-Masonic and anti-Semitic material while at the same time cultivating an interest in Grail and Hermetic lore. Those who defend Plantard's politics claim that it was a wartime cover for his work in the French Resistance, but this is unproven. However, he is acknowledged by some as 'Pierre de France' due to his patriotism at the time.

I have no intention of apologizing for Plantard's actions or condoning his apparent anti-Semitism, but I would not dismiss him out of hand as, for a time, he became very useful to Sion. His intentions in launching the Rennes-le-Château and Sion affair of the late 20th century appear to be based on the necessity to reveal a truth.

While researching I contacted Pierre Plantard's son, Thomas, via an intermediary, offering him the opportunity to set the record straight on his father. However, the invitation was politely, and understandably, declined. At the time Thomas Plantard claimed to have no interest in these matters. Ultimately, readers will view Pierre Plantard how they wish. However, we should bear in mind that he clearly did not exploit his position or potential fame for wealth.

By registering the Priory of Sion his aim appears to have been to gather together the remaining adepts and bloodline members in order to manipulate a shift in society and ensure a continuation of Sion's ideals.

This might be where the confusion surrounding the different Grand Master lists stems from (see Chapter 3). The underlying concerns and ideals of the Priory of Sion have existed since antiquity but only when necessary do these concerns and ideals coalesce in the form of a functioning group. Added to this, the loss of libraries and of Sion's network of associates due to wars and other upheavals greatly diminished the order. Hence Plantard's first attempt at a list of Grand Masters is wildly optimistic but useful as a basis to attract other members/ archivists with more accurate information.

Later, Plantard considered Gisors as a possible conduit for the information he was to make public, but finally settled on Rennes-le-Château. While Gisors had documents and other connections to the Templars, Rennes-le-Château provided far better material with which to communicate the cause.

Through the mystery of Rennes-le-Château, Plantard brought many new ideas to light. The belief in the bloodline of Jesus, while being present in the region (*see* Chapter 14 Heresy and History), was not his prime purpose, but it caught the imagination of the authors of *The Holy Blood and the Holy Grail* and attracted far more publicity than anyone had imagined. If Plantard's aim was to get certain information into the public domain and to make the masses conscious of it then he was fantastically successful. As I write this on a train the woman sitting opposite me is reading *The Da Vinci Code*, a worldwide bestseller that sparked a legal spat between Dan Brown and *The Holy Blood and the Holy Grail* authors, who unsuccessfully claimed that Brown had plagiarized their book. The court case made national news as far away as South Korea.

The bloodline idea is central to the Priory of Sion but incidental in terms of its purpose. It is taken as a given within the Priory and at this point in time has little meaning to those of us not of the bloodline families. In fact, in this respect Plantard was almost too successful in his dissemination.

Through the mystery of Rennes-le-Château, Plantard has invited us to consider all manner of arcane matters for research and discussion. However much we try to refute his claims and dispense with his evidence we have to concede his success. Plantard was no fool and at his core it seems he was an alchemist, given to transformation. His achievements have set things in motion – but it is only the beginning.

The Holy Blood and the Holy Grail came as a great shock to many when it was released, but it also proved that society could withstand these heretical and historical revelations. Sion intended that after allowing a period of time for its ideas to be absorbed into society, further information would emerge. This book is a part of that continuing release. We are currently entering a new circuit, a new cycle.

Like Sion today, Plantard directs our attention to locations, events, art and historical figures. He charges us with unravelling Sion's history and making its aims known to the world. As Nic Haywood said in an interview:

> '[Plantard's release of information] was timely; the goals of the
> Priory of Sion are spiritual and cultural, and Pierre was a genius
> – he was aware that Rennes-le-Château would filter into the
> public domain, and what had happened there opens a whole new
> chapter.'

In Sion's current ranks there exists an undercurrent of 'old school' machinations among Plantard's circle from the 1970s. Some members, such as Gino Sandri, seem unable to let go of Plantard's time or its shadier aspects, such as links to the secret service and behaviour akin to the French resistance work Plantard was credited with during the Second World War. But we cannot join Plantard's 'underground stream', as that time has passed: the path, in spite of Sandri's efforts, is no longer available to us. The current cycle of information-revealing adds some details to elaborate on Plantard's period, but there are also plenty of new revelations that are more appropriate to our time. For other members the feeling is that the sense of opportunity has returned. They are optimistic that Sion is once again moving forward.

THE PRIORY OF SION TODAY

Recent books such as *The Holy Blood and the Holy Grail* and *The Da Vinci Code* have entirely focussed public awareness on the bloodline aspect of the Priory of Sion. But Sion would have us believe that the bloodline is peripheral, having little meaning in the current world beyond its theological implications.

There seems to be much more to the order and I have discovered that Sion is very active in many parts of the world at present. The scope of its activities vary from the occult to Middle Eastern politics. The political weight of Sion cannot be underestimated. We have seen how it has a penchant for employing from within the secret service and other secret societies. To achieve its aim of a marriage of Eastern and Western philosophies it is increasingly involved in Arab-Israeli politics with the intention of putting an end to the infighting among Christians, Muslims and Jews.

This seems to be a continuation of the work of the Templars, who sought common ground with Muslims in the last days of the Crusades.

As well as the intelligence service mentioned earlier, it is Sion's devout Catholic/Christian element, known internally as the 'Italian contingent', that is identified today as the primary cause of any delay in Sion's release of information. Understandably it does not suit the Catholic Church to hurry along its own potential demise, which is what the revelations ultimately imply. In addition to this element Sion's membership also embraces the old families of the bloodlines as well as more alchemical members. It must make for an uncomfortable crucible to work in.

In spite of this the aim of Sion in the present day – the release of certain religious truths, artefacts and knowledge – is all in service of a greater cause. Indeed, possibly the greatest cause of all. As Nic put it:

> 'The fundamental goal of the Priory of Sion is the unification
> of mankind by means of engendered cultural and spiritual shifts
> in perceptions and values. It is for this reason that Sion's name
> appears to be appended to so many seemingly disparate causes.'

CONCLUSIONS

This chapter has served as a general introduction to the Priory of Sion. But to achieve a deeper understanding we must explore further some of the themes and aspects that make Sion what it is. Let us recall the biblical quotation at the head of Chapter 1 (Isaiah 28.16):

> 'I lay in Zion for a foundation a stone, a tried stone, a precious
> corner stone, a sure foundation.'

We can now view this quotation in a new perspective. The use of the word 'Sion' or 'Zion' is not merely a reference to a physical location in history, it is an ideal, a place of complete fulfilment and freedom, and perhaps this describes what lies at the heart of the Priory of Sion. There is a regressive risk with this outlook – a stultifying harking-back to a supposed 'Golden Age' – that has stalled many societies through history, as we will see later. But the Priory of Sion is moving forward, not backward, and its 'Arcadian' ideals stem from its knowledge of human potential, not from some rose-tinted nostalgia for lost glories.

There are also a number of theories regarding the transmission of Sion's core secrets. There seems to have been a loss and subsequent rediscovery of the information at certain points in history, for example prior to the time of the Templars and the Cathars, after the French Revolution and during the Second World War. From this angle, Sion often appears as a loose group of adepts passing on knowledge and secrets down the centuries. In this form, Sion can remain a meme (something that identifies ideas or beliefs transmitted from one person or group of people to another) from age to age until the mid-20th century, when it was regrouped to serve a purpose. By regrouped I mean that all those diverse individuals and groups who could be considered 'adepts' of the various branches of ancient esoteric and spiritual knowledge were brought together – conceptually if not literally – under a single name: the Priory of Sion.

At one level, therefore, we have to accept that the Priory of Sion exists. It is possible to meet members, read their documents and publications and learn a great deal from them. As just mentioned, Sion as an organization is currently very active. It has a headquarters in Paris and members all over the world including in France, the US, the UK, Canada and Egypt. I have not been party to their 'ultimate secret', should such a thing exist, but this does not devalue the organization as a force for better or worse in the world. And it is very much a force.

In the same way that Sion uses other vehicles of dissemination to further its message it could well be that Sion itself is a method of delivery for knowledge that predates the Crusades. This will lead us inevitably to the Sion's main point of departure: the mystery of Rennes-le-Château, where the church has amazed and baffled researchers since it came to wider public attention in the 1950s. The Priory of Sion uses Rennes-le-Château as a vehicle to disseminate certain truths, both historical and spiritual, and as explorers of Sion we are obliged to investigate this mystery in its many forms.

PART 2

THE MYSTERIES

CHAPTER 5

RENNES-LE-CHÂTEAU: THE FRENCH MYSTERY

Full knowledge of the secret at Rennes-le-Château confers a very real and potentially world-shattering power, were it ever in the wrong hands.

The Priory of Sion

ARRIVING AT THE MYSTERY

The tiny French hilltop village of Rennes-le-Château carries the weight of a mystery that haunts Christianity.

I first climbed the hill to Rennes-le-Château in the early 1990s, having read the many and varied books about the village that had appeared in the UK over the previous decade. I arrived just after sunset, during a storm, and traversed its few streets in search of a hotel or café. There was nothing to eat and nowhere to stay, but a local gave me lift down to the nearby town of Couiza. The next day I climbed the hill again and immediately faced the same issue. In a town that was central to a burgeoning publishing industry and tourist trade, it was impossible at the time to buy so much as a glass of water. There were no hotels, no restaurants and no sense of being welcome.

Today, however, this has changed and in Rennes-le-Château one gets the impression that there is an uneasy tolerance of tourists, with a small café and a bookshop to cater for the inquisitive.

On my first day there I stood on the threshold of the church and looked up at the inscription above the door and the sight filled me with a sense of amusement. Carved into stone it reads 'Terrible is this place'.

But before we can dive headfirst into this fascinating church we must understand something of the context in which it stands.

A SENSE OF PLACE

The quiet village of Rennes-le-Château is situated in the Languedoc region of the southwest of France. In the view across the landscape you can clearly see the Pyrenees erupting in the south, and this region provides a gateway to Spain. The village lies 30 miles (50km) south of Carcassonne in an area where farmlands have given way to the fault lines that cross the southwest amid rolling hills and the occasional mild earthquake. The soil is red, rich with iron, and covers a shattered bed of limestone and granite riddled with caves and crevasses from a turbulent past. The abundant seashells to be found on these hills remind us that at one time the entire area was beneath the waves of what is now the Mediterranean Sea, and that time, though slowly here, moves ever on.

Here and there water rises from the ground as natural springs, many of which are warmed by the core of the Earth. Geologically, the water table is higher in this area than anywhere else in France and it was the abundance of water and rich soil that probably led the first settlers to stop here rather than attempt to negotiate the Pyrenees. As civilization advanced, strategists would have realized the defensive value of the area and no doubt many of the hilltop locations would have begun in pre-Roman times as Celtic enclosures and forts. Rennes-le-Château was especially viable for fortification as there is a lake inside the mountain to supply any settlement with water.

A BRIEF HISTORY OF THE LANGUEDOC

The earliest known settlement near Rennes-le-Château was a Neolithic burial site dating from c 3000 BCE discovered in a cave on the hillside. Evidence of continual settlement in the region can also be seen in nearby Rennes-les-Bains, where there are many half-buried walls of terracing. Ruins litter the landscape from all eras and standing stones, both natural and contrived, run like teeth across the hills. At the time of the Celts the area was known as Areda, or Rhaeda, names thought to be derived from the red soil or possibly, as the Priory of Sion maintains, a variation on *reda*, the Celtic word for chariot.

The Romans occupied Gaul – roughly what is now France – for 500 years, leaving their mark indelibly on the landscape. Old mineshafts and worked caves remind us that they mined the area extensively for jet and possibly gold. They also made use of the hot natural springs at Rennes-les-Bains and built communal baths. In Roman times it is estimated that some 30,000 people lived in the area. There are walls, ruins and paths that date from this time and an old Roman bridge recently collapsed into the River Sals at Rennes-les-Bains during a storm.

The south of Roman Gaul provides the setting for an old French tradition, dating back at least as far as the 13th century, that after the crucifixion of Jesus, Mary Magdalene fled Judea in a boat that sailed via Greece to Marseille. It is said that Mary Magdalene remained in the region, initially teaching but later becoming a recluse and finally being buried there. The Catholic Church has produced a number of her alleged relics, which are on display in Aix-en-Provence.

In 410CE the western Roman provinces, including Gaul, were under assault from various German tribes. One, the Visigoths, looted the city of Rome and then migrated west to settle in the Languedoc. Their capital was 50 miles (80km) north of Rennes-le-Château in Toulouse, but it is thought that they built a great fort in the area. This has never satisfactorily been identified, but high on the hills overlooking the area are the remains of huge walls and fortifications that served some long-forgotten purpose.

A point of interest is the ingenious manner in which the Visigoths buried their dead kings. Whereas many cultures create great monuments and tombs that are subsequently looted, the Visigoths would dam a river and bury their king and his treasures in the riverbed. The dam would then be removed and the king would lie hidden from looters indefinitely. This is seen as a possible cause of treasure in the area, which had come to Rome from the East, then been looted by the Visigothic chiefs and taken to Gaul.

The theme of the bloodline of Christ arises in 428 with another Germanic tribe, the Salian Franks. Merovech or Merovius (Mérovée), or perhaps his predecessor Chlodio, established the Merovingian dynasty in parts of Gaul and was said by Pierre Plantard to have been descended from Jesus and Mary Magdalene. The genealogy of the Merovingians was also present in the *Dossiers Secrets* as mentioned in the previous chapter. The Franks were united under Merovech's descendant, Clovis I, who in 486 overthrew the last remnant of Roman rule in Gaul and established his capital at Paris. Ruler of most of Gaul, Clovis is usually regarded as the founder of the kingdom of France, the 'Land of the Franks'. In 678 the Merovingian king Dagobert II is thought to have been assassinated in the Ardennes forest. There exists a French myth that states that one of Dagobert's sons, Sigisbert, was smuggled away to the Languedoc by soldiers and survived to continue a secret royal bloodline.

During the Middle Ages the Languedoc was under the control of the Counts of Toulouse. A cosmopolitan region, it possessed a number of Jewish settlements and is thought to be the origin of several alchemical and Kabbalistic schools.

During this period the Templars, as mentioned earlier (*see* Chapter 2), also took up residence in the Languedoc. They had a number of commanderies in the area including Arques, Blanchefort and Le Bezu to the west of Rennes-le-Château.

It was also a time when heresy swept through the region. There is not the space here to fully explore the Cathars and there are already many excellent books on the subject should you wish to follow this theme further. There will be more on their beliefs later in this book. The Cathars were a Gnostic dualist sect and their popularity drew many converts from Catholicism, even priests. Dualism is the idea that light, or 'good', is trapped in matter and is to be liberated and can be found in Zoroastrianism dating back to the second century BCE. Undoubtedly much of the attraction of Catharism was its tolerance and the fact it did not tax the common people. The simplicity and moral example of the lives of the Cathar priesthood, the *Perfecti*, would also have been appealing to those who wished for a Christianity that appeared closer in practice to the actual example of Christ.

Catharism had its roots in the Bogomils, who were centred at the time around the Bulgarian empire. The empire had been Christianized in the late ninth century but many invasions and missionaries had forayed into the Balkans leaving a mix of culture and beliefs. The Bogomils claimed to have maintained a true and hidden form of Christianity and their dualist religion spread south as far as Greece and into Western Europe. By the early 13th century its own missionaries had found many converts in the southwest of France.

It would be wrong to think that the beliefs carried from Eastern Europe remained unchanged. Dualism was developing from town to town and evolving over time. It was a living religion, growing to fit the needs of its followers. From this tradition came the Cathari, meaning 'pure ones'.

The Cathars had no churches of their own, they owned no buildings or land but they were permitted to reside in premises afforded them by sympathetic local dignitaries and lords. They worked among the people and lived simple lives, gathering in fields and barns to preach.

With such a stark contrast to the wealth and power of the Catholic Church it was inevitable that the Cathars would eventually force Rome to act. A crusade was declared against the Cathars (the Albigensian Crusade, *see* page 29) and they were forced to seek refuge in castles such as Montségur, west of Rennes-le-Château.

The siege of Montségur is worthy of our attention. According to one story, three Cathars were lowered down the cliff of Montségur just before the end of the siege. Whatever they took with them could not have been very big or heavy so a physical treasure such as gold is unlikely. The Cathars were believed to be in possession of some heretical secret. Some have surmised that it was the Holy Grail, with Montségur being synonymous with 'Montsalvaat', refuge of the Grail in Arthurian legends. For example, Wolfram von Eschenbach's *Parzival* places the castle of Montsalvaat in the Pyrenees. There is an issue here as to the nature of the Grail, as the Cathars did not believe in venerating objects. They renounced their possessions, which makes them an unlikely order for guarding an artefact. Documents would seem more likely, and potentially more important. In spite of the actions of the Catholic Church against the Cathars the scent of heresy has never left the region.

After the Albigensian Crusade the Languedoc became much less independent, as the French kings increasingly muscled in on the region. And the crusade was not the last time that religious intolerance was inflicted on the region. Prior to rounding up the Templars in 1307 (*see* page 27), King Philip IV had seized the wealth of the Jewish communities, and as late as the 16th century there were witchcraft trials in Toulouse.

An event in 1633 has generated much speculation among adventurers. In that year a gold mine was established at Blanchefort, the hill opposite Rennes-le-Château. However, it was rumoured that what was brought from the mine and subsequently smelted were not natural gold deposits but a hoard of Visigothic treasure. German miners had been brought in to recover the gold, leading to speculation that the language barrier was used by the Blanchfort family to prevent them from sharing their knowledge with the local population.

Another local myth, published in 1832 in *Journey to Rennes-les-Bains* by Labouïsse-Rochefort, tells of a shepherd boy called Ignace Paris who is said to have lost one of his sheep in the hills near the town. The sheep had fallen into a hole and the boy lowered himself by rope to retrieve it. When he landed he followed the sheep along a fault that led to a cave filled with treasure. The boy filled his pockets and returned to the town to announce his find only to be accused of stealing and hanged before he could reveal the location of the cave.

It must also be noted that on a broader scale few countries have undergone such a sudden political and social upheaval as France did during the French Revolution. In ten years at the end of 18th century the *ancien régime* – the old ruling classes of royalty, nobility and Church – was rapidly and violently deposed. As a result many of the nobles in the Languedoc would have been forced to hide their wealth and family histories. Any treasure they may have inherited would likely have been buried and as local Priests were often their sole confidants important documents were placed with the local clergy for safe keeping.

A representative of the Templars of Portugal told me that during the Second World War the Germans had tunnels dug back and forth beneath the valleys in the area of Rennes-le-Château and beneath the town itself. He would not reveal what they were looking for, but said that when the prisoners who were used to do the digging found nothing they were buried alive in these tunnels. I was once advised by a local that if I were to find a hidden wall in the mines I should not to go beyond it as the bodies of those prisoners were entombed there.

Several decades earlier, in 1885, François Bérenger Saunière (1852-1917) took up the post of priest in the church at Rennes-le-Château, and it is here that our particular story begins. Saunière restored the church and funded several expensive building projects in and around the parish that seemed impossible on a meagre priest's salary. Rumours spread that he had located a horde of treasure and he was known to have given valuable stones and other items to local residents as gifts. Amid an episcopal enquiry into alleged fraud, Saunière eventually resigned from the parish in 1909.

The story of the Rennes-le-Château mystery began to surface in the mid 1950s when Noël Corbu, who had bought Father Saunière's estate in 1946, sought publicity for a new restaurant. In 1956 the local press ran Corbu's claim that Father Saunière's wealth had derived from lost Visigothic treasure hidden in the local hills and mountains, which he had exploited to decorate his church and build his fanciful house and garden. Although Corbu's intention – to drum up tourism for the remote village – was a success, he seems to have been out of his depth in regards to grasping what he was sitting on. *How* Father Saunière had spent his money is just as important as how he came by it, if not more so. Corbu's publicity set the story in motion and treasure-hunters and mystery seekers have flocked to the area ever since.

The story of treasure stems from a claim that Father Saunière had discovered parchments containing coded messages leading to a specific location. In the 1970s, Pierre Plantard influenced author Gérard de Sède in his writing of *The Accursed Treasure of Rennes-le-Château*. This book further publicized the mystery of Father Saunière, taking his sudden wealth and strange church as an example of Sion's mythology. The book contained copies of parchments that the priest had supposedly found and decoded. They contained obvious codes but these were ignored in the book and left to the reader to discover. One such reader was researcher Henry Lincoln, who made three documentaries on the mystery in the 1970s and then went on to co-author *The Holy Blood and the Holy Grail* (1982), which first brought the mystery of Rennes-le-Château, Pierre Plantard and the Priory of Sion to the English-speaking public. The book claims that Father Saunière discovered an astonishing secret: that Jesus and Mary Magdalene were married and had produced children. Since its publication it has sold 18 million copies worldwide.

On first reading *The Holy Blood and the Holy Grail* I found the links between the Rennes-le-Château mystery and the 'bloodline of Jesus' theory a bit of a leap. I asked Nic Haywood if Sion had been happy with the book and its bloodline theory. His reply:

> 'We found *Holy Blood, Holy Grail* [the book's US title] a little too
> ambitious, but we were glad they did it. That Jesus married and
> had children, there is evidence beyond doubt.'

I have no doubt that the Priory of Sion used the Rennes-le-Château mystery as a dissemination tool for their beliefs and aims. It is a vehicle that contains a myriad of esoteric links that can be used to carry a number of messages from antiquity. It was a matter of synchronicity that Noël Corbu had begun to publicize the mystery at the same time that Sion was choosing to go public.

It could be said that there are three levels to the mystery. There is an underlying truth; there is the Priory of Sion, who claims to be communicating that truth; and there is the mystery of Rennes-le-Château, which is the vehicle for that truth.

The mystery of Rennes-le-Château should be a simple one, easily answered and discarded, but there is so much baggage attached to this little town with its allegedly errant priest that one wonders where to begin. Even during the height of summer the little town of Rennes-le-Château is buried in fog – a fog of human creation. As you try to make sense of the patterns that appear in the swirling clouds there seems to be endless possibility for interpretation, countless distractions and many images that are no more than a trick of the light.

THE SAUNIÈRE MYSTERY

Let us look at the controversy surrounding Father Saunière's tenure in more detail. At the end of the 19th century the town of Rennes-le-Château had 200 inhabitants. In 1885 Father Saunière, aged 33, was installed as the new priest at the little church of St Mary Magdalene. The eldest of seven children, he had been born in the nearby town of Montazels and raised in a house that overlooked the town square with its unusual fountain surmounted with Tritons.

When Saunière arrived in his new parish, the church was in a dilapidated state. The roof leaked and the structure was all but derelict and desperately in need of renovation. Saunière had no money of his own and was paid a meagre wage, making him dependent on his parish for handouts. A local girl was put into his care as housekeeper. Marie Denarnaud was 18 when she joined the priest and she stayed with him throughout his life.

For six years he survived on the goodwill of the townsfolk. Apparently he spent much of his spare time hunting and fishing. He also read widely, studying Greek, Hebrew and Latin.

In 1892 he applied for and received a small loan from the bishop of Carcassonne for restoration purposes. During these restorations a broken flagstone was lifted in order to be replaced. Beneath it was discovered a bag of gold coins and a chalice. The chalice has survived and was gifted to Abbé Grassaud, priest of Amélie-les-Bains, where it is still kept. (Although the chalice is in the medieval style it does not look older than the 19th century so it may not be the original or it might be something that Saunière purchased as a gift that has since become confused with his original find).

Work began again on the renovation of the church and over the next few years Father Saunière spent much of his time exploring the countryside with a sack to 'collect rocks for his garden'. According to Sion, this was a cover story for his search for a specific location.

He replaced the altar, which had rested on two Visigothic-style pillars and used one of these pillars as a plinth in the garden. A statue of Our Lady of Lourdes was installed on the plinth, an event accompanied by a procession through the town.

The interior of the church at this time was a building site and one evening a local bellringer noticed a fallen wooden balustrade. It had a slot in the top of one pillar and in this there was a glass phial containing a piece of parchment. Though this discovery is accepted – and the nephew of the bellringer is still alive to support it – what the parchment said is a matter of contention. However, it seems likely that it was a plan of the church's hiding places. We can ascertain this from Father Saunière's actions following this event.

It is said that Saunière had two workers assist him in lifting another flagstone, this time in front of the altar. On turning it over they discovered a worn carving on the underside that appears to show two archways with an adult and child on one horse following a single adult on another horse. The style of the carving is Visigothic, like that of the altar pillar, but it has not been accurately dated.

The two workers were quoted as saying that beneath the flagstone (since known as the 'Knight's Stone'), 'there were a number of shining objects showing through the earth'. The priest immediately sent them away, closed the church and refused entry to anyone else for a number of days. It seems likely that Saunière was excavating during this time. He himself is quoted as explaining the find as a large pot filled with 'bright objects' (he never explained further), 'worthless medallions', and a few skeletons.

It is thought that a number of items were hidden in the church either at the time of the French Revolution, when many churches were plundered, or by Saunière's penultimate predecessor, Antoine Bigou, who according to Nic Haywood was 'a brother of the Rose+Croix'.

Whether beneath the Knight's Stone or via another route, a crypt was also uncovered at this time. The tombs in this crypt would have belonged to the lords of Rennes, ruling nobles from the late Middle Ages. In fact there are two crypts, one of which was opened and then resealed by Saunière. The other was not sealed until after his death. Older members of the community, such as the Captier family, remember playing in the second crypt and accurately describe where the entrance was. This entrance is still visible in the hidden room at the back of the church. It is uncertain whether Saunière discovered or just re-opened the first crypt. The second one he reopened.

In a diary entry for this period Saunière also states simply: 'Found a tomb'.

At around this time it is said that he discovered further documents with encrypted text. Local stories claim that these came from the same wooden pillar as the first. The pillar still exists in the small museum adjacent to the church but from the size of the hidden compartment it seems unlikely that anything other than a small scrap of paper in a tiny glass phial would have fitted into it.

It is possible that further documents were found in the crypt and that the two discoveries became confused over time.

In his interview for the *Bloodline* movie, Gino Sandri claimed that the texts found by Father Saunière were in fact carved on stone. This idea is echoed by Nic Haywood, who has also mentioned the existence of inscribed tablets in the church, so it is possible Saunière made copies of these.

It is claimed by Sion that after failing to make sense of the texts Saunière applied to the bishop of Carcassonne and received permission to take them to Paris to get them deciphered. The visit to Paris is undocumented, though Sion hinted that the records of Saint-Sulpice church are worth checking, if not for Saunière himself then for others in his circle. It is possible that Saunière's mentor, Henri Boudet, went on his behalf.

It is difficult to say whether Father Saunière actually went to Paris or if this trip is a myth aimed at drawing our attention to Saint-Sulpice, linking the discoveries of one to the knowledge of another. Had Saunière visited, the director of Saint-Sulpice seminary, Abbé Bieil, would have introduced him to Emile Hoffet, an authority on old manuscripts and secret societies.

Saint-Sulpice is an interesting choice of destination, for at this time, as we have seen, it is thought to have been frequented by members of secret societies and it also produced such occult-orientated people as Eliphas Lévi, author of *Transcendental Magic* and one of the most influential occultists of the 19th century. (*See* Chapter 3 and also Chapter 2.)

Father Saunière is also attributed with a visit to the Louvre, where he supposedly bought reproductions of three paintings, including the legendary *Et in Arcadia Ego* (*The Shepherds of Arcadia*) by Poussin, a portrait of Pope Celestine V, and a work by David Teniers. These are covered later in the chapter on art and symbolism (*see* Chapter 16).

During his presumed time in Paris, Saunière is said to have been introduced to the occult establishment and secret societies, a scene very much in vogue with elitist groups formed of artists and the aristocracy. Sion speaks of an exchange, a sharing of information, that involved twelve parchments or documents passing through Saunière's hands. His find, according to Sion, had opened a doorway to a greater mystery.

Among the people it is claimed he spent time with in Paris around 1892 are opera singer Emma Calvé and composer Claude Debussy. At the time Calvé was a world famous opera star and had recently returned from one of her frequent performances for Queen Victoria. Both Calvé and Debussy are considered to have been highly respected members of Paris occult circles. Calvé is said to have befriended Saunière and visited him at Rennes-le-Château, but there is no solid evidence to support this.

To the south of Rennes-les-Bains is a cross beside the road with the name 'Calvet' carved on its base. Mélanie Calvet was the witness of the Virgin Mary apparition at La Salette and Emma Calvé was born Calvet and the two may be distantly related. The link to visions will become an important factor in the mystery later.

The parchment theory claims that among the encoded manuscripts discovered by Father Saunière were two genealogies dating from 1244 and 1644. These have never been seen since their alleged discovery, or adequately described. There are also said to have been another two pages of parchment inscriptions, either one double-sided sheet or two single-sided pages. Two supposed parchments were published by Gérard de Sède in his book *The Accursed Treasure of Rennes-le-Château*. Saunière's parchments are further explored in the following chapters but for now suffice it to say we know that the two texts in de Sède's book were fabrications, either pure invention or, as Sion would have us believe, modified versions of the originals. Certainly, the text in which the 'codes' are embedded clearly derives from a 19th-century version of the Codex Bezae, a widely circulated reprint of a 5th century collection of Greek and Latin passages from the New Testament. Nic Haywood has commented that an associate of Pierre Plantard, Philippe de Chérisey, is known to be the hand behind their augmentation. I cannot confirm or refute the fabrication claim as the original parchments have not been released.

French researcher Gérard Thome is in possession of similar parchments – all variations on biblical passages with additional hand-drawn maps. The passages include such embedded phrases as 'come to the tomb' but the manuscripts, although on vellum, do not appear in any way older than the 1960s.

Whether the alleged parchments (and the trip) were genuine or not, on his return to the parish Saunière began to order materials for restoring his church.

He continued excavations and local people complained when he was seen at night tampering with graves in the graveyard. During this time he chiselled the inscription off at least one gravestone. One of these is the gravestone of Marie de Negri d'Ables, Countess of Blanchefort (died January 17, 1781), whose entirely defaced remains can still be seen today in the church museum. The countess was the owner of Château Blanchefort in the 18th century, and her marriage joined the family of Blanchefort with that of Hautpoul, owners of the old château from which Rennes-le-Château's name derives. A 'copy' of the original inscription has been circulating for a number of years but is possibly a fake.

Author Gérard de Sède claims that Saunière opened bank accounts in nearby towns, including Perpignan and Toulouse, and later in other countries, notably Austria-Hungary. According to de Sède one of these accounts was opened adjacently to an account belonging to the Hapsburgs, the Austro-Hungarian ruling dynasty, giving some credibility to Sion's claim that he was being funded by them in exchange for the information he was discovering or to fence valuable objects that he had located.

In 1896 the complete redecoration of the church began. With garish taste, Saunière ordered many statues and lavish frescoes to clutter the little church. The chessboard floor, statues, water stoup with attendant demon and the inscriptions all hail from this time. At this point the bishopric began to ask questions about the sizable sums that Saunière was spending – evidently far in excess of the restoration grant. The entire church was renovated and refurbished and Saunière began buying up more land to expand his domain. He built a garden with a curved promenade on the crest of the hill. This was flanked by twin structures, a stone Gothic-style tower called the Tour Magdala and an identical (but mirrored) greenhouse, which he used as an orangery. He added a fountain to the garden. The Gothic tower afforded superb views across the surrounding valleys and of the Pyrenees and was used to house Saunière's expanding library, which included *The Prophecy of the Popes attributed to St Malachi* by Joseph Maître and *Celtic Monuments* by L F Alfred Maury (both of which researcher Benoist Rivière traced to a bookshop in Lyon).

Saunière also erected a two-storey guest house, the Villa Béthania. He never lived there but was said to have used it to entertain the many guests who visited Rennes-le-Château in the years that followed and was always well stocked with expensive food and wine. These guests included, it is claimed, Emma Calvé and the Hapsburg Archduke John, cousin to the Austro-Hungarian emperor. Saunière's public excuse for building this guest house was recorded in a letter in 1910: 'I built the house completely independently. It was not for me to get rich and live in comfort. I was intending to offer it as a house for elderly and sick priests.'

In 1897 the restored church was reopened. Among those attending this event were Father Antoine Gélis, priest of Coustaussa, the small town on the hill opposite Rennes-le-Château. His visit to the reopening of the church would have shocked him as he was a local historian and it is likely he recognized what Saunière was trying to convey. As we will discover later, the overwhelming symbolism in the church is not Catholic but blatantly heretical and having appeared to have been on the payroll Gélis may have had a change of heart and decided he had to report Saunière for his actions.

Four days later Father Gélis was found dead, his head beaten in by an axe with his arms across his chest. He is known to have been cautious to the point of paranoia, never opening the door to anyone except his daughter, so the murderer was likely to have been someone he trusted. There were no signs of forced entry into his house and no money was taken, but the place was searched so documents may have been removed.

Father Gélis left over Fr. 11,000 of unexplained funds and was known to be using others to invest money on his behalf. He was clearly part of Saunière's coterie and was possibly being paid to keep silent about his colleague's discoveries at Rennes-le-Château.

Gélis is buried beneath a gravestone surmounted with a rose cross and the grave is facing north, a direction usually reserved for suicides. A more thorough account of this incident has been compiled by Gérard de Sède in his book *Rennes-le-Château*.

Saunière's mentor, Father Boudet at nearby Rennes-les-Bains, also had money and he is said by Gérard Thome to have paid for the refurbishment of a number of churches in the area. Indeed, Sion claims that it was Boudet who was the main force behind the redesign of Saunière's church (*see* below, page 80).

After Father Boudet died in 1914 a new priest, Father Rescanière, was installed at Rennes-les-Bains. Father Rescanière took a strong interest in the local mystery surrounding Saunière's actions. A year later two people were witnessed paying Rescanière a visit and he was found murdered later that same day.

Saunière continued to spend money. While there is some dispute as to whether he was responsible for having the main road up to the town paved, he did finance the installation of running water in the town for the first time, unusual then for a town of that size. He may have had more than simply altruistic motives for doing this; he seemed to believe that people would come to Rennes-le-Château as if they were on a pilgrimage to a holy shrine. He is said to have claimed it would be 'like a second Lourdes'.

Saunière also built a 'water tower' with an office above it, but when a fire started in the town he refused access to it, arousing suspicion that it served a secondary purpose, as Nic Haywood claims:

> 'That "water tower" served as a ventilation shaft for a pre-existing mine (perhaps several centuries before). The Blanchefort mine extended right over [to Rennes-le-Château]. [Saunière] dipped into those reserves [of gold, whose location he had] foreseen and known about early on.'

Inside the church Saunière included the inscription from the New Testament: 'My house shall be called the house of prayer' and this continues: 'but ye have turned it into a den of thieves.' Saunière's housekeeper, Marie Denarnaud, is recorded as stating to townspeople: 'You are walking on gold'. This also giving credence to the idea that the Blanchefort gold mine had been rediscovered.

Despite his alleged and largely inexplicable wealth, at various points during his various projects Saunière seems to have run short of funds and owed money to his builders. He also made gifts to parishioners of semi-precious stones, some of which are still in the possession of relatives in the area. This might also indicate that Saunière had intermittent access to his source of wealth, which was perhaps a hidden tomb or treasure trove.

Eventually Saunière was called before the local bishop to explain his wealth and actions. In particular he was accused of selling hundreds of masses – receiving money in return for saying mass for a living or deceased person – that he had never performed. Saunière refused to cooperate with the enquiry and was relieved of his duties. Sion claims the selling of masses was a cover for more covert actions.

> 'Saunière... was paid large sums of money – the Priory of Sion has two examples from the Hapsburgs and others. He became proud and thought he was untouchable by the Church. His position went to his head.'

Saunière remained in the presbytery and built a small altar there. The locals were so committed to him that they stopped going to the church for mass and attended a private one in his house instead. He also received many letters of support from other local priests, copies of which are still in circulation, and which contained statements praising, for example, 'all the wonderful things you have achieved.' (Letter of January 22, 1908.)

In a letter dated December 24, 1909, Saunière admitted to selling masses at two francs per mass, ten for the Sister Superior of the Hospital of St.-Joseph in Paris, which he confirms he actually celebrated. The selling of masses is claimed by some to be the sole source of Saunière's wealth. Extracts of his accounts in circulation do show a multitude of entries for very small sums of money received for masses. However, these sums are not substantial and would not have covered the cost of Saunière's spending – let alone that of Fathers Boudet and Gélis in the neighbouring parishes, who also appear to have been receiving large sums at the same period.

Another issue with the selling of masses is that it in no way explains the décor of Saunière's church, nor his actions such as defacing gravestones or distributing precious stones as gifts. From a conversation with Nic:

> 'Saunière's money was not from simony – you couldn't do that
> many masses. The account books may be an attempt to cover up,
> especially with the programme of works planned for later that
> were never completed.'

A letter from Saunière dated July 15, 1910, states that 'after your interdiction [suspension by the bishopric] I did not offer to say any masses, even if certain details in my file appear to prove the contrary.' This supports the idea that Saunière used the selling of masses as an excuse as a cover for some other activity that was generating his wealth.

Saunière continued to plan lavish creations, including a second tower much taller than the first. But this was not to be.

THE DEATH OF SAUNIÈRE

Father Saunière had been ill for some time when, on January 13, 1917, his housekeeper Marie Denarnaud ordered his coffin. A few days later another local priest was called to administer the last rites. After hearing his confession it is reported that the priest refused absolution and left the house looking deeply shocked by what he had heard. On January 17, 1917, Saunière died. The date of January 17 recurs throughout this mystery – on the Marie de Negri d'Ables tombstone, for example – and its significance will be summarized in a later chapter, so to me this initially appeared to be fictitious or merely symbolic. But then Sion put forward the idea that Saunière was in fact murdered:

> 'It is not inconceivable that the Priory of Sion killed Saunière. At
> that time it consisted of noble families and illustrious people in
> the arts; Saunière was arrogant, it had gone to his head.'

Gino Sandri echoed this opinion:

> 'Saunière was murdered – hit over the head in the tower. He got
> too demanding for money.'

While his mentor, Father Boudet, would use the money that he, too, was
evidently receiving to fund the restoration of churches and other charitable
causes, Saunière generally spent it on himself. He lived an expensive, ostentatious
lifestyle and as a result, according to Sion, may have been eventually murdered. I
was given the impression that Saunière considered himself to be in an untouch-
able position, that he saw his role as too important. Others thought that he had
not executed the instructions he was given as he was meant to and that he was
extravagant and took liberties with the money he received.

After Saunière's death his housekeeper Marie is said have told people in the
town, 'He has died. It is finished'. His body was placed in a chair on display
outside his church. His body sat there for three days wrapped in a shawl covered
in tassels. The people of Rennes-le-Château and others who knew him queued
to view the corpse and each removed a tassel from his cloak. This is an unusual
practice, especially for a Catholic priest. True, the display of the corpse happens
to popes when they die, and viewing the deceased is common in Catholic
countries. But the issue of removing tassels seems a unique and slightly bizarre
way to pay respect to one's priest. I mentioned this trivial issue to Nic and got
the following response:

> 'Given that the ancestors of King Merovius came, it is maintained,
> from the Middle East via Greece, we should not be surprised at
> an interesting coincidence which I now relate. The chronicles
> maintain that when a Merovingian king died, before being buried
> along with his scrying crystal, etc., he lay in state and his subjects,
> in paying their respects, filed past and pulled off a tassel from his
> burial robe. This tradition, it is said, harks back to the cutting of
> a lion's tail when it had been successfully fought and killed. A
> trophy, if you will permit.'

It seemed a small, almost insignificant piece of the jigsaw but it indicated a lot
about Sion's knowledge in these matters. Sion also clearly states that the driving
force in the redesign of the church of Mary Magdalene at Rennes-le-Château
was not Saunière himself but his mentor, Father Henri Boudet.

HENRI BOUDET

According to Nic Haywood, an archbishop once made an interesting comment: 'The Abbé Boudet is in possession of a very old and very powerful secret.' On arriving at Rennes-le-Château, Saunière met and befriended the Abbé Henri Boudet, the priest of the neighbouring town of Rennes-les-Bains. Boudet was key to Saunière's learning and is said to have become his mentor and guide. Boudet told Saunière to 'research local history'. From an interview with Nic:

> 'Boudet was a Rosicrucian and a card-carrying member of the Priory of Sion. He was trusted to work on his own accord and was not run by the Priory of Sion. He was in possession of something quintessential to what Sion is about. Bérenger Saunière was not trusted which is why it played itself out the way it did.'

I requested proof of this.

> 'Other than a certificate bearing his name, along with copies of his signature, etc., held in the order's archives, Boudet's allegiance to Sion is mostly evidenced by the private company he kept and the friendships he maintained. Most, if not all, have direct connections with the order [and they include] Doinel, Debussy, Péladan and numerous others. Boudet's predecessor [as priest] likewise had clearly discernible connections. We have made it perfectly clear that a document linking the Abbé Boudet directly with one of the body of Sion might be made available for physical inspection.'

As yet, however, this documentary 'proof' remains on my list of outstanding items. Should it arrive I will publish it on my website.

Sion states that it was through Boudet's tireless enthusiasm and willingness to act in the capacity of private tutor that Saunière learned phonetic Arabic (it was not essential for him to write it), along with increasing his knowledge of English and learning some ancient Hebrew.

The link between Rennes-le-Château and the Priory of Sion during the time of Saunière and Boudet therefore remains unproven. The abbreviation 'A.O.M.P.S.' inscribed on the base of a cross outside the church was claimed by many to stand for *Antiquus Ordo Mysticusque Prioratus Sionis* ('Ancient and Mystical Order of the Priory of Sion'), yet it also exists on an obelisk outside the Vatican where it stands for [*Christus*] *Ab Omni Malo Populum Suum* [*Defendit*] — 'Christ Protects His People From All Evil'.

It is worth noting once again that it was the fashion, certainly during Saunière's time, to be a member of more than one esoteric group. Even today both of my main Priory of Sion contacts are affiliated with other groups such as Freemasonry and Martinism. Many of those listed on the Priory Grand Master list (*see* Chapter 3) will also have been members of numerous other orders and groups.

It seems that over time Boudet became unhappy with the way that Saunière was handling the resources that were coming his way. He tried to reason with him, causing a feud between them. Boudet's own wealth has never been fully explored and certainly little has come to light of Boudet's finances. However, unlike Saunière he appears to have spent his income on more charitable works. According to Gérard Thome, Boudet paid for a number of renovations of other local churches, notably one in Limoux that was fully refurbished in the early 20th century and contains many heretical images among its stained glass windows. Thome gave me a personal tour of the church and brought to my attention the following scenes: Jesus and Mary Magdalene sitting together on thrones; the wedding ceremony of Jesus and Mary Magdalene; Jesus and Mary Magdalene with a child; and the inscription 'Woman, I give you a son'. These are all depicted in stained glass within a Catholic church.

Another church linked to Boudet contains a small porcelain relief showing the Last Supper in the style of Leonardo da Vinci. In this the person to the right of Jesus is female (she clearly has breasts) and is resting her head on his shoulder. I was asked not to reveal the name or location of the church as this would most certainly attract theft or vandalism. Should you happen to find it yourself, please do not publicize its location.

The evidence of the works in these churches is proof that a group of heretical priests were working in the area at that time and such a group may still exist today. As mentioned previously, the heretical Cathars of the medieval Languedoc believed that Mary Magdalene and Jesus were married.

Sion also maintains that Boudet was an alchemist:

> 'Henri Boudet was undoubtedly a true adept of the alchemical
> art, whatever else may be said of him. He did possess the
> [Philosopher's] Stone, having discovered it for himself.'

My source went on to stress that alchemy 'is at the heart of the entire secret' of Rennes-le-Château. A number of researchers have focussed on a book written by Boudet and published in 1889 that appears to the casual eye to be a work of outright folly. *The Language of the Celts and the Stone Circle of Rennes-les-Bains* is a weighty study of language that makes little sense on the surface. Boudet's book appears to be a study of the roots of the Celtic language, and maintains that the names of places are derived from modern English. By word association and puns Boudet derived 'hidden' words from seemingly innocuous terms. The book looked preposterous to those who encountered it and was unsuccessful. It remains a dense and difficult work even for those versed in the local dialect. I think Boudet understood only too well that his theory was a nonsense but used the book to pass on ideas in code, which was practised in Masonic publications of the time.

The second part of the book talks about cromlechs, or prehistoric stone circles, and covers the natural standing stones, mostly caused by erosion of limestone on granite, that litter the region. Boudet goes so far as to provide a map. He also refers to a circle of churches in the area, which will be covered in the later chapter on landscape (*see* Chapter 7).

Many researchers have devoted years to decoding the wordplay in Boudet's work. They employ numeric and linguistic codes, bouncing them back and forth through the book, but I have yet to see any real sense made of it. It is possible that he used what is termed the 'Phonetic Kabbalah', or 'green language', which appears in the works of Fulcanelli and other alchemical authors. This is a method of writing that groups words together that sound phonetically like other words when spoken aloud.

It is possible that the book's apparent failure to enthuse either historians or the wider public inspired Boudet to choose a more direct means to communicate his message. According to Sion, he oversaw the redecoration of Saunière's church at Rennes-le-Château and employed the same 'Phonetic Kabbalah' in the Stations of the Cross. We will explore this in detail in the following chapter.

Marie Denarnaud

Saunière's housekeeper, Marie Denarnaud, may have had a more important role to play than previously thought. Sion has stated directly to me that it is a fact that Marie was provided as housekeeper, and in due course banker, by Henri Boudet. He was most adamant, and her position as such appears to have been crucial to the entire sequence of events.

Marie Denarnaud's importance has always been underplayed by previous writers and commentators, as has the Denarnaud family's status, which seems to have continued a tradition whereby the family were looked after: not in a lavish manner, but certainly their comfort was assured. This seems to have stretched back to times well before Boudet's immediate predecessors. With this in mind it would seem likely that she was placed in a position of influence over Saunière in order to monitor his progress on behalf of Boudet and Sion.

CONCLUSION

It appears that three priests – Saunière, Boudet and Gélis – all benefited from the wealth that was being generated or recovered in the region. Abbé Boudet, according to researcher Gérard Thome, gave much to the poor and funded the renovations of other churches, and there is evidence of this in the nearby town of Limoux. He was a humble man and discreet with his resources. Abbé Gélis increasingly became a recluse and privately invested his money – some Fr. 20,000 according to Gérard de Sède. Abbé Saunière was the youngest and most extravagant of the three. He spent his wealth on high living, fine food and wine, entertaining, and the garish refurbishment of his church and property. This is why Saunière garners the most attention in the mystery of Rennes-le-Château and it may also have been the cause of his demise.

The local bishop, Félix-Arsène Billard, was also implicated. He lived a poor life but is said to have left millions in his will.

Researcher Nicole Dawe related the following:

> 'Marie Denarnaud did apparently say things like "there is enough gold for the whole village to live on for 100 years", and "the villagers are walking on gold". She did make it sound as though it was a hoard of treasure. There was also the incident where she was seen burning wads of notes in the garden of the Villa Bethany after a currency change, when money exchanged had to have its provenance justified.'

So far the threads of the mystery revolve around where Saunière got his money from, what he discovered, with a few unexplained deaths thrown in for good measure. This is the foundation for the mystery; a simple enough issue that would have quietly gone the way of speculation were it not for how Saunière spent his money.

It is also clear that the Priory of Sion brings an entirely new level of meaning to the mystery of Rennes-le-Château. It may have seized upon the existing mystery and used it to promulgate its own agenda and like some other authors you can, if you wish, attempt to separate the two and review the 'French mystery' only as it relates to Saunière. But Sion's agenda gives a far broader context to the mystery, and one that makes it relevant today.

One thing is clear: the area of Rennes-le-Château contains more than one mystery and the Priory of Sion pertains to more than one secret. The church at Rennes-le-Château extends the mystery in many directions and, unlike some of Saunière's other actions, every inch of it remains intact and available for inspection.

CHAPTER 6

THE CHURCH OF MARY MAGDALENE

As to the nature of the 'treasures' at, and in the environs of, Rennes-le-Château, they are fivefold.

The Priory of Sion.

SACRED SPACE

A church is a temple, a holy place. The idea of a space set aside for sacred purposes spans history and cultures, as across the world and through all ages people have raised monuments to their gods. Whether in caves or cathedrals, congregations have gathered to learn rituals and chants and to hear laws and teachings passed down through priests – special individuals who serve as intermediaries between the human and divine realms. Regardless of their complexity of structure, all places of worship adhere to the same basic usage. Often the strongest building in a community, they would be the sanctuary, a safe place from attackers, the elements or evil spirits. The church or temple would often be placed on the highest point in a community, closer to the perceived divine abode. Even now, in spite of all that space exploration and astronomy has discovered, it is difficult for some to shake the childhood image of heaven as a place beyond the clouds.

Reaching up to the sky like a path to heaven, mountains too became sacred, and traditionally gods have often resided on the summit of a sacred peak. There is a well known example of this in the biblical Book of Exodus, when Moses climbs Mount Horeb to converse with Yahweh and receive the Ten Commandments.

Owing to its hilltop location the church at Rennes-le-Château fulfils the role of a holy place built on the peak of a mountain. It is a modest structure that from the outside looks ramshackle and slightly dilapidated. However, on entering the church we are greeted with a wonderland in miniature, a trove that draws visitors from far and wide to marvel at the wealth of symbolism on offer.

When Father Bérenger Saunière refurbished the church (see Chapter 5) he did so in an absurdly ostentatious manner for such a small parish. Not one inch of the entire structure is without decoration and it is not just the garishness that catches the eye. Saunière's choice of décor raises many questions and for me is one of the most important aspects of the Rennes-le-Château mystery.

Perhaps the church is meant to overwhelm the senses, to drive out all distractions and flood the mind in imagery. It might be an attempt to be truly awe-inspiring, to 'blow the mind' into an empty space for prayer and contemplation of God.

When I began to investigate the mystery of Rennes-le-Château I was convinced there was no single underlying answer to all aspects of the enigma. The multitude of threads would not be woven into some great tapestry but must be separated out and researched in isolation. A risk for researchers at this stage is to attempt to fit all the pieces into a single theory by either ignoring anomalies or desperately hammering square pegs into round holes. So rather than imposing an absolute view, what follows are a list and explanation of some of the elements of the church that appear to be incongruous with Catholic symbolism. Let us begin with an overview and brief history of the church itself.

THE CHURCH OF MARY MAGDALENE

Many who come to study this little temple are amazed by the wealth of apparently unorthodox symbols that furnish the church. Many of the objects on display have more than one meaning, and more than one influence on their design. If we can split these strands into separate theories then we may stand a chance of seeing clearly the messages left to us by Saunière. First and foremost Saunière and his colleague in the neighbouring parish, Henri Boudet, were Roman Catholic priests and therefore it would be wise to consider the Christian use of the symbolism in the church before leaping to more outlandish conclusions.

Much of what we see can be recognized from other churches, and some may be surprised to learn that the pentagram and the 'Star of David' are not entirely uncommon in Christian churches. Sometimes a church will have features that may seem to a greater or lesser degree at odds with the Christian surroundings:

examples are the 'pagan' symbols of Rosslyn chapel, the zodiac of Santiago de Compostela, and the labyrinth of Chartres. Even with this in mind the church at Rennes-le-Château stands out simply because there is so much incongruous décor that it is at risk of overwhelming the Christian message entirely.

History

The church of St Mary Magdalene (Sainte Marie-Madeleine) was consecrated in 1059 and the apse dates from the ninth century, but it was not the first church to stand on the hilltop. There are a few remaining stones from an earlier church of St Peter in the wall of an old garage nearby. Part of a crypt of this earlier church is still rumoured to exist, but the current owners of the plot on which it is said to sit deny this, and a concrete floor currently prevents any further investigation.

The church is basically Romanesque in design and the date 1646 is inscribed on the porch which might indicate a previous restoration. The altar until the time of Saunière was said to be Carolingian, dating from the eighth–ninth centuries.

Today the church is desperately in need of renovation. There are many cracks in the walls and plasterwork, damp has seeped into the painted stars on the ceiling and to the right of the main door a crack runs up the wall, caused by a previous neighbour attempting to dynamite his way into the crypt. Flagstones are broken and loose, and the head of one of the statues was replaced in recent years after some unknown vandal removed the original. With the church being the focus of so much speculation, so many stories of treasure and secrets, such physical damage is unfortunately inevitable.

In 1994 the Vatican received permission for a team of archaeologists under Dr Eisenmann to do a ground scan of the church. The group arrived with ground radar equipment and locked themselves in the church for a number of days and also spent time in the graveyard. They left refusing to discuss anything that they may have found.

The fact that the Church are still looking, long after Saunière's death, means either that they have lost something or that they believe something to be hidden there. A Catholic priest once told me that I should be careful about what I say about the Catholic Church while in the area of Rennes-le-Château because they have people working there and consider the work important.

Inside the church

Nic Haywood stressed the church's significance:

> 'It is an initiate's church, not for the profane; there are many
> anomalies. [For example,] the Latin inscription ["By this sign you
> will conquer"] and water stoup – there are messages hidden in
> there. It has a Masonic resonance.'

The contents of the church and the surrounding buildings are the only solid
evidence we have of anything unusual having occurred at the time of Saunière.
The politics, secret societies and mythology of this area are difficult to substantiate but the church is real, and open to viewing by all.

It was made clear to us by Sion that much of the church was neighbouring
priest Henri Boudet's design, but to avoid confusion I will refer to it as Saunière's
church as it was in his parish and domain.

'Terrible is this place'

As we approach the church the first item that catches our eye is the Latin inscription above the door: *Terribilis est locus iste* ('Terrible is this place'). Although
somewhat alarming at first sight – and the source of many wild theories – this
is simply a quote from the Bible (Genesis 28.17). When Jacob lies down to sleep
he witnesses a vision of angels ascending and descending a ladder.

> 'How dreadful is this place! This is none other but the house of
> God, and this is the gate of heaven.'

In this context the words *terribilis* and 'dreadful' mean 'awesome', 'terrifying' or
'inspiring dread' rather than 'terrible and 'dreadful' in their modern negative
senses. Whether or not Saunière imputed another meaning to this phrase, it is
used in the standard service for the dedication of any Catholic church, however
modest in size, and is also quite a common Catholic inscription.

We shall return to the visionary aspect of this biblical quotation, but for now
it is interesting to note that the passage about angels ascending and descending
a ladder also has a Kabbalistic echo as the Tree of Life is sometimes described
as 'the ladder of lights'. This is revealed to Jacob once he has placed a stone
beneath his head as a pillow. Afterward he sets this stone up as a pillar, anoints
it with oil, and names the spot Bethel – House of God. The perfect stone is a
possible Masonic connotation. The first Masonic tracing board has a ladder that
represents Jacob's Ladder and the way back to God.

The ladder also features heavily in the ritual of the 18th (Rose+Croix) Degree, where the candidate is instructed to ascend a ladder that is adorned with a rose. This is the Rose of Sharon, a symbol of love (Song of Solomon 2.1) and also, according to some Masonic researchers, of Jesus. There is ambiguity in this as the candidate might also be ascending the ladder in order to re-enact the crucifixion. I think that the main issue of contention with such interpretations for the Catholic Church is that the ladder symbolizes humankind's ability to ascend to an experience of the divine directly.

Water stoup

On entering the church we are greeted by the gaze of a demon, the star of many photos on websites, books and articles about Rennes-le-Château.

The statue itself supports the water stoup and is part of a larger sculpture representing the elements. The demon is the earth, shouldering a small font in the shape of a scallop shell. This holds [holy] water for those entering the church to dip into and bless themselves with the sign of the cross. Above the shell are two salamanders, symbols of fire, forming part of a plinth that carries the French inscription *Par ce signe tu le vaincras* ('By this sign you will conquer [him or it]'). Four angels stand above the inscription, each making part of the gesture of blessing oneself with the sign of the cross. The angels represent air.

The demon

The statue of the demon is most likely to represent Asmodeus, a character from the *Book of Tobit* in the Catholic Old Testament; the Talmud; and various apocryphal works. He is identified as such in the Priory of Sion publication *Le Serpent Rouge*, which is covered later.

Prof J R Porter's *The Lost Bible* contains many scriptures that were excluded from the final Bible. One of these is the *Testament of Solomon*, a Christian work of the early centuries CE, which tells how Solomon 'harnesses a succession of demons to help build the Temple'. Porter writes (p.76):

> 'In the Bible, Solomon's wisdom is said to consist primarily of knowledge about natural phenomena, plants and animals (1 Kings 4.29–34). Extrapolating from this passage, the rabbis credited Solomon with a vast store of astrological, magical, medical, and especially demonological lore, which enabled him to compel evil spirits to work on the Temple.'

The demon is a grotesque statue, with mouth open and eyes bulging and was probably based on Bernini's *The Damned Soul* sculpture in Rome, which is fitting. His posture is crouched, with one hand pointing toward a section of floor and the other gripping what must have been a staff or pole, long since removed.

Note that the posture of Asmodeus is a mirror image of the statue of Jesus being baptized, on the other side of the church. In this context the scene is entirely reminiscent of the medieval Kabbalistic dualistic pairing of good and evil couples. It is a theme that links Kabbalah to the Gnostic dualist faith of the Cathars (*see The Other God* by Yuri Stoyanov).

Asmodeus is the *Deus Invertus*, the inversion or reflection of God, and this is why he can be seen mirroring the statue of Jesus in every way. This mirroring appears throughout Saunière's domain and we will return to it as a theme later.

Also of note is that according to local researcher Gérard Thome, Asmodeus is said to follow the Ark of the Covenant wherever it travels. Briefly, the legend of Solomon and Asmodeus is as follows:

Solomon intended to build his Temple but was instructed by God that he must neither use tools nor make any sound. In order to find a silent cutting tool he sent for Asmodeus, the 'king of the demons' who, as a magical creature, could work without making a sound. Asmodeus lived high on a mountain, where he had dug a deep pit to use as a water cistern. Solomon's servant drained the water and filled the cistern with wine. When Asmodeus became drunk, the servant captured him and led him back to Solomon.

On the journey back, Asmodeus jeered at a magician. When asked why, the demon said it was 'because at that very moment the magician was sitting upon a vast treasure hidden in the soil underneath him, and yet he knew not, although he pretended he could foretell the future and unravel mysteries.'

Later Asmodeus was summoned again, this time using Solomon's ring, the seal of which is described as five interlaced A's (this forms a pentagram, not the hexagram of the traditional 'Seal of Solomon'). He told Solomon that he was the offspring of a marriage between an angel and man: 'I am of celestial origin. Is my star not bright in heaven, the star which some men call the dragon's child? The archangel capable of frustrating my designs is Raphael.' Asmodeus asked not to be made to work with or in water, so Solomon made him carry water in order to frustrate his designs on humankind.

It may seem strange that Solomon chose to summon a demon and not an angel to do his work but in Christian theology angels serve only God and no mortal has power over them. Solomon was able to compel demons to work for him, thereby showing his power to subdue evil.

It is also possible to understand this relationship in terms of psychology. There are methods for identifying, accepting and working with our own inner demons in order to bring them under our control and ultimately transform them and integrate them back into our self.

Perhaps Solomon subjugated his own, lower unconscious aspects, symbolized by the demon, with the water of his emotions. This frees his inner fire (symbolized by the salamanders) to rise up as creativity to higher states of consciousness (symbolized by the angels).

As the details of the story of Solomon and Asmodeus exist not in the Bible but Judaic folklore it would seem strange that a Catholic priest would employ it at all.

The truth is that the significance of Asmodeus is neither Jewish nor Christian in this context. Asmodeus as the builder of Solomon's Temple is central to Freemasonry and their Templar predecessors. As all Masonic temples are fashioned on Solomon's blueprint it makes Asmodeus especially important to the Freemasons. The presence of Asmodeus adds weight to idea that either Father Saunière or Boudet was influenced by quasi-Masonic groups.

One of the Jewish traditions surrounding Asmodeus is that he was a keeper of treasure and beside his statue a fresco of the Sermon on the Mount includes a prominent bag of gold spilling out from a depiction of the local landscape. Sadly, this alone has been responsible for attracting a fair number of treasure hunters to the region.

Scallop shell

Shells were used as a motif of pilgrims who had visited the Holy Land, where shells were said to have been in abundance on the shores and could be used to drink and eat from (see Whone, *Church, Monastery, Cathedral*). The words 'shell' and 'skull' are thought to be related and both were also used as drinking vessels. Later, the scallop shell represented the pilgrimage to the shrine of St James at Compostela in northeastern Spain. Rennes-le-Château is close to a major pilgrim route to Santiago so the most likely reference is to St James. However, there is also a scallop shell in Saint-Sulpice, Paris, that serves as the baptismal font, so it is a common enough design.

Salamanders

The link between alchemy and salamanders is well known and often this interpretation is given. Salamanders are small lizard like creatures considered to represent fire because of their legendary natural ability to withstand it. Even in classical Christian symbolism they are seen as representing 'enduring faith and the righteous man who cannot be consumed by the fires of temptation' (*Symbolism* by J C Cooper).

'By this sign you will conquer'

The French inscription *Par ce signe tu le vaincras* above the water stoup is relevant in two ways. Firstly, there is a rare Rosicrucian alchemical manuscript called the *Codex Rosae-Crucis* (*Book of the Rosy Cross*) that includes a collection of alchemical engravings. The final plate, and culmination of the alchemical workings, includes a Kabbalistic Tree of Life, at the foot of which is a circle cut into the four elements, earth, air, fire and water, overwritten with the inscription 'By this sign you will conquer'. This is the first of many references to the Rosicrucians in the church.

Second, the inscription has exactly 22 letters, a number that we find repeated throughout the Rennes-le-Château mystery. The Kabbalistic Tree of Life has 22 paths that correspond to the 22 letters of the Hebrew alphabet. The Tree is represented in the Bible by Jacob's ladder. There may also be a clue here as to how to read the Stations of the Cross (*see* page 94).

Associated with the Kabbalah and alchemy are tools to reinterpret language. This may be by the numeric values attributed to letters (numerology) or through puns using the 'green language'. Both methods are thought to have been employed by the Abbé Boudet in his book *La Vrai Langue Celtique* (*see* above, page 82).

The second, and more usual, interpretation of 'By this sign you will conquer' comes from the legend of Emperor Constantine I's vision before the battle of Milvian Bridge on October 28, 312CE. It is said that the night before the battle, the emperor saw an image of the cross and Christ appeared and spoke to him and said: 'By this sign you will conquer'. Constantine adopted the cross for his monogram and had the shields of his army painted with it. He won the battle and this event is said to have helped persuade him to legalize Christianity in 313. Constantine himself is said to have converted fully only on his deathbed.

Saunière also had his initials, BS, carved between the salamanders, though some interpret the letters to indicate the place where two local rivers, the Blanc and the Sals, meet at a spot known as Le Bénitier ('Holy Water Stoup') just north of Rennes-les-Bains.

Four angels

The four angels make the sign of the cross but the anomaly here is that the tallest angel is not touching his forehead but shielding his eyes, as if looking into the distance in the direction of Rennes-les-Bains. Strangely, there is a hole in the top of his head that seems to serve no known purpose. It would be impractical as a candleholder and unlikely for affixing some form of headwear or halo as he has the only hole. I suspect that at some point in recent history the hole was made to check if Saunière had hidden anything .

Chessboard floor

Moving on into the nave, the full impact of the church becomes apparent. Here we are surrounded by murals, carvings, paintings, statues and stained glass, all in the space of a small parish church. It would be interesting to think that the priest had intended to overwhelm the senses of the visitor, rendering them open to the grace of God, but unfortunately I suspect that he simply got carried away with tasteless interior decorating and did not know when to stop.

Originally the area of chessboard floor created by Saunière in the nave was like a true chessboard, a perfect square of only 64 black and white tiles, giving the game away as to the use of the church. However, in more recent times the entire floor has been tiled, masking the original chessboard square. The chessboard floor of light and dark squares is a requirement of all Masonic lodges, and can take the form of carpet if it is a temporary lodge. In Saunière's church the chessboard is laid in tiles in the floor and is placed so as to be 'contemplated' by the statues of both Jesus and the demon Asmodeus. It is instantly recognizable and proof that the church is a Masonic/Rosicrucian temple in its décor. Bernard Giscard, a local architect and sculptor of the renovations, was a known Freemason but could not have created a working lodge without the agreement of the priest, Father Saunière.

The chessboard also appears in one of the decoding methods of the de Sède parchments that were published in the 1960s (*see* page 289). This involves a knight's tour where a single knight follows moves around a chessboard by landing on every square only once. Letters can be added to the board in the order they are discovered in the text and as the knight follows the tour he spells out a secret message.

Symbolically, the black and white squares of a chessboard represent duality in all its forms. In his book on Chartres cathedral, the author Louis Charpentier makes a very subtle link between the chessboard, the Chartres labyrinth and alchemy by using the knight to 'square the circle'.

THE STATIONS OF THE CROSS

Many churches contain interpretations of the Stations of the Cross. These are the fourteen key events that mark the Via Dolorosa or Way of Sorrows, the route taken by Christ from the site of his judgment to his crucifixion at Calvary (Golgotha). The reputed locations of the Stations were sites of pilgrimage in Jerusalem, and the Franciscans installed representations of them in European churches to allow congregations to follow the Via Dolorosa in spirit. A number of Catholic churches still hold Easter services where parishioners are taken from Station to Station in remembrance. In many churches you will find the Stations marked by simple Roman numerals but occasionally they are a little more elaborate, either paintings or, as at Rennes-le-Château, sculptured reliefs. There are in fact two versions of the Stations of the Cross but the following is the more popular and can be found at Rennes-le-Château:

1. Jesus is condemned to death by Pilate.
2. He is forced to carry his own cross.
3. He falls for the first time.
4. He meets his mother.
5. Simon of Cyrene helps Jesus carry the cross.
6. St Veronica wipes his face.
7. He falls for a second time.
8. He speaks to the daughters of Jerusalem.
9. He falls for the third time.
10. He is stripped of his cloak.
11. He is nailed to the cross.
12. He gives up the ghost.
13. He is taken down from the cross.
14. He is placed in the tomb.

The Stations here are quite large and ornate, with each one surmounted by a cross with a rose at the centre. As already mentioned, the rose-cross symbols are indicative of the Rosicrucians and of the higher Rosicrucian degrees of Freemasonry.

The actual framed carvings depicting Christ's journey are of a standard design for the region and like much of the church they were created by Bernard Giscard. The originals were supplied unpainted and examples of these exist in the church of the nearby town of Couiza. From this we know that any modification made by Saunière or Boudet lies in the painting of these carvings. According to Sion, 'much may be had from Boudet's Stations of the Cross if one is adept in Phonetic Kabbalah.'

Phonetic Kabbalah, known in alchemy as the 'green language' (*la langue verte*), was explained by the alchemist Fulcanelli as a way of inscribing symbolic puns into buildings, and a language peculiar to individuals who wish to communicate their ideas without being understood by outsiders. These word games sometimes appear in Freemasonry as well but are mostly linked to the Rosicrucian and alchemical tradition. The term 'Rosicrucian' is itself part of this tradition since the name of the mythical founder of the tradition was one Christian 'Rosenkreuz', a symbolic surname simply meaning 'rose cross' in German.

Such images allow the viewer to re-interpret what they see by breaking the words up to form different words or to render a phrase that sounds alike yet contains a different or deeper meaning. Without knowing how to interpret the symbols, researchers can get lost in a maze of verbal simulacra.

True Phonetic Kabbalah is said to work in most languages but is best rendered in French, Arabic and Hebrew. My French does not stretch as far as Boudet's Occitan word games, but I do have some thoughts on the Stations of the Cross. To begin with, the Stations of the Cross at Rennes-le-Château also illustrate a ritual of initiation. This initiation is the same one as the route that *Le Serpent Rouge* takes through the surrounding landscape, which is covered later. The lesser reflects the greater in true Hermetic fashion. It is alchemical in nature and in some ways resembles the Rose+Croix 18th Degree of the Ancient and Accepted Scottish Rite of Freemasonry. I will cover here the outstanding points of interest but bear in mind that these interpretations are a work in progress.

Station 1: He is condemned to death by Pilate.

Pilate has red hair and is waited on by a black boy. This feature is also present in Chartres cathedral, where a black boy at the feet of the Queen of Sheba is thought to indicate that she was from Ethiopia and has been linked to the Ark of the Covenant (*see* Hancock, *Sign and the Seal*). There is also a gold gryphon, a mixture of eagle and lion. The eagle symbolizes vigilance and the lion courage, and during the Middle Ages the gryphon was considered a symbol of good and evil. That it is rendered in gold next to the black boy might indicate the *nigredo*, the 'blackening' stage of alchemy often shown as an 'Ethiopian' boy. There is also perhaps a reference to the local noble family of de *Negri* d'Ables, residents of the Château Blanchefort. Their name is also written 'Nègre', which is identical to the French for 'negro'.

The black boy carries a "white plate" of water with which Pilate washes his hands. This is a likely allusion to Le Plateau Blanc between Rennes-le-Château and Blanchefort. Pilate is also wearing a veil.

Station 2: Jesus is forced to carry his own cross.
A boy in the foreground picks up a stick as if taking up the baton. This appears in other renditions in the region so it is not unique to this church.

Station 4. Jesus meets his mother.
In the nearby town of Couiza lives the artist Alain Féral, a former student of Jean Cocteau. Féral once painstakingly produced a scale model of the church and also illustrated a beautiful plan of the layout, copies of which are on sale at the little bookshop in the town. Féral makes much of this particular Station. He points out that it is the only one with a black shape beneath the picture. This, he tells us, is also a reference to the de Negri d'Ables family. They are important to the mystery as they would have been the source of the documents that Saunière is said to have found. As mentioned earlier, they claimed that their land contained a goldmine but rumours abounded that they were mining not gold but an ancient hoard of treasure (*see* page 68). As I have indicated, the name 'de Nègre' can mean 'of [the] Negro' and is traditionally said to derive from the family's intermarriage with non-Europeans. Possible interpretations of the root of this name will be covered in the bloodline chapter (*see* Chapter 15).

Also linked to this is the theory that a cousin of Marie de Negri d'Ables of Blanchefort, Jacques-Etienne Marconis de Nègre (1795–1865), who lived at Rennes-le-Château, created the Rite of Memphis, a precursor to the Ancient and Accepted Scottish Rite that later merged with the Rose+Cross degrees.

Station 7: Jesus falls for a second time.
As Jesus stumbles again, St Simon of Cyrene once more takes up the Cross in order to assist him. According to Sion,

'References to St Simon, as portrayed in the Stations of the Cross, (see Station 7) are to Henri de Saint-Simon (1760–1825), a brother of the order.'

Henri de Saint-Simon was very influential on both socialism and sociology and formed a semi-mystical order of scientific priests, which he intended to replace the clergy in the industrial age. He is said to have attempted suicide, but Sion denies this, claiming his injuries were 'an act of retribution' by those who opposed his work.

Phonetic games can be played with this as with all Stations of the Cross. For example, there is a soldier holding up a large shield with around its edge an arrow design pointing anticlockwise and running halfway round it. This shield obscures one half of a tower in the distance. In French, this can be understood as *haut bouclier et demie tour* ('raised shield and half a tower'). However, in Phonetic Kabbalah (*see* page 95) this can be understood as the phonetically identical *au bout clier et demi-tour* ('at the bottom [of the] enclosure and a half-turn [ie anti-clockwise, to the left]').

St Simon seems to be looking out into the distance to one side of the station and St Veronica crouches holding the cloth. Not only are they rendered in an irregular fashion, but they are also overemphatic gestures and/or symbols. In Phonetic Kabbalah one could read *Simon regarde* ('Simon looks') as *cime on regarde* ('[the] summit one looks at') and *Veronica au lin* ('Veronica with the cloth') *ver en nid kaolin* ('worm in [the] nest [of] kaolin'). 'Worm' here could be understood in the sense of serpent. If one goes to the bottom of the churchyard (the 'enclosure') and makes a half turn, the crest one sees is the 'Eagle's Nest' (*Nid d'Aigle*) a local term for Pech Cardou, which is formed, in part, from kaolin clay.

Station 8: Jesus speaks to the daughters of Jerusalem.

A child accompanying Jesus is dressed in a tartan sash. Due to the overriding Masonic nature of the church's décor, this is likely to be a reference to the Ancient and Accepted Scottish Rite of Freemasonry. The Masonic notion of 'protecting the widow's son' comes to mind, and some interpret this as a reference to the child of Mary Magdalene and Jesus.

Station 10: Jesus is stripped of his cloak.

The Roman soldiers strip Jesus of his cloak and play dice to determine who should take the spoils. The dice are displayed with three and four on adjacent sides and a five on a separate die. In fact three and four are *never* on *adjacent* sides of a die, whose opposite sides always add up to seven. The same device appears in both *Le Serpent Rouge* and in a mural painted by Jean Cocteau in London, both of which are covered later. The numbers 3/4/5 are also Pythagorean. The ancient Greek mathematician Pythagoras discovered that in a right angle triangle, the square of the hypotenuse (long side) equals the sum of the squares of the two shorter sides. Hence $3^2 + 4^2 = 5^2$ (9+16=25).

Station 14. Jesus is placed in the tomb.

The image for the final Station traditionally shows Jesus being taken to the tomb, but the Station in this church is unusual in that this scene takes place at night. Some authors, such as Michael Baigent in his excellent *The Jesus Papers*, claim that this is evidence that Jesus survived the Crucifixion. Baigent asserts that because the scene takes place at night Jesus is not being taken *to* the tomb (since Jewish law required burial before sunset, the start of the Sabbath) but is being smuggled away *from* it under cover of darkness. However, this theory ignores the previous two Stations, which clearly show the sky darkening and the sun setting, as described in the gospels, which state that it was supernaturally dark when Jesus died (Station 12): 'There was darkness over the whole land until the ninth hour, while the sun's light failed.' (Luke 23.44; compare Matt. 27.45, Mark 15.33). The night aspect of Station 14 is a natural extension of these scenes.

It was also claimed that as it was against Jewish law to touch a dead body on the Sabbath (after sunset on a Friday, the day Jesus died) and during Passover, Jesus must have been alive when being carried. While this is true it ignores the fact that Saunière was a Catholic priest and had no reason to take Jewish laws into account when having the Station painted; indeed he may simply have been ignorant of them. The scene may still depict the living Jesus being smuggled out of the tomb, but the evidence is not conclusive.

STATUES

As well as Asmodeus and the angels, the church has a collection of works depicted in wood and plaster. This is not unusual though why these particular saints were chosen is unclear: clues may be found in their acts and lives but it is possible that the statues were selected simply for their names alone: Germaine, Roch, Anthony, Anthony of Padua and Luke. St Germaine and St Roch are covered individually below. The statues are laid out in such a way that the five saints' initials spell out the word *Graal*, the French for Grail, in the form of a letter M.

The statue of Mary Magdalene is positioned at the centre of this design, at the top of the M, so this reference could not have been accidental. The idea of Mary *as* the Holy Grail might have more to do with an archetype of the 'divine feminine' than with the bloodline, but even so, it would be no less important.

St Germaine de Pibrac

This local saint was a shepherdess born on a farm near Toulouse. Her grave at Pibrac has been a site of pilgrimage and host to a number of recorded miracles. Her feast is celebrated on January 17 – the date of the defaced de Negri d'Ables tombstone (*see* page 74)

St Roch

A local saint, native of Montpellier in the Languedoc, St Roch was thought to have healed the sick through supernatural means. Accounts of his life claim that he was on a pilgrimage to Rome when struck by illness and had to return to France, where he was accused of being an impostor and died in prison.

St Roch was a favourite of Bernard Giscard, the supplier of these statues. He appears in many of the local churches, including Limoux (with its Black Madonna), Rennes-les-Bains and Couiza. St Roch is the patron saint of lost items, especially treasure, and Saunière may have installed the effigy for this reason. St Roch is also depicted lifting his robe to reveal his right knee, a known reference to Masonic ritual.

St Mary Magdalene

St Mary Magdalene's statue here is accompanied by a book and skull. The book is open and has a pattern on the pages but no writing. Skulls feature in Masonic rituals and are used in conjunction with a book in the Chamber of Reflection but they may also indicate the presence of a corpse. Mary is covered at length in a later chapter.

The Holy Family

Both St Joseph and the Virgin Mary are holding children, each having different coloured hair. This possibly indicates that Christ had a brother, perhaps even a twin – a notion accepted by some schools of esoteric thought. The other child could also represent a brother of Jesus, who is described in the Bible as having brothers and sisters including James, Mark, Judas and Simon. Roman Catholicism traditionally explains these siblings as being children from a supposed previous marriage of Joseph, allowing Mary's virginity to remain intact.

Sermon on the Mount mural

The church has a large mural depicting the Sermon on the Mount, the classic depiction of Jesus preaching during his ministry. The main feature of this work is the detailed landscape surrounding his figure. To the left we can clearly see features local to Rennes-le-Château, such as the nearby town of Coustaussa where the priest, Father Gélis, was murdered (*see* page 75), and local flowers, notably the one known as Seal of Solomon (*Polygonatum*). There is a bag of gold in full view on the hillside, hinting at treasure as the simple answer to the mystery of Saunière's wealth. But if it *is* treasure, where did it come from: ancient Israel, the Celts, Romans, Visigoths, Templars or Cathars?

There is also a tract of land covered in roses.

> 'If one considers the image carefully, one can clearly see a pointed mount to the left of the composition. This steep mount is covered with roses. Likewise, if one looks down the valley, with Coustaussa to the right, one clearly observes this geological outcrop which, on paper, is a separate tract of the Fleury lands.'

Sion's mention of the Fleury lands highlights that areas of land in the area can be traced to old families who in turn can be traced back to the Templars.

Also visible in this mural is an image of the top of the pillar in which parchments were said to have been found (*see* page 72). This has pomegranate leaves growing from it, symbolic of immortality and resurrection. A bush on the right of the painting contains a hidden spyhole that links through to a bedroom in the church presbytery. It is not known what purpose it served though it might simply have allowed Saunière to keep an eye on his replacement when he was suspended from duty.

THE ALTAR

This is the only item in the church that is strongly considered to be by Saunière's own hand. It depicts Mary Magdalene kneeling in a cave beside a cross made from two branches. One of the branches has sprouted two live shoots and this is sometimes interpreted to signify the descendants of Jesus and Mary Magdalene.

The cave, with its hill formation in the background, bears a resemblance to a cave opposite Rennes-le-Château known as the Magdalene Grotto. There is a view from the road looking east as you approach Rennes-le-Château from Couiza that is a good fit for this image. On the left is the ruin of Coustaussa, and the peak opposite is Pech Cardou, beyond Blanchefort. This matches both the Sermon on the Mount depiction of Coustaussa and the statue of the standing angel looking east. A photograph of both the altar and the comparative view are included in the plates section.

The figure of Mary is seated with her hands in her lap, the fingers interlaced. In the Rose+Croix degree there is an instruction about the 'Sign of Adoration' that begins with the interlacing of the fingers.

This image serves a second function. It explains the Magdalene Grotto as a Masonic room of contemplation. The presence of the skull and the cross could be evidence that this cave was used as such. But in simple terms the local landscape, the grave and the skull may also allude to traditions that either Jesus or Mary may be buried in the vicinity.

WINDOWS

The stained glass windows are pretty but of little interest. There are examples of the mission of the apostles Martha and Mary, and Mary Magdalene wiping the feet of Jesus with her hair. However, there is an effect that seems to occur every year – on January 17. It is said that at noon on this day, light through the windows casts blue spheres on the wall. Witnesses gather every year to view this phenomenon and photographs exist to back this up. From one of the parchments released by de Sède in the 1970s we are told that these are 'blue apples'. The phenomenon seems to exist in other churches, including Saint-Sulpice in Paris, though the blue glass has recently been removed from this church so it cannot easily be verified. The windows in the church at Couiza also cast strange forms but I have yet to witness anything more revelatory than a Rorschach test.

THE HIDDEN ROOM

To the right of the altar is the sacristy, a small office with cupboard set into the eastern wall. The cupboard has a false back – amusingly reminiscent of *The Lion, The Witch and The Wardrobe* by C S Lewis – that leads to a hidden secret room, the semicircular shape of which can be determined from the outside of the building.

In Freemasonry, the Rose+Croix degree is prefaced by spending time alone in a 'chamber of reflection' or room of contemplation. These are small rooms adjacent to Masonic lodges where the candidate prepares for ritual by contemplating objects such as the skull and the cross. Secret chambers are not exclusive to Freemasonry but in the context of the church and Saunière's work this was likely to be one of its uses. The chamber has its roots in Judaism, where a small room or part of a room is put aside for prayer, and this fits in with the Masonic 'Temple of Solomon' design for the church. As this room can be used to attain gnosis, direct communion with the divine, it ironically has no place within a Catholic church and possibly reveals Saunière's heretical leanings.

The chamber of reflection often includes a number of alchemical symbols such as triangles representing the elements, plus sulphur, salt and the acronym VITRIOL – *Visita Interiora Terrae, Rectificando Invenies Occultum Lapidem*. This is usually translated as 'Visit the interior of the earth, purifying to discover the hidden stone'. It is advice for the person meditating, though I think *rectificando* meaning 'purifying' or 'rectifying' works better if translated as 'making straight' in terms of psychological distortions. VITRIOL also appears on a number of Sion's publications.

These alchemical elements are covered later in the section on alchemy but for now they indicate the broader origins of this room beyond Freemasonry.

A second feature of the hidden room is that at one point it contained steps leading down to the crypt beneath the altar.

THE CRYPTS

There are two closed chambers beneath the church. At the planning stage of the *Bloodline* documentary, producers Bruce Burgess and René Barnett had reached an agreement with the mayor and the council of Rennes-le-Château to fund some of the much needed rewiring of the church. This would have required excavating the floor in certain places, giving access to the crypts. Unfortunately the government department that oversees all work on national monuments in France vetoed the work. However, there are records of others having had access to the crypts, notably Claire Captier, who remembers accessing the stairs and the vault beneath the church as a child. Researcher Nicole Dawe also tells us that another local priest Abbé Mazières (1909–1988) also claimed to have been inside the tomb, which apparently lay beneath the famous 'Knight's Stone', near the altar.

According to the Priory of Sion two vaults beneath the church contain two important items placed there by Saunière. He had originally found these at the back of the church, and in one of the vaults there is imagery – a carving on a wall or on the floor – indicating something important in the local landscape. Over time Sion made a number of further comments about the objects in the crypt that can be summarized as follows.

> 'The objects may go unnoticed and be stepped over. The two objects belong with the 'body of evidence' but are not body parts and should be reunited with a third item in the museum in Carcassonne. They would also have been used during the Cathar *Consolamentum* ritual.'
> 'Two out of three items deposited around Rennes-le-Château before the siege of Montségur during the Albigensian Crusade, were concealed in two locations. Saunière put those two items for safe keeping beneath the church. The décor, at Boudet's behest, was to leave signposts for others to follow. Part of the tradition is that you leave a sign.'

It was also said that there were bodies at Gisors that were moved to Verdun and then to the Rennes-le-Château tombs. The treasure of Gisors went to the Vatican and included two fonts dating from 1350. The impression given was that these were Templar treasures, but to this day the crypts remain sealed.

THE TOWER, GUEST HOUSE AND GARDENS

From the church interior we move outside to the grounds and gardens of Saunière's personal property. After the visual bombardment of the church it is somewhat relaxing to amble through the rest of Saunière's domain. The approach to the church is flanked by two small gardens.

Calvary

To the right is a small triangular garden with a Calvary and a grotto, that was rebuilt after visitors raided the original for souvenir stones. The orthodox view of the grotto is that it represents the cave where Mary Magdalene spent the final years of her life when, according to local tradition, she came to France. There is also a depiction of the Crucifixion in the centre of this garden with the inscription: A.O.M.P.S. As mentioned previously, this was claimed by Pierre Plantard to mean *Antiquus Ordo Mysticusque Prioratus Sionis* (Ancient and Mystical Order of the Priory of Sion) but a similar inscription exists on an obelisk in Rome that translates as 'May Christ protect his people from all evil'. I tend not to believe Plantard, who I think was struggling to attach Sion's name to the Rennes-le-Château mystery because it served other purposes. However, it is a claim the order upholds to this day.

In the corner opposite the grotto, beside the entrance to the graveyard, is Saunière's small office. Carved into the wood is a reversed N as seen in the paintings of Emile Signol in Saint-Sulpice and said to be a sign of an adept (*see* page 170) but this might be a recent addition. Excavations beneath this office have led to a tunnel system and witnesses who have gained limited access to this area can support this.

Small garden

To the left of the path is another, smaller garden containing a short pillar supporting a statue of Our Lady of Lourdes, the Virgin Mary. The pillar is said to be Visigothic in design and is a copy of the one that supported the altar in the church when Saunière began his restorations (*see* page 71). (The original exists but does not look old enough to date from the Visigothic period so it may also be a copy.) The pillar has a cross carved into it with the Greek letters alpha and omega but it has been inverted so the cross and symbols appear upside down. Into the base is carved the word 'Mission'.

Presbytery

Beside the garden is a gateway to a small courtyard and the presbytery, which currently houses a small museum of Saunière's possessions. There is said to have been a tunnel from the presbytery to the nearby Château Hautpoul, but from the dilapidated condition of the château it would be difficult to know if this was still intact.

Installed in the presbytery was a private altar used by Saunière following his expulsion from the church. Here we find another statue of the kind made by Giscard. The statue, which was never on public display, is of Joan of Arc in full armour and bearing a standard.

The graveyard

You enter the graveyard through an arch surmounted by a skull and crossbones. A simple emblem of death, this was also a symbol of the Templars and is better known for its adoption as a pirate flag. Gérard Thome insists that these indicate that the church contains a way into an underground system of tunnels. There are other tunnels in the area, including one that commenced at a now bricked-up archway in the small town of Serres to the east, which is said to have collapsed when a nearby road was built. The skull and crossbones may have their roots in a Templar symbol that appeared in the Middle Ages.

Within the graveyard itself exists evidence of one of Saunière's most baffling and disturbing actions. In the ossuary lies a broken gravestone, one of two that Saunière removed from the grave of Marie de Negri d'Ables, countess of Blanchefort, and chiselled completely blank to remove the inscription. According to a version in circulation of the original inscription, the letters 'Et in Arcadia Ego' can be discerned among the text, the same inscription that appears on the painting of that name by Nicolas Poussin (also called *The Shepherds of Arcadia*).

I have received an old map of the graveyard via Nic Haywood detailing who is buried where, but I choose not to make this public at this time as it is likely to attract further vandalism and treasure hunters to the location.

VILLA BÉTHANIA

Saunière's guesthouse, the Villa Béthania or Bethany, continues the Mary Magdalene theme. According to one tradition Bethany, near Jerusalem, was her birthplace, and she is identified with 'Mary of Bethany' in John 11. The guesthouse has two stained glass windows above the front door depicting two slightly different sacred hearts.

The garden to the rear of the villa was lovingly restored by Saunière and originally housed a menagerie. It would seem that this was a reference to Noah's Ark and the Royal Ark Mariner degrees of Freemasonry.

The garden is enclosed and has a fountain to the rear of it. In Christian symbolism this is usually said to represent the Virgin Mary, the legend being that only a virgin could tame a unicorn. But in medieval tapestries Mary Magdalene was also depicted in a closed garden with a unicorn. The biblical Song of Solomon, or Song of Songs, attributed to King Solomon, has the verse: 'A garden locked is my sister, my bride, a garden locked, a fountain sealed.' (Song of Solomon 4.12).

TOUR MAGDALA

This little stone tower built by Saunière appears at first to be a folly. Said to have housed his library, the inside is a tiny space, ornately decorated but cramped. The tower is steeped in duality: it is repeated and reflected a number of times in both name and architecture. The angle of one of the windows was said to have been changed on Saunière's instruction. According to Nic Haywood, 'changing the angle of the window meant altering the vision; a shift'. Again, as with the figures of Asmodeus and Jesus (*see* page 90), we find mirroring. Magdala (Migdal), was the town on the shores of Lake Galilee from which Mary Magdalene is named (Luke 8.2). *Migdal* means 'tower' so the building is actually called 'tower tower'. It is also said that the gardens are designed to mirror the layout of the church. The meaning of reflection in this context will be further explored later.

According to information quoted by author Patrice Chaplin in her book *City of Secrets*, the tower is linked to visits that Saunière made to Gerona, where an almost identical tower, also called Torre Magdala, existed until the late 1950s. The version in Gerona is a possible source for both the name and the design of the tower.

ORANGERY

This is a further example of reflection. Curving round the edge of the hilltop like a battlement is a balustrade with the Tour Magdala at one end and at the other another tower designed as a mirror image of it. There is one difference: the second tower is an iron-framed greenhouse that originally housed an orangery. In every other respect, however, it perfectly reflects its stone counterpart. The point exactly midway between the two towers is the fountain in the garden. This is important, as there is a broader alchemical tradition of water reflecting the inverse that pervades other aspects of this mystery.

By tracing Christian symbolism we find that the tower is also symbolic of the Virgin Mary. This pairing of the two Marys is a consistent theme, however you interpret it. It is very reminiscent of Jean Cocteau's work in the French Church in London, where he painted an image of Mary Magdalene and the Virgin Mary facing away from each other but linked by their hair. Together the two figures form a letter M, containing both Marys.

The structures and buildings of note at Rennes-le-Château bear more than a passing similarity to what remains of Old Jericho (*Ar, City of the Moon*), in that, at Old Jericho, there stands a prominent tower, the remains of an ancient church and a house or large villa built to house visitors of importance.

Jericho, it will be recalled, was the site at which the Ark of the Covenant was employed by the Israelites, during the biblical battle.

THE VIEWS

We cannot leave the sites of Rennes-le-Château without admiring the wonderful views that surround the town: the Pyrenees to the south, Pech Bugarach to the southeast and Blanchefort, in the shadow of Pech Cardou, to the east. Looking south from the Tour Magdala, we see the Grotto of Mary Magdalene cut square into the opposite cliff, which rises above the Ruisseau des Couleurs, the 'River of Colours'. Below is a slope leading down to a plateau on which Saunière intended to build another tower. According to Sion, the plans for this exist and show the immense height he wanted the tower to be. This would have afforded views far and wide across the landscape and we can only wonder today what other purpose this tower was intended to serve.

Saunière himself apparently claimed that people would one day come to visit his parish as if it were a second Lourdes. The idea of Rennes-le-Château as a pilgrimage site is covered in more depth later. Suffice it to say that to become one it would need to have a holy relic or some other form of unique religious attraction.

For now let us leave Father Saunière's domain and explore the surrounding landscape.

CHAPTER 7

LANDSCAPE

Anyone researching the mystery of Rennes-le-Château should visit the area and walk the land to get a sense of place. Much is invisible to 'armchair archaeologists' and only a direct experience of the landscape gives a true feel for the mysteries of the region. As we will see, it is a landscape that bears all the hallmarks of a ritual space – on a grand scale.

Even in the harsh light of the day it is a romantic land, in places possessing a mythical feel, like a lost world. When I first planned to visit I looked over the map of the region and delighted in the bizarreness of names and locations. The Dead Man, the Devil's Armchair, the Valley of God, the Valley of Paradise, the Fountain of Love, the Circle, the town called the Serpent, the River of Colours, the town called Light and the Farm of the Dead. The place names read like one of Charles Perrault's fairytales, among an ancient landscape of standing stones and ruined fortresses. The region is evocative, beautiful and harsh to traverse. With so much in one small area you can understand why authors have claimed this as the home of everything from King Arthur to the cult of Isis.

I return time and again to the region. Like nowhere else on earth it resonates with some deeper peace within me. A local man once told me that the land calls to it those who were here before, like Cathars and Templars reincarnated, whose memories are stirring in the blood.

But if you too are drawn to explore this area, take heed. There are rules to adhere to for those who visit:

- Take nothing.
- Leave nothing.
- Change nothing.

However much a part of you this place may seem, it also belongs to others yet to come. Anything found here belongs here and anything taken should be returned. The reason why will become apparent over time to those who have contemplated the meaning of the landscape.

VIEWS AROUND RENNES-LE-CHÂTEAU

For a moment let us return to the church of Rennes-le-Château. Father Bérenger Saunière was said to have put his hand to only one work of art in the restoration of his church – the altar painting showing Mary Magdalene in a cave with a landscape visible in the background. Many take this location to be the Grotto of Mary Magdalene, a square cave in the cliff to the south of the town. It is visible from the Tour Magdala and very prominent above the Ruisseau des Couleurs or River of Colours. The grotto itself is quite shallow and has been well dug in the past. If you choose to visit be prepared for a slightly precarious journey; access is probably easiest from the plateau above.

In the altar painting the landscape beyond the grotto directs us to a different location. It shows a low hill to the left with a ruin and sharp peak beyond and to, the right. Upon leaving Couiza for Rennes-le-Château if you stop and admire the view east from the second turn in the road you will see to the left the ruined château of Coustaussa, and to the right the peak of Blanchefort and beyond to Pech Cardou. The view can be aligned to match the image on the church altar (*see* plates section).

Coustaussa is also visible in the church's fresco of the Sermon on the Mount. This tiny village was the residence of Father Gélis, whose demise was covered in an earlier chapter (*see* page 75). The importance of this view will become apparent later.

Blanchefort is the site of a château that was home to the Blanchefort and de Negri d'Ables family. Its ruins can still be seen along with the remains of what looks like a watchtower. The 'white tower' of Blanchefort is mirrored by the 'Black Rock', Roc Nègre, a little way to the south. At Roc Nègre there is land known to have been owned by Pierre Plantard in the 1970s. There is a small cave and a chamber of sorts here that could have been used in past times. It is known that the area is riddled with caves and that mines were cut beneath Blanchefort.

If you walk from Rennes-le-Château toward Blanchefort and Rennes-les-Bains you will likely encounter some strange stone 'igloos' scattered on the hillside. There are over a hundred of these, many in good condition, but they are difficult to date as they consist of natural flat stones piled high into domes. They are known as 'Les Capitales' and have so far confounded any attempt to explain their purpose. Explanations range from grain storage and sheep shelters to hermitages, but the inconsistent design and lack of proximity to one another seems to exclude these ideas. Some have clearly defined doorways, others have windows and some have neither. I suggest not getting too attached to these as a part of the mystery as they could have been reused and modified many times and in some cases they may have served simply as a way to gather the stones that litter the farmlands hereabouts and impede the plough.

The circle of churches

The 'circle of churches' is another pattern on the landscape and was first publicized by Father Henri Boudet in his book *La Vraie Langue Celtique* (*see* page 82). This was also picked up by David Wood in *Genisis* [sic], which presents his own theory of the design and purpose of the circle.

More work needs to be done to interpret the circle of churches in the impenetrable text of Boudet's book, but an important feature of the circle is Espéraza, a small town to the southwest of Rennes-le-Château. Espéraza has recently become notorious in the region for its installation in the church of an ambiguous sculpture of Jesus in a grotto tomb. Designed as a cross-section it looks more like a burial in a mountain cave, a more natural-looking site than the traditional depiction of Christ's tomb, squared off with a lintel and a door. It is a sizable piece of work, around ten feet (3m) across and six feet (2m) high. Also of note in Espéraza is the statue of St Roseline, whose feast day is on January 17 – that date yet again. She is explained further in the chapter on Art and Symbolism as she also appears in a relevant painting (*see* Chapter 16). For now it is enough to say that the statue is in keeping with the style and design of those commissioned by Saunière for the church of Mary Magdalene and can therefore be considered contemporary. Also, the name 'Roseline' is more than a coincidence for the 'Rose Line', which runs parallel to the Paris Meridian (*see* page 53) near Rennes-les-Bains.

A final point about Espéraza is that opposite the 'grotto' sculpture is a particularly good rendering of a skull and crossbones, an emblem of death also used by the Templars. It also appears above the entrance to the graveyard at Rennes-le-Château and as Gérard Thome has pointed out, it could also be employed to signify the entrance to a tunnel (*see* page 105).

Lavaldieu

Lavaldieu or 'La Val Dieu' translates as the Valley of God. It is located southeast of Rennes-le-Château toward the Château des Templiers (Templar Castle) and consists of a single road lined with occasional farms culminating in a small farm estate perched on an outcrop of rock. The recent collapse of part of this outcrop revealed an underground chapel. Should you be tempted to explore it I must stress that it is both empty and on private land.

I have a pilgrim's badge that was discovered near Lavaldieu during the filming of the *Bloodline* documentary, buried close to a water source near Rennes-le-Château. The small metal badge features the head of the crucified Jesus. Badges were often sewn onto the pilgrim's robe and deposited near or in water once their destination had been reached to signify the end of the journey. (When the River Thames in London was dredged, thousands of pilgrim badges were found near the bridges). Pilgrims en route to Santiago de Compostela would usually wear a scallop shell, the symbol of St James, and one of these can be found in use as the smaller font in the church at Rennes-le-Château. By coincidence, at our first meeting with Nic Haywood for the documentary, he gave producer René Barnett, a small metal badge that illustrates the 13th Station of the Cross. It is a *pietà*, depicting the Virgin Mary cradling the body of Jesus in her arms, flanked by two palm trees that form a natural arch. This is a copy of an original *pietà* that was also found near Rennes-le-Château.

The Priory of Sion gave many indications about the site of what may have been a Roman-era necropolis at Lavaldieu. However, we undertook no exploration or excavations, having received strong warnings that any such structure would be prone to collapse, so any work undertaken here would need to be a professional affair. I identified the location as a shrine based on its proximity to the natural spring close to where we found the pilgrim's badge. Much of this area is also private land, so if you go exploring you must again seek permission and respect the privacy of those living there.

To the south of Lavaldieu is a field with a pagan-style circle of bushes with an old tree at the centre and a standing stone to the east. This is visible from the Château des Templiers. Although its date cannot be easily ascertained there is no reason to suspect it is a recent addition to the landscape. The field looks contrived and I think the bushes have been maintained from an earlier site.

The sacred pool

Heading north from the location of the badge, we were directed by Sion to a secluded pool among some trees. Old photographs of this location can be seen in the updated edition of *The Holy Blood and the Holy Grail*, whose authors originally seemed at a loss as to why they had been directed here. At the head of the pool is a sizable stone, often mistaken for an altar. The truth of the matter is that the stone was used to re-enact, possibly symbolically, the Flagellation of Jesus by Pilate's soldiers, an event marked by the First Station of the Cross in the Via Dolorosa. In former times this place was clearly used as part of a wider initiation and this will be covered in the chapter on pilgrimage (*see* Chapter 9).

The pool has a second function in that the copse it sits in was entirely contrived. As Sion put it:

> 'We must conclude its importance by virtue of its blatantly
> man-made/man-sculpted surroundings for, if you permit yourself
> to wander [?wonder], you will doubtless forge a connection
> between the Sacred Coign of Vantage, the All-Seeing Eye – the
> reality of which is but the reflection of one's self in the eyes of the
> Beloved – and the notion of a sacred pool. It is the Underground
> Stream made manifest, risen from the ground. It is a fittingly
> sacred place.'

The 'Coign of Vantage' or 'All-Seeing Eye' is represented by an eye in a triangle: the pool is in a field that is triangular in shape. It is a symbol that appears in Freemasonry to represent God, but it is also known to have been in earlier use by the Rosicrucians and alchemists. The meanings of the eye in the triangle are many, but in churches it usually represents the Eye of Providence or God. In alchemy it is the eye of God in which the alchemist sees himself reflected. The symbol suits the Masonic concept of God as expressed through geometry and architecture. Unfortunately the pool is also on private land so permission is needed to access it.

Old photographs show the pool as being surrounded by trees and having a stone altar at one end. However, this formerly sacred and secluded place is now a sad sight to behold. The land around the pool has been developed, the trees that surrounded it have been cut away to a bare few and the pool itself has been lined with concrete and fenced in. The plinth or 'altar' that stood at the head of the pool has been removed. On discovering the site it looked so far removed from anything remotely sacred that I ignored it completely until I confirmed its location with a map. The destruction of the site came as a surprise to Sion but it is further evidence that the sands of time are shifting, slowly covering what had been revealed among these hills in times gone by.

Jaffus
A little further to the north there is an area of land marked on the map as 'Jaffus'. This is due west of Rennes-le-Château and its similarity to the Jaffa Gate in the Old City of Jerusalem seems more than a coincidence. From Jaffus continuing east one climbs the hill to the ruins of the Château de Blanchefort. There was once a row of carved stone heads on Blanchefort, and there still exists a rock named 'head' here. But of the original carved heads I know only one that has survived. This is kept in private hands at a house in a nearby town. It cannot be reinstated for fear of theft or vandalism but should probably make its way to the Carcassonne museum to be shared with the public. Stone heads are often a feature of Celtic finds, the ancient Celts having great reverence for the severed head, believing the head to be the source of spiritual power in humans.

The heads of stone may be linked to the summit of Blanchefort, which appears on the map as Caput, Latin for 'head' or 'skull'. It is not a stretch to see the link between this and the name Golgotha or Calvary, the 'Place of the Skull', where Jesus was crucified.

Looking east we face Pech Cardou, the mountain that overlooks much of the area, situated just north of Rennes-les-Bains. Here is another pointed reference to Jerusalem: the word 'Cardou' is of similar origin to Cardo, the main street of Roman and Byzantine Jerusalem. This street, with columns along its entire length, was a long avenue that crossed the whole city from north to south.

As Nic Haywood warns, we can go too far in our quest for links between the region and Jerusalem. There are a few pointers, enough to indicate the existence of a symbolic route through the area. The landscape was adapted, certain features added, others modified to create a mirror of Jerusalem. The importance of the location would have been well established prior to the crusades, but the Middle Ages saw the area revived. 'Such locations', said Nic, 'are but vehicles used to carry a timeless truth'.

Blanchefort
It is at the ruins of the Château de Blanchefort that we begin the most esoteric aspect of this journey, as it is the starting point for *Le Serpent Rouge*, 'the Red Serpent'. This is the name of a Sion publication where all the threads of the

mystery come together. It is cryptic and strange and I consider it the most important document of the entire mystery, and I have devoted a whole later chapter to its meaning (*see* Chapter 10).

For now, it describes a journey through the landscape as an initiation, with the church of Rennes-le-Château acting as a place of initiation and its plan being mapped onto the landscape as if it were a vast temple:

> 'That whole area [around Rennes-le-Château] was elaborated and carved out and added to and sculpted in order to allow a three-dimensional journey, as Masonic lodges enact rituals in lodges, but in the real world. The labyrinth [an underground system of mines and tunnels] is Rennes-les-Bains, the 'Devil's Armchair' is where it finishes – that is where your feet are washed; it involves crossing a river. It is an initiation into a mystery – the closest Masonic ritual is the AASR [Ancient and Accepted Scottish Rite] Rose+Croix degree, alluded to in the church by the plaid.'

The Rose+Croix degree is said to be the closest ritual to enacting the Via Dolorosa, the re-enacting of the journey that Jesus took from his judgment by Pilate to his crucifixion and placing in the tomb. It is this journey that is mapped out in the Stations of the Cross in the church with anomalies including the presence of tartan as mentioned above (*see* page 97).

Rennes-les-Bains

Following the crest of the hill south we pass Rennes-les-Bains in the valley to the east. This is the site of the Roman baths, still in use today and close to the old Paris Meridian. It is also home to the church where Henri Boudet, apparently the leading light behind Father Saunière's restoration of Rennes-le-Château, was priest. Boudet's own church has a few interesting features including what appears to be a compass design in the floor beneath the altar. The outstanding items of interest here are in the graveyard. There are two graves bearing the name Paul-Urbain de Fleury, each marked with different dates. One is inscribed with 'he who passed in doing good', a phrase used to describe Rosicrucians, as do the grave's symbolic roses. The tomb of Boudet's predecessor, Father Jean Vié, can be read in such a way as to be '*janvier* 17' (January 17) – In French, Jean Vié and *janvier* are homophones. The graveyard also once held a grave marker for a plot owned by Pierre Plantard, but this was lost during a storm in the early 1990s.

The Devil's Armchair

Continuing south from Blanchefort down past Rennes-les-Bains we come to a large carved rock called Le Fauteuil du Diable, the 'Devil's Armchair'. On the hillside is a natural stone, partly carved to represent the shape of a giant chair. Its origins are unknown but other features of the nearby landscape, such as the terracing further south, are likely to have been Celtic. The 'chair' is situated beside an iron-rich spring that can be used to bathe the feet of anyone sitting in the chair, presumably an initiate.

Carved into the chair's weathered stone are a number of devices, the oldest of which appear to be an alpha and omega (AΩ). As seen on the Visigothic pillar at Rennes-le-Château church, this symbol – the first and last letters of the Greek alphabet – represents the beginning and end, marking a circular route that we will explore in *Le Serpent Rouge*. There is also a triangle that may relate to the triangular field with the pool (*see* page 112), although as a general symbol it usually represents a mountain. It is possible that the pool itself is a representation of a location within the mountain – an image, in cross-section, revealing where something important is buried. There are two notable mountains in the vicinity. Facing north is the sharp peak of Pech Cardou, visible in the Rennes-le-Château altar painting (*see* Plates).

As for the name 'Devil's Armchair', it serves to remind us of Saunière's demon Asmodeus, the keeper of secrets, but it also relates to the archetype of the Trickster or Fool, who undertakes a journey of spiritual awakening – from alpha to omega.

According to Sion, the view from Le Fauteuil du Diable at full moon of a Lammas Eve was 'a sight to behold', with the area's many streams and rivers brightly illuminated. Unfortunately a programme of tree planting and the advent of artificial light have polluted the view at night.

Château des Templiers

Looking south from the Devil's Armchair we follow the River Sals as it snakes its way to the foot of another mountain. On the crest of this stands the ruin of an old Templar outpost, the Château des Templiers or Templar Castle. Between the château and the Devil's Armchair is a place called the Dead Man, which hints that someone is buried nearby.

The château is one of a number of structures in the region credited with being a Templar fortress after their return from the Crusades. Sion claims that it was Templar stronghold, although locally some argue that it belonged to the

Knights of St John (the Hospitallers). However, both are possible, since most Templar lands and properties were eventually handed to the Hospitallers. Its location, on a hill to the south of Rennes-les-Bains, is important for a number of reasons. It commanded views over Rennes-les-Bains and Lavaldieu, and during the time of the Templars, Château Blanchefort would also have been visible to the north beyond the Devil's Armchair. Rennes-le-Château can be seen to the northwest. The significance of this will become clear in later chapters, but for now it is sufficient to remark that the castle presides over the entire landscape and is, according to Sion, directly linked to the Templars. The secret of this landscape, which we will come to later, was known at least as early as the time of the Templars.

According to Sion a second Templar keep was located at Arques to the northeast, providing comparable views across this region. The impression we get is that the Templars knew the area's secret and for a time kept watch over it.

On their return from the Holy Land, a number of Templars took up residence in the Languedoc and much of the region's land was owned by Templar families. Following their persecution and dissolution in the early 14th century (*see* Chapter 2), Templar lands were confiscated and distributed to other orders, notably the Knights Hospitaller, who later became the Knights of Malta.

We cannot tell for sure exactly which sites were occupied by the Templars, but from the echoes of Jerusalem in several place names it would seem possible that they greatly influenced the landscape.

CONCLUSION

The land sometimes holds our memories, the traces of those who came before us in sediments of society through the ages. The landscape of Rennes-le-Château has changed and every excavation brings into the light of the present day traces of ancestors who once stood in these same fields. In the last hundred years, centuries of slow progress have given way to an onslaught of development and the landscape has changed dramatically. Old roads are remade in concrete and tarmac and old tracks are lost to the plough; clear crests punctuated by outcrops of rock are now obscured by forestation; markers have been moved or become buried and broken; and at night the amber glow of electric street lighting obliterates many of the stars and the moon no longer brings the rivers to glistening life like serpents of mercury. When everything is lit, it seems the way is lost.

The last word on the ritual use of the landscape is bound up in a tract called

Le Serpent Rouge, a text that marks the link between what has passed and what we are about to discover. But before we embark on the next stage of our journey we should pause to consider what we have learned so far. Looking back over the past few chapters we can see a number of themes emerging that we can use as a foundation for the thoughts and ideas of subsequent chapters.

CHAPTER 8

EMERGING THEMES

INTRODUCTION

Father Saunière's church and the surrounding landscape embrace a number of themes of the mystery that we are dealing with. At some point in the future these themes may converge under a broader canopy that links them all together, but at the moment any all–encapsulating answer remains elusive. Until such an answer emerges we must presume that there may be more than one mystery involved. Certainly, the themes are easier to identify and pursue as individual threads. For now, my intention in this part of the book is to summarize the background, clues and information available on a number of paths and some possible conclusions. There are also a few new ideas and recent developments that have enriched the mystery. Much of the existing evidence is subject to more than one interpretation and where possible I will explore the alternatives.

FATHER BÉRENGER SAUNIÈRE

Saunière's role at the centre of this mystery appears to be one of both explorer and gatekeeper. His discoveries and his sudden wealth (*see* Chapter 5) placed him in a position to communicate, through the physical fabric and décor of his church, a number of different ideas. In this he was assisted by those around him and by others in the region who supported and directed his actions. Sion informs us that:

> 'An important letter was sent to Bérenger Saunière from Granes informing him that a symbol or small marker had been located there. A line drawn directly from this to the vaults at Arques (derived from "a chessboard" in Arabic – *ar-qa, ruat* – also the origin

of Arlakeen or Harlequin, and also meaning "confused speech", "great doorway or entrance") passes right through the Tomb!'

We will learn more about the 'tomb' in Chapter 11 but Sion is implying that a fellow priest based at Granes helped Saunière locate a tomb. This tomb may have been the direct source of his wealth or may have contained documents, information or treasure, that he exchanged for money. This money, and possibly items from the tomb were shared between Saunière and two other local priests, Father Gélis and Father Boudet. Gélis invested his share in business, Boudet funded the refurbishment of a number of churches in the region and other charitable causes, while Saunière spent his on refurbishing his church at Rennes-le-Château, a guesthouse and luxury items. Saunière's church and gardens were developed to include esoteric and sometimes heretical symbolism. The most prevalent of which came from the Freemasons and Rosicrucians.

FREEMASONRY

Whatever Saunière discovered as a source of wealth, his church décor (*see* Chapter 6) first struck me as something like a Masonic theme park. As if to emphasize this link, a party of Freemasons from the US visited while I was there, clearly delighted by the abundance of their own symbols. Other Masonic groups are known to travel from Paris and England to marvel at what appears at first sight to be a Masonic lodge hidden within a church. But although it has much in common with the standard Masonic temple, in truth the church is a creation of Rosicrucianism, the spiritual arm of the Priory of Sion, as Sion confirmed:

'The church at Rennes-le-Château was undoubtedly used as a preceptory – a lodge for the purposes of high meetings of the Rose+Croix – and its refurbishment attests to that fact.'
'Furthermore, it was also used to celebrate elevation/initiation into [the Rosicrucian higher] degrees (17 to 33).'

Superficially there is little difference between the two types of lodge, since Freemasonry's rituals and regalia were largely adopted from Rosicrucianism. Masonic lodges are built in the image of the Temple of Solomon and this church is no different. Inside the door is a statue of Asmodeus, the demon summoned and bound by King Solomon to build his temple in silence. Solomon bound Asmodeus using water, which is why the statue crouches beneath the water stoup. The demon contemplates the chessboard floor, itself a feature of every Masonic temple. In Saunière's time this pattern was limited to the correct 64 squares, but has since been expanded to cover the entire floor, presumably in an attempt to hide its presence.

The church at Rennes-le-Château was a place of initiation, of ritual and mystery. The teachings imparted there were under the guise of Rosicrucian Freemasonry. From a Christian perspective, the 18th (Rose+Croix) Degree is the closest to the Passion of Christ and its initiation rites follow the Stations of the Cross. As mentioned earlier, in the Eighth Station a boy can be seen dressed in tartan, a reference to the Ancient and Accepted Scottish Rite of Freemasonry (see Chapter 6). Many of the higher, or *ecossais* [Scottish], degrees have their origins in the old aristocratic families of Europe. This Eighth Station has also been linked to the local noble family of de Negri d'Ables (also spelled de Nègre) and it was Jacques-Etienne Marconis de Nègre who created the Rite of Memphis – a precursor to the Ancient and Accepted Scottish Rite. Jacques-Etienne de Nègre was an ancestor of Marie de Negri d'Ables, countess of Blanchefort, who was buried in the church.

> 'The fusion between the Scottish Rite and the Rose+Croix had created an additional 17 Degrees, increasing the total number to 33. The truth of the matter is that the Priory of Sion needed a safe repository for its inherent knowledge and an unquestionable source for recruits – somewhere secure, secret and well-protected. What better place than the upper echelons of a secret institution that they had themselves created and, for the best part, monitored?'

The emblems of the Rose+Croix degree are the rose, the cross, the eagle and the pelican. The pelican is seen feeding its young from its own breast, in an act of self-sacrifice. The small museum at Rennes-le-Château displays Saunière's cassock with this image embroidered on the back (see Plates).

In the Rosicrucian degrees a 'room of contemplation' was used to prepare the candidate for rituals, and this can be identified as the secret room hidden by Saunière behind the cupboards in the sacristy.

The symbol of the rose on the cross on the pulpit and above the Stations of the Cross also remind us of the Rose+Croix degrees and link the Freemasons to the Rosicrucian movement, Sion's spiritual arm.

The rose cross alone can be absorbed into a Christian setting without raising eyebrows as it can be interpreted as Jesus as the 'Rose of Sharon'. However, so much Masonic and Rosicrucian symbolism in one place is overwhelming evidence of the influence of secret societies.

There ritual also uses three chambers coloured black, white and red– the classical stages of alchemical transformation. These can also be experienced as stages of meditation. The 25th (Rose+Croix) Degree confers the title 'Knight of the Brazen Serpent' upon the candidate, symbolized by the title of Sion's document *Le Serpent Rouge* ('*The Red Serpent*').

The symbol as used in the 25th degree, a serpent draped across a Tau cross, will be familiar to those who have viewed the images from Nicolas Flamel's book.

The text of *Le Serpent Rouge*, which is fully explored in a later chapter, shows that the ritual was not limited to the church but was recreated on a grand scale in the surrounding landscape: a place of mass initiation not beneath the painted stars of the church/lodge ceiling but beneath a real starry canopy.

No record of Saunière's Masonic/Rosicrucian membership has been made public, but at the time priests were forbidden to join the Freemasons so he would certainly have kept it quiet. Even the story of Saunière's actions may be based upon the instructions in a Masonic ritual. During the ritual of the 17th (Royal Arch) Degree the candidate is taken through a re-enactment of the uncovering of Solomon's Temple, itself based presumably on the Templars' return to the Holy Land and residence on the Temple Mount. At a specific point in the ritual the candidate symbolically prises the Temple vault open with a crowbar and discovers a secret scroll – in much the same way as Saunière is said to have discovered parchments.

It may be tempting at this stage to write off the entire mystery as a Rosicrucian folly. But that is only part of the story. Secret societies are a perfect vehicle for transmitting heretical ideas and the abundance of symbolism in this church indicates the possibility of some greater secret.

TEMPLAR LAND OWNERSHIP

The Knights Templar are often seen as precursors to the Freemasons. Certainly a number of Masonic rituals re-enact scenes from Templar history, such as the excavation of the Temple Mount during the 17th Degree. The Templars had a strong connection with the region around Rennes-le-Château. On their return from the Levant the majority of Templars relocated to this region and we are told by Sion that at one stage they were attempting to create their own principality, resurrecting the ancient region called Septimania, part of the Visigothic kingdom in post-Roman times. This incorporated much of the Languedoc, including the region of Rennes-le-Château.

If areas of this region once belonged to the Templars then among the items that may have come into Saunière's possession via his predecessor from the local nobles of Hautpoul and Blanchefort are the title deeds for Templar land, which would have been in the name of the old families that had links to the Templars. Sion claims that deeds granting the entire region to the Templars did exist, and constituted part of Saunière's find. According to Nic Haywood,

> 'It is no secret that Septimanie [Septimania] was to have been the self-governing principality of "the Order of the Poor Knights of the Temple", and that all the requisite documents had been signed and sealed to that effect prior to their arrest. Did this include the land and environs of Rennes-le-Château? If so, it is a fact that neither France nor Rome ever revoked those deeds.'

The Templar order fell in 1307, when King Philip IV of France ordered the mass arrest of the knights on suspicion of heresy. Philip seized Templar territory and wealth, and although many Templars escaped the persecution and much was lost, scattered or hastily buried, their lands, including the Languedoc, were taken from them. These lands would have been given over to the Knights Hospitaller (also called the Knights of St John and, later, the Knights of Malta).

THE CHINON PARCHMENT

We covered the Chinon Parchment when discussing Sion's history in relation to the Templars (*see* Chapter 2). Before its discovery in 2001 this papal decree, which explicitly absolves the order of heresy, had been lost in the Vatican Secret Archive for centuries. Its existence throws new and invaluable light on both the Templars and the Rennes-le-Château mystery.

> 'Despite the existence of this authenticated document, Benedict XVI – like his predecessors – refuses to back a pardon [for the Templars], the proclamation of which would negate the tenancy of both the Knights of Malta and those of the Holy Sepulchre [an order founded in 1099 and later merged with the Hospitallers].'

Aside from the placing of the land deeds in the vicinity of Rennes-le-Château and the exoneration of the order, of interest to us here is that land belonging to the Templar order and Templar families should have remained under their control. As mentioned above, following the trial of the Templars their land and possessions passed to the Hospitallers, the current Knights of Malta. In the light of the Chinon Parchment all property that has survived should be returned to its rightful owners.

Having such a direct interest in this affair it is no surprise that some active members of Sion are still located in the region, or that their former Grand Master, Pierre Plantard, also possessed land in the vicinity of Rennes-le-Château. Earlier I also mentioned lands belonging to the noble de Fleury family, which are visibly highlighted in the Sermon on the Mount mural in the Rennes-le-Château church (*see* page 100). I have also identified the Rosicrucian reference on the tombstone of one family member. Sion states:

> 'Specific lands in the environs of Rennes-le-Château/Rennes-les-
> Bains are held by families with discernible links to the 20th-century
> Priory of Sion, to the Rose+Croix or to Cathar tradition.'

The importance of the issue of who owns the land is not entirely political. The real significance is that whoever owns the land owns whatever lies buried beneath it.

> 'As to quite what it is that Sion believes to be buried in the
> environs of Rennes-le-Château is an entirely different matter
> indeed. *Le Serpent Rouge* alludes to "embalmed corpses and
> precious metals too heavy to carry, etc." There are several "acute"
> items stored down there, which may include human remains in
> a state of preservation (specifically a head), that have, by virtue of
> their existence, been used as "leverage" in times past.'

The treasure aspect of the mystery makes for quite a distraction for many people. The possibility that Saunière discovered, and looted, a horde of Templar or Visigothic treasure is exciting but we should not let it distract us. There are far more interesting avenues to be pursued. As the items can be used as 'leverage' against the Church they must have some religious meaning that is at odds with orthodox Christianity.

SACRED GEOMETRY

Building techniques and traditions may travel the globe, like those of the cathedral-builders of the Middle Ages. Their cathedrals and many later constructions were adorned with rose windows that are in effect mandalas, or cosmic diagrams, illustrating a subtle cosmology, while their structure in general expressed the concept of the square of matter containing the circle of spirit. All these aspects have their roots in Eastern philosophies. This is especially true of domed structures. During this time some places of worship, such as some of the Templar churches, were constructed in the round, reflecting the shape of the world. They had transcended the idea of a square earth with 'four corners' in the Middle Ages, perhaps from something that was learned in the Holy Land.

Sacred geometry was applied to these cathedrals, having declined after ancient Greek times only to be rediscovered in the East by Europeans during the early Crusades. The functional Romanesque style, which derived from late Roman models, was suddenly imbued with a new sense of awe as meaning and balance were restored to architecture. In medieval European towns and cities, where few buildings were more than two storeys high, these new 'Gothic' monoliths towered above the people, demanding that they look ever upward at a spectacle of power and beauty. Even today, the scale of these structures has the power to overwhelm us.

Geometry carries its own secrets; it encapsulates growth and evolution in the patterns of nature and can be seen as an expression of the divine order within apparent chaos. The word 'rational' comes from Latin *ratio* – reason, or the right vision of things; it is not just logical but meaningful. At Rennes-le-Château geometry is especially important as it used to portray deeper mysteries. As Nic Haywood confirmed for me by email, 'geometry is an essential key to all that appertains to Rennes-le-Château's "mystery"'.

The pentagram

Two authors in particular have explored the physical geometry of the region. In *Genisis* and *Geneset*, David Wood maps a complex pentagram and hexagram onto the landscape, while in *The Holy Place* and *The Key to the Sacred Pattern* Henry Lincoln also finds a perfect pentagram, with each of the five points of the star marked by a mountain peak. Both cover the land between Rennes-le-Château and Rennes-les-Bains.

A few other authors have included Rennes-le-Château in geometric alignments and there are also a number of unpublished or privately printed works, including Ron Weighell's *Angles of Coincidence*, but these mainly draw heavily on Lincoln's geometry and try to interpret it in a different manner or have it point to a specific location.

Although David Wood's complex, Egyptian-themed *Genisis* was published first, it was Henry Lincoln's simple pentagram that caught the imagination of the public. Lincoln's pentagram links the Château des Templiers to the south with Rennes-le-Château and Blanchefort in the north and two other peaks on the map. These structures were built on peaks that appear natural, which means the underlying pentagram was formed either when the Pyrenees rose up from the earth or when the region was extensively worked to produce such an effect. Even the otherwise dry book on Rennes-le-Château by Puttnam and Wood concedes the accuracy of the pentagram on the landscape. Probability dictates that with so many peaks the form of a pentagram was bound to appear somewhere, but it makes for an interesting coincidence that it happens here and linking these locations.

Like all symbols, the pentagram, or five-pointed star, is prone to many interpretations but most people would recognize it as a symbol of the occult. King Solomon, whose Temple is emulated by Freemasons and referred to in the church of Mary Magdalene at Rennes-le-Château, is described in Jewish and Christian traditions as wearing a ring inscribed with a magical seal. The seal is often depicted erroneously as a six-pointed Star of David, when it is correctly described as five interlocking A shapes, in other words a pentagram. This tradition, transmitted through history by people like Saint-Sulpician occultist Eliphas Lévi, can often be seen as a basis for modern magical working.

The pentagram itself is often associated with evil or the devil but as such was either consciously or unconsciously part of the campaign to discriminate against the feminine within the Catholic Church. In its most primitive form the pentagram describes the path of Venus in the night sky. This would have been recognized by the ancients and passed down through history as a feminine archetypal design, the planet being identified with powerful pre-Christian goddesses of female sexuality (variously called for example Aphrodite, Venus, Astarte and Ishtar). The Church naturally sought to suppress such a powerful pagan archetype, and this clear but complex symbol of the feminine was mis-appropriated as a sign of evil. (Its appearance on the forehead of the 'Sabbat Goat', as designed by Eliphas Lévi, may have more to do with the relationship of Venus to Capricorn than to the 'Devil worshipping' of popular conception.)

In occult magic the pentagram is used both to invoke spirits and to banish them. It can also be used to create a protective barrier around the enquirer. Whether or not one considers magic to be nonsense, the psychological effect of the pentagram transcends the medium of the occult. If the landscape is marked with the five points of a pentagram in the peaks of the hills it represents a feminine and protective symbol.

One line of the Lincoln pentagram links Rennes-le-Château to Blanchefort, which is also depicted in the view in the altar painting in Saunière's church. Following this route we arrive at the Paris Meridian and the 'Rose Line', just beyond Pech Cardou. This is marked by the remains of a tomb at Les Pontils, which originally looked very similar to the tomb in Poussin's *Et in Arcadia Ego*. Poussin used the pentagram to create the form of this famous and enigmatic work, and Lincoln uses the painting as the basis for his design.

The presence of the Rose Line in the region allows us to make further links with the Lincoln pentagram. Like many other researchers I have drawn endless lines on the IGN maps of the area, studied the angles and searched the hills. As there is nothing at the centre of the pentagram and no other single discernible focal point it is difficult to prove that the pentagram has some directional purpose. Perhaps it simply exists to draw people to the area as a whole and signify its importance. There is likely to be a key to unlocking the pentagram, as I received the impression that it is used to indicate specific sites using a simple set of rules. I will explore this later, but for now we are at the mercy of those who either constructed the pentagram or made use of a natural pentagram to reveal their purpose.

Many see the geometry of this area as a sideshow, a distraction from the principal mystery, for lines alone could not make a poor French priest rich unless they pointed to a specific location. A second problem is that the same geometry can often be found to fit many other locations or cities (*see* for example Chris Street's *Earthstars*, which finds a correlation between complex geometric patterns and the placement of churches across London).

Also of interest is a work of limited publication called *The Secret of the Templars* by Patricia Villiers-Stuart. Sion supplied us with a partial copy of this and I will explore this further in the chapter on documents (*see* Chapter 10). Like Henry Lincoln, Villiers-Stuart uses Poussin's painting as the basis for her designs. As shown by Lincoln, the pentagram was also used by Jean Cocteau when he designed the Crucifixion scene in the French Church in London:

'Jean Cocteau had prepared a series of drawings, based closely
upon pre-existing progressions of geometry, which were
themselves the basis for a revised Tarot. These were highly
minimalist, almost bare glyphs, which suggested an object, the
formation of which followed closely the underlying geometric or
glyph. It was progressive.'

Sion supplied me with a selection of these Tarot cards (*see* pages 290–1). I have
already referred to Cocteau's links to Sion and we will encounter him again later.

On a broader scale, Greg Rigby's *On Earth as it is in Heaven* maps the stars
of Ursa Major to the several cathedrals dedicated to Notre Dame ('Our Lady')
across France. The only star not represented by a cathedral, and the southern-
most point of this design, is represented instead by Rennes-le-Château, where
the church is dedicated to Mary Magdalene.

Energy will organize itself into straight lines and take the form of geometric
patterns. There remains another feature of the landscape that would greatly assist
in the aligning of energies: magnetism.

LANDSCAPE ENERGY

The land around Rennes-le-Château has magnetic properties. The soil of the
region contains so much iron and so many natural springs that the entire area
is a dowser's dream. There are areas that are said to be 'no fly zones' because
of the effect the magnetism in the land has on aircraft instruments. I have also
been told by various sources that when one stands in the doorway of the church
of Mary Magdalene, an old-fashioned metal compass will spin wildly out of
control. From the interview with Nic Haywood:

'The treasures, things buried [in and around Rennes-le-Château]
to be discovered, they are an aside. There is an energy. The land is
ferrous, often said to be the site of the largest lodestone known to
man. Lodestones – magnetite – are nature's natural magnets, and
navigators would rely on it for navigation without stars.'

The dozens of pagan standing stones, both man-made and naturally occurring,
scattered throughout the landscape around Rennes-le-Château also serve as
a link to this magnetic field. They are reported by dowsers to channel earth
energies. Even if you do not believe in dowsing, the idea of earth energies or

'telluric currents' has plenty of followers and if enough people subscribe to an idea – much like religion – it will be influential irrespective of whether it is actually true. (For another view on these 'telluric currents', Umberto Eco's entertaining novel *Foucault's Pendulum* has a lot of fun linking earth energies with the Templars.)

The idea of currents in the earth that can be harnessed is ancient and occurs in a number of cultures. According to this idea, the earth's magnetic field can be used to act upon the individual at an energetic level. Everything vibrates on a molecular level and would respond in some way to strong magnetic fields. In theory the vibration of a vast magnetized rock will affect an individual who has been prepared in the right circumstances to be open to these energies.

I am neither a channel nor a dowser but have witnessed both channelling and dowsing at work. Dowsing in particular is easy enough for most people to experience at least some indication that there is a biological response to geological entities. From speaking to people in the Rennes-le-Château region, I received the sense that the energy here can amplify either positive or negative traits in an individual and so must be protected from misuse. In this context, I will quote a strange missive that I received from Sion:

'I was also drawn by chance to open a certain old volume at this page:

"For in brain and heart and loins/Gates open behind Satan's seat to the subterranean city of 'Golgooza', which is the spiritual fourfold centre in the heart of Arcadia." Arcadia is the spiritual home of arts and crafts. Its eastern gate holds the key and is guarded by the messengers of "Los", the personification of creative energy. The four-dimensional "Golgooza" is modelled on Jerusalem – Sion – the place of complete fulfilment and freedom.'

This enigmatic text links the Devil's Armchair ('Satan's seat'), Poussin's *Et in Arcadia Ego* (*The Shepherds of Arcadia*) and creative energy. It identifies the mountain of Blanchefort with Golgotha ('Golgooza'), the Place of the Skull, and on this mountain there is indeed a peak called the 'Caput' or head. The idea leans towards an initiation and this will be seen later in the chapter on *Le Serpent Rouge*.

The analogy of an underground city based around creative energy also leads us toward other realms of possibility. As with many aspects of these mysteries just when we become rooted in the reality of the soil and rocks we find another level of meaning bubbling up like a stream from beneath the ground. The energies in the region would seem to go beyond magnetic disturbances toward something altogether stranger.

A PORTAL IN TIME?

On the subject of the idea of energies in the region, there is something else that might be linked. In the late 1980s I came across the idea of a 'portal' at Rennes-le-Château. Author Elizabeth van Buren had described this as a doorway into time, hidden in the landscape. The idea of such a 'portal', though seemingly bizarre, has some supporting accounts. There are two separate stories of visitors to the town of Rennes-le-Château experiencing what seemed to be a shift in time.

In one clearly described account, a local resident recounted the story of a woman who had visited her on a bright summer day. The visitor followed the road to the church up through the town in the late morning, only to find the entire town closed. The church was locked and the streets deserted. The visitor left and returned the following day – only to discover that at the time of her visit on the previous day there had been a parade with hundreds of visitors lining the streets and the church packed to capacity. The visitor also noted that on her first visit to what looked like an abandoned town it looked strange, old fashioned, as if stuck in the 19th century. There is no evidence to support this account but it is not in isolation.

I know of at least one other person's similar experience in the region in the 1980s, and further rumours circulate of more recent incidences.

Having followed the notion of a portal for many years I asked Sion if such a place exists. This was Nic Haywood's response:

> 'The Priory of Sion are, for the most part, aware of such a specific
> site – a place. Its purpose is that of gnosis and total edification.
> This, in the main, constitutes the essential core of the initiatory
> experience, but it could be said to be easily prone to misuse.'
>   'I should clarify that the very idea of a "portal," a "doorway,"
> an "entrance", however fantastical, is not far off the mark.'

Another member of the Priory of Sion, who chooses to remain anonymous, had also commented on this phenomenon, bringing to light a much wider scheme within the landscape.

'There is a place of gnosis, spiritual experience, at night. To be influenced by vibration will enforce the positive or negative, so it is kept hidden.'

It was made very clear to me that if I were to try to locate this 'portal' I would be prevented from doing so. This was the only time Sion restricted my actions and the closest they had come to issuing a threat. There have since been a number of other claims of experiences of some kind of 'portal' in this region but as far as I can tell, these differ to what is being alluded to here.

VISIONS

Another theme at Rennes-le-Château is that there are a number of references to visions, as seen in the statue in the garden of Our Lady of Lourdes. This was an apparition of the Virgin Mary that appeared at Lourdes in 1858 to a girl named Bernadette Soubirous. Lourdes rapidly developed into a major pilgrimage destination.

Saunière was a regular visitor to Lourdes, especially in his later life, and he clearly put some faith in the importance of visions and the information they conveyed. As we have seen (*see* Chapter 6), the inscription above the door of his church reads *Terribilis est locus iste* and is taken from Jacob's vision of angels travelling between earth and heaven. Inside we see above the stoup the French inscription 'By this sign you will conquer' which appeared in the sky in Emperor Constantine's vision of a cross with the alpha and omega suspended beneath. This image of the cross also appears on the presumed Visigothic pillar supporting the Our Lady of Lourdes statue.

One of the many interesting coincidences in the Rennes-le-Château affair is found just south of Rennes-les-Bains, where a stone cross on a plinth is carved with the name 'Calvet'. There is no date on the cross but it looks contemporary to Saunière and Boudet. 'Calvet' is both the original surname of Emma Calvé, a famous singer of the time, and the name of a girl, Mélanie Calvet or Calvat, who had a vision of the Virgin Mary in La Salette. 'Our Lady of La Salette' was sighted in 1846 and the site became a focus point of pilgrimage (*see* page 74). Both Lourdes and La Salette remain important pilgrimage sites to this day.

Within the church of Rennes-le-Château the scallop shell of water supported by Asmodeus (*see* page 89) represents St James and is often worn by pilgrims on their way to Santiago de Compostela. One route to Santiago passes within sight of Rennes-le-Château. Both the visions and pilgrimage are covered elsewhere in this book but for now it is enough to recognize that they are represented in the church.

My own interest in visions stems from personal experience in the region.

A few days into my first visit to Rennes-le-Château I was sitting in my hotel room in nearby Couiza, perched on the end of the bed. The light was fading and my mind was awash with all the places I had visited that day, including the church and the grotto of Mary Magdalene. It was early evening and the daylight was fading when I became aware of something moving behind me in the shadows at the head of the bed. I turned slowly and saw what looked like vines emerging from the wall. The vines had green leaves and were rapidly growing, becoming intertwined as they spread up the stone wall from behind the headboard. I am not easily surprised by phenomena, so I sat and calmly watched a mass of vines growing up and through the wall. They brought to mind many things, including the jungle creepers of an old Tarzan movie. They were strong and tall, eventually reaching the ceiling. I felt no sense of threat so I continued to watch, bemused by the realistic quality of the image my imagination had conjured. After a few minutes the vines faded back into the wall.

I had read enough books and seen enough of the Rennes-le-Château mystery to relate the 'I am the true vine' statement by Jesus (John 15) with the idea of a bloodline and consigned the whole episode as an example of active imagination. It was very lucid and interesting and all looked real enough, but probably no more real than the effects of a psychotropic compound, such as ergot (found on mouldy rye and a fairly common cause of hallucinations), and therefore nothing the human brain is not capable of manifesting in certain circumstances. What I took away from the experience was that it might be possible to induce gnosis or other transpersonal and mystical experiences by applying the right kind of information in the right environment. A ritual of some kind might achieve this.

Three days after this event I met the author Elizabeth van Buren for the first time. She was then living in the amusingly named 'Farm of the Dead'. She entertained me with stories of her adventures and was kind enough to provide a wonderful lunch and a cassette narrating her interpretation of the Rennes-le-Château church décor. At one point late in the afternoon she recounted the true story of a couple who had come over from England, intending to drive to a holiday destination in the south of France. Having a read a book mentioning Rennes-le-Château, the husband had insisted they stop there on the way. When they arrived at the village they stepped out of the car with the intention of seeing the church, but the wife immediately began screaming and insisted that they get back in the car and drive home to England at once. With their holiday cancelled, the husband obviously wanted to know what had bothered her so much. She claimed to have seen what looked like vines coming out of the ground toward her.

Such events can be seen as coincidence and it is ultimately up to you how you interpret them. For me, they cemented something of my attachment to the area as a place of amplified energy.

JANUARY 17

Another vision during the lifetime of Father Saunière was the appearance of the Virgin Mary at Pontmain in the Loire. The apparition of Our Lady of Hope occurred on January 17, 1871. The date of January 17th occurs repeatedly in this mystery and leads to a number of ideas that expand on some of the themes hinted at in the Rennes-le-Château church. There are such an overwhelming number of references and layers of relevance to this date that I think it poses one of the true examples of how important the Rennes-le-Château mystery is. From the perspectives of psychology and alchemy the meaning of synchronicities is always worth pursuing. They are evidence of something of the holistic nature of the universe.

I asked Sion if January 17 was important to them, and received this response:

> 'January 17 is, as you are doubtless aware, the date of Nicolas Flamel's "Gift from God", and certainly marks the commencement of his extraordinary wealth and philanthropic career.'
> 'His diary speaks clearly of his transmutation taking place at midday. It is no coincidence that, as we have previously reminded, all Masonic meetings, especially the higher degrees, take place at "virtual noon".'
> 'In addition, this date also marks the feast day of St Anthony of Egypt, the sainted alchemist. It was by design that the feast day of St Sulpitius [the seventh-century patron of Saint-Sulpice church in Paris] coincided with that of St Anthony.'

The first alchemical transmutation of Nicolas Flamel took place at noon on January 17, 1382, as recorded in his own journal. In 356CE St Anthony died aged 105 and January 17 is his feast day. As we have seen it is also the feast day of St Sulpitius as well as of St Germaine (who features in the church) and St Roseline, of whom we will learn more later.

There is also a possible link with the last of the original nine Knights Templar, André de Montbard, who died on January 17, 1156. He was succeeded by Bertrand de Blanchefort, who hailed from the Bordeaux region of France. As yet I can find no direct link other than in name between him and the noble Blanchefort family of Rennes-le-Château, though some researchers do consider him related. Perhaps the name was adopted by the later family as a symbolic gesture of respect.

As for Freemasonry, the 17th Degree is the precursor to the 18th Rose+ Croix Degree, though as Sion affirmed:

'The controversial and initiatory [17th Degree] rite as a prelude to the alchemical Rose+Croix is not the sole explanation of the relevance of January 17. There are many other facets to that date.'

We have also seen that at Rennes-le-Château, January 17, 1781, is given as the date on the tombstone of Countess Marie de Negri d'Ables and is also the officially recorded date of Father Saunière's fatal heart attack in the Tour Magdala in 1917. And it is on that same date that the stained glass windows in Saunière's church produce an image of blue apples. The date is also said to be the day on which the future Sigisbert IV, the surviving son of the Merovingian king Dagobert II, arrived in the Rennes-le-Château region in 681, as mentioned in the *Dossiers Secrets* that Sion circulated in the late 20th century.

According to researcher Nicole Dawe, this day also saw the visit of the Archduke Rudolph of Hapsburg (1919–2010) to the church at Rennes-le-Château as recently as 1975.

It is difficult to tell which event, if any, is the key to these occurrences of the date, or how many of them are merely coincidence. I consider the date to be a marker, a way of making links between distant events that have some underlying correlation with Sion's aims. It may be that January 17 is important to all levels of the mystery and therefore resonates on all levels in an alchemical fashion. That Nicolas Flamel noted it as the date he achieved the Great Work is of particular significance.

THE MIRROR

'When we look into a mirror we rarely see through the glass to
the tin beyond.'

Wolfram von Eschenbach, Parzival

Another alchemical effect that is of interest here is mirroring. There are two
aspects of mirroring at work in the mystery of Rennes-le-Château. The first
is a physical representation, as Father Bérenger Saunière placed objects in the
gardens that were to reflect the contents of the church, inverted. In this way
he created a mirror-image of the church, both upside down and reversed. The
Visigothic pillar supporting the Virgin Mary statue outside the church has also
been inverted. Many individual features have a 'reflection', for example the
statues of Christ and Asmodeus perfectly mirror each other both in posture
and the focus of their gaze within the church. The Stations of the Cross are also
displayed in reverse order, and in addition to this Saunière's Tour Magdala is
mirrored in his glasshouse/orangery tower at the opposite corner of the garden.

Why did Saunière work with reflection? Given the strong strand of heretical
and unorthodox beliefs of the region it is entirely possible that this church of
Mary Magdalene has been used as a focus to uphold and express the importance
of the hidden feminine as a mirror and counterbalance for the all-male establishment of the Catholic Church, just as the female moon is traditionally the
reflection of, and necessary balance to, the masculine sun.

Further afield, in England, Shugborough Hall has a statue sculpted after
Poussin's *Et in Arcadia Ego* (*Shepherds of Arcadia*) painting, but carved as a mirror
image. This is seen in an alchemical context as having been reversed because it
is on the opposite side the water (the English Channel) of the original tomb in
the painting, which is located near Rennes-le-Château.

In the broader sense, the Rennes-le-Château mystery also appears to have
the psychological effect of acting like a mirror on some researchers.

THE MAGIC MIRROR AND SYNCHRONICITY

Aside from the physical evidence for reflection there is also the idea that the
mystery of Rennes-le-Château is like a mirror in that it reflects and amplifies
what visitors already know. Many seem to discover an angle on the mystery
that perfectly fits their own prior knowledge or issues, to the extent that when

exploring the mystery they find what they bring to it.

To some extent this happens in many aspects of life but at Rennes-le-Château it seems especially prevalent. When I put this idea to Sion, this was their response:

> 'Whilst archaeological digs would yield certain things (some of great importance), the reality was such that one would be likely to "turn-up" whatever one was looking for by virtue of Rennes-le-Château's unique status, it being a place and a "mystery" that was "created" many moons ago by magi who sought to utilize its geological and locational significance.'

This may not seem possible, but when we examine some of the authors and researchers who have written on the subject we often discover that whatever their field of interest they have been able to find evidence for it in the region. Likewise some of the critics who seek only to negate the mystery are equally prone to fall into the same trap. I use the word 'trap' because I believe this effect to be just that. Apart from the fascinating bizarreness of the phenomenon it can only act as a barrier to the truth. If all we attain is our individual need, then we fail to see the real secrets of Rennes-le-Château.

The idea that we in effect create our own reality is well documented in psychology (and is also current in some aspects of modern physics) as a form of projection. I have never known a place to invite so much projected material. It is as if Rennes-le-Château can be experienced as an external manifestation of the collective unconscious. So much so that it makes for an excellent psychological 'sand box' for experimentation.

An example of the effect at its most basic can be seen in some of the Rennes-le-Château treasure hunters. In its adult form the juvenile urge to find 'buried treasure' is likely to be a prompt to search the self and redeem emotional material that is lost to the unconscious. This search can be projected onto the outside world in the form of a quest to find hidden Visigothic gold, or any other 'treasure hunt'. An image of this can be seen in Plate 5 of the *Splendor Solis*, a 16th-century alchemical manuscript famed for its rich engravings, where the figures dig deep to explore the underworld for treasure.

In my experience Rennes-le-Château does seem to accelerate and heighten this process of projection and it has been described by Sion as a 'magic mirror'. Whether or not one accepts this notion, it does no harm to realize that the path of the mystery of Rennes-le-Château is fraught with distractions. Rather than decreasing the mystery, however, in my view it only adds to it. As Sion put it:

> 'Did you never wonder just how it was that everything of
> consequence relating to the place would appear as if Rennes-
> le-Château were some immense magic mirror; a wonderful
> reflecting, Hermetic, looking-glass?'

ALCHEMY

Both the physical and psycho-spiritual forms of mirroring are also a part of a greater work at play here: the work of alchemy.

> 'You enquired at the outset as to whether or not the "secret" is
> in any way connected with alchemy, and our answer is in the
> affirmative.'

The underlying theme that touches every aspect of the mystery in some form is alchemy. This will be covered at length later, but for now it will suffice to remind ourselves of the presence in the church of salamanders, which represent fire and sulphur in alchemical symbolism, while the Rose+Croix symbols on the Stations of the Cross also have their roots in this tradition.

A local resident once stated that 'there is a cave near Rennes-le-Château that has all the elements needed for alchemy' and we will return to this subject at great length later, after exploring much more of the mystery.

SUMMARY

Linked directly to alchemy is the attainment of communication with the divine. This experience is known as gnosis, literally 'knowledge' – that is, direct knowledge of God. Gnosis can be induced, and this has been the aim of the Priory of Sion, the Rosicrucians and many of the mystery schools of antiquity. In the Rose+Croix degrees of Freemasonry, the Chamber of Reflection is used to attain a state of gnosis. It is considered a place to commune with the 'Inner Master', the divine, or in psychology, the Higher Self.

The area around Rennes-le-Château has been used and modified over time to serve a number of purposes and local resources have been adapted accordingly. The overall impression we receive from Sion is that near Rennes-le-Château is a route that enables one to undertake the spiritual journey of the Rose+Croix, a mystical re-enactment of the journey of Christ as he approached the cross. The steps along this journey, and its many levels of meaning, are narrated by the Priory of Sion in a text called *Le Serpent Rouge – The Red Serpent*.

With this in mind let us now join the tradition of which this land is a part and look at pilgrimage, and then take up the challenge of unravelling the Red Serpent: Sion's symbolic spiritual quest, enacted through this region.

CHAPTER 9

PILGRIMAGE

INTRODUCTION

Pilgrimage is a theme that pervades the area of Rennes-le-Château. To undertake a pilgrimage is a humbling experience, be it to the tombs of Christian saints or the Hajj to Mecca, as pilgrims neither expect nor want recognition for their endeavour. They are often called or compelled to journey great distances from their homes and families to a place that resonates with them, and yet the journey is often more transformative than the arrival at their goal. At the core of pilgrimage is the desire to journey to sacred sites, and this responds in some way to an innate urge to connect with the divine. By undertaking a journey of contemplation toward a sacred goal we hope to become attuned to receiving an experience of the divine. The achievement of completing such a journey compounds the relationship between the pilgrim and the sacred object or location, allowing it to act as a physical amplifier for spiritual energy.

Believers have long been drawn to their chosen holy site. In ancient times it may have been the temples of Egypt or the oracle at Delphi in Greece, and today pilgrimage remains a feature of Christianity and most of the world's other major religions, including Islam, Buddhism and Hinduism. Some journey to ask favours and some to ask for healing, while others see their journey as an act of pure devotion, a sign of respect for whatever waits at their intended destination.

THE INNER ASPECTS OF THE QUEST

The outer journey of pilgrimage is also reflected in an inner journey of self-discovery.

There are ways to experience some of the religious aspects of pilgrimage symbolically. For example, a believer may follow the Stations of the Cross in churches in the order that Jesus experienced the events at the time of the cruci-fixion. Moving from Station to Station and contemplating each one allows for an empathic response to the suffering and trials of Jesus.

Following a labyrinth can perform a similar function. The labyrinths set out on cathedral floors, such as at Chartres, can be walked by believers as symbolic journeys to Jerusalem, the Holy City. But the labyrinth may also be used by those outside the Christian ethos. By contemplating the path of this device you can spiral down toward the 'source' and then return, having witnessed many revelations. So too in the Tarot, the journey of the Fool (representing the holy innocent or spiritual seeker) through the cycle of the Major Arcana is an explo-ration of the archetypes that can be contemplated and worked with as tools for self-development. Even rituals of the Masonic variety can act as condensed pilgrimages.

The journey, whether real or symbolic, serves as an important part of the spiritual path. Ascending a mountain to a church or temple may represent the exploration of higher consciousness – the realm of Higher Self and the path to gnosis. Many religious sites were situated high on mountains, close to 'heaven'. The act of climbing the mountain symbolically re-enacts our spiritual ascension toward an experience of the divine. This is borne out not just in theology but can also be found in transpersonal psychology, mythology and literature.

The routes of Christianity

Christian pilgrims may visit a vast array of relics and holy sites scattered throughout Europe and the Middle East. Spiritual pilgrimage has come back into fashion in recent years, with increasing numbers choosing to explore the journeys to sacred sites in a traditional manner. In a way they are taking back the term 'pilgrimage' from its broader misuse and reclaiming the sacred places from the tourists who rush from pillar to post for their next photo opportunity. Just a single day's walk with an open mind to a holy place may present oppor-tunities for a spiritual experience.

Christian pilgrimage to the Holy Land, culminating in the many holy sites of Jerusalem, began as early as the fourth century CE. By the Middle Ages, the popularity of the major routes from Europe had exploded. Regardless of the authenticity of the site or relic they were visiting, the growing trend of undertak-ing a long journey to a holy site had become an important spiritual expression for kings and peasants alike. This is where the roots of modern tourism as we know it began, with many pilgrims who had previously lived entirely within the boundaries of their home area, or even village, suddenly traversing Europe and the Holy Land.

The secret diversion

Within Europe itself, medieval pilgrims headed for two principal destinations. One of these was the ancient imperial capital of Rome, the seat of the Church and site of the martyrdom of many famous saints, including the apostles Peter and Paul.

The other site was the shrine of the apostle St James (Santiago) at Compostela in northern Spain. The *Guide for the Pilgrim of Santiago*, written in the 12th century, states that there were four main routes to the shrine at that time. From these stemmed a number of lesser routes such as the 'wet' and 'dry' routes via land or sea, which denoted an alchemical dimension of the journey.

> 'It was always stated that the pilgrimage of St James, undertaken by many well-known visionaries and artists of all disciplines, was important because the route involved the pilgrim being "both pedestrian and *nautonnier* (helmsman)".'

The section between Toulouse and Oloron-Sainte-Marie traditionally passed close to Rennes-le-Château. As on many other routes, a number of sites along the road are significant as part of the spiritual journey undertaken by the pilgrim. However, Sion believes that this section of the road to Santiago was used as cover for a secret destination, a diversion that took seekers into the region of Rennes-le-Château:

> 'The true and ancient alchemists such as Flamel journeyed under the aegis of the *Camino de Santiago* [Road of St James], thus preserving their true intentions and the real place to which they made pilgrimage.'

The alchemist Nicolas Flamel is recorded as having undertaken this pilgrimage and, as we will see later, this is alluded to in *Le Serpent Rouge*.

To the south of Rennes-le-Château passes an old Roman road that is known to have been used as a route to Santiago de Compostela since the Middle Ages. I have walked a part of the route, though at the time I was unaware that I had joined such a sacred path.

INITIATION

Having left the main pilgrimage route a winding path would pass a number of important sites. There is a fork in the path near the Grotto of Mary Magdalene, and at this point the exoteric and esoteric routes diverge. The entire area was modified, carved and sculpted to allow a three-dimensional journey in the same way that Masonic lodges enact initiation rituals – but in the real world.

The Masonic Rose+Croix degree is said to be the closest ritual to enacting the Via Dolorosa, the journey that Jesus took from his judgment by Pilate to his crucifixion and entombment. It is this journey that is mapped out in the Stations of the Cross in churches. The versions of the Stations at Rennes-le-Château have a number of anomalies including the presence of tartan, as mentioned above.

We know that the Templars, having been expelled from the Holy Land, settled in large numbers in the Languedoc. It is entirely possible that they would have attempted to recreate their beloved Jerusalem locally in order to continue the traditions that they had learned and developed in that city, thus creating a 'via dolorosa' that mirrors the journey Jesus takes in the Stations of the Cross. This would then have been adapted by Sion as an early form of initiation into the Rosicrucian degrees of Freemasonry. As Sion says:

'The environs of Rennes-le-Château were most definitely used for the purposes of induction – induction on a very grand scale.'

The pilgrimage route at Rennes-le-Château visits locations that derive their names from places in Jerusalem. The route is also in view of Father Saunière's Tour Magdala, which acts as a beacon at various points on the journey. After the tower had been erected, the angle of one window was changed at great expense to both provide a better view of the route and to symbolically recall that Mary Magdalene was considered repentant: a woman who changed her view. This links the route of both the pilgrimage and initiation to Mary Magdalene.

It is likely that the route has varied and developed over the years with the ever-changing landscape, but there would seem to be some key aspects that have survived from as far back as the Templars.

Important though the ritualistic aspects of the journey are, one must not lose sight of the destination. Every pilgrimage must have a goal, a final location of great religious or spiritual significance, and this one is no different.

In search of this final destination we emerge from the Grotto of Mary Magdalene and follow the Ruisseau des Couleurs (the River of Colours, itself symbolic of the iridescent 'peacock' or 'rainbow' stage in alchemy), due east toward Lavaldieu, the Valley of God. Here there are a number of sites of interest but for the most part they are on private land. They include the pool with its 'Pillar of Flagellation' (the Sixth Station of the Cross) and a labyrinth at Rennes-les-Bains that harks back to the old design. on cathedral floors. The route finishes at the Fauteuil du Diable (Devil's Armchair), where the initiate's feet are washed, reminiscent of Mary Magdalene washing the feet of Jesus. But to truly understand the depth of what is being presented here – the many levels of being that a true initiation works upon – we must immerse ourselves in what I consider to be Sion's most important release: *Le Serpent Rouge*. There we may find some clue to the secret that is revealed along the way.

CHAPTER 10

LE SERPENT ROUGE

Le Serpent Rouge encapsulates all aspects of the mystery.

The Priory of Sion

In the late 20th century the Priory of Sion circulated a small publication entitled *Le Serpent Rouge* (*The Red Serpent*). At its core is a mystical poem in thirteen stanzas in which all the threads of the Rennes-le-Château mystery are drawn together, including a route through the landscape; symbolism; alchemy; bloodlines; art; literature; and the Paris Meridian. It touches upon every level of the mystery while encrypting its secrets in strange, symbolic language.

It was *Le Serpent Rouge* that first really attracted me to the mystery of Rennes-le-Château and the Priory of Sion. The document is drenched in esoteric symbolism yet contains directions and references to real locations in the valleys surrounding Rennes-le-Château. The 'red serpent' of the title is both the alchemical salamander (a creature once believed to be impervious to flames, and hence a symbol of fire) and the River Sals, which turns red from the iron-rich soil as it runs through Rennes-les-Bains. Sion confirmed that '*Le Serpent Rouge* does indeed draw attention to the environs of Rennes-le-Château'. The entire symbolic journey is mapped onto a real symbolic landscape to create a journey of initiation.

On first encountering this work I suspected that its authors were trying to communicate something of great importance. In my twenty years of research that suspicion has never wavered. It is clear that *Le Serpent Rouge* works on a number of levels. On the surface there are references to the physical aspects of the Rennes-le-Château church and the surrounding landscape. Beneath this are direct references to alchemical processes, which lends the entire document the feeling of a dream. It calls to mind the alchemical journeys described in *The Most Holy Trinosophia* (a work attributed to the legendary Comte de St Germain) or the process of the 16th-century *Splendor Solis*. According to Sion, *Le Serpent Rouge* 'intermixed the whole crucible of information, the secret itself, in alchemical allusion.'

Like all alchemical texts we are taken on a journey of initiation that acts on both the physical and spiritual levels of being. The initiation that it describes can be undertaken as a pilgrimage, a spiritual journey or a ritual much like the 18th (Rose+Croix) Degree of Freemasonry. It can also be studied remotely and used for visualization of the kind that appears in guided meditations.

KNOWN HISTORY

Although the current edition of *Le Serpent Rouge* first went into public circulation in the late 1960s, its true origin and age are unclear, as Sion gives the impression that it has been changed and updated to reflect changes in the landscape over time. According to Sion the original, which 'was never intended for the public eye', existed in French, Arabic, Catalan, German and also Provençal, a dialect of Occitan, the language of southern France which is still widely spoken in the Languedoc and elsewhere. But none of these versions have been made available, and given that the bulk of the poem is devoted to the renovated church of St Mary Magdalene at Rennes-le-Château, I think it is safe to say that *Le Serpent Rouge* as we know it originated in the 20th century. The current version may have several predecessors, each of which was subsequently expanded or elaborated. Sion claims that the text has a long and distinguished history; allegedly used by Renaissance artists, philosophers and metaphysicists, it has a core-message that may well stretch back as far as the early medieval or Gothic period.

It is a beautiful poem in its own right, and its authorship is still in question. Pierre Plantard was capable of writing it, as was Jean Cocteau. Certainly, parallels can be seen in Cocteau's own exploration of the journey into the underworld in his film *Orphée*.

The work originally consisted of a single piece of prose, the thirteen stanzas representing an expanded zodiac. Some parts of the poem are said to have been compiled from other texts, including the diaries of Nicolas Flamel and parchments that originated with the St Hillier family. Flamel is a recurring figure in many of the alchemical references made by Sion. As we have seen, he is said to have achieved the Great Work at noon on a January 17 and is considered one of history's leading alchemists. But his published writings reveal little of his actual knowledge. The 'genuine' diaries that have influenced *Le Serpent Rouge* are not publicly available. Sion would also have us believe that Flamel received much of his alchemical knowledge from a book that he was given while undertaking a pilgrimage that included the Rennes-le-Château diversion (*see* Chapter 9). This might simply be a further allusion to Flamel's importance, but we will return to this idea later.

According to the cover of the current (1960s) edition, the authorship of *Le Serpent Rouge* was originally attributed to three men who were said to have been found hanged following its publication. The story is spurious but exists to indicate that something important and esoteric is being revealed, and is akin to the Masonic threat of hanging for the revelation of secrets. The myth of the murders also serves to generate interest in the document while hiding the identity of the true authors.

Louis Vazart, an archivist and antiquarian member of Sion's second level, was known to have circulated copies to prospective members of Sion toward the end of the 20th century. Vazart had revised an earlier version of the text which he distributed unsolicited to those who Sion thought might be interested or of use to them. These copies were given a fictitious publisher and had a red binding.

The booklet was also used as a form of signpost by the Priory of Sion. It is worth noting that they tendered to potential recruits an invitation not to join the Priory of Sion directly but to join 'the mystery of Rennes-le-Château'.

It is no surprise that the Priory of Sion used *Le Serpent Rouge* as a circular in order to attract people who would be interested in its work. It is the most perfect invitation to join an esoteric society since the Rosicrucians published the *Fama Fraternitatis* and *Confessio Fraternitatis* in the early 17th century (*see* page 32). The Priory was moving to make public some of its knowledge and had begun to disseminate something of the organization to the outside world.

THE ORIGINAL TEXT

The first public appearance of the publication was a copy deposited in the Paris National Library in the late 1960s. The cover was titled *Le Serpent Rouge* and subtitled *Notes on St.-Germain-des-Prés and Saint-Sulpice of Paris*. Also on the cover is the publication date of January 17, 1967 – January 17 being the date found as a signpost throughout this affair – and a price of three francs, along with the spurious author names plus a reference to Pontoise as the publisher's location. Pontoise is the birthplace of Nicolas Flamel, and another subtle reference for alchemists to recognize. These details convey the overall effect of making it appear a normal publication while subtly highlighting the content for the intended audience.

The cover bears a hand-drawn shield device depicting a horse with the inscription 'LENE BUXEUM-EOUS SCAPH FE'. This phrase may seem impervious to translation, though in Latin *lene* (short for *plene*) translates as 'completely' and *scaph* (short for *scaphium*) as 'bowl', so it may be an allusion to the biblical phrase 'my cup runneth over' (Psalms 23.5).

There is also a circular device of three concentric rings. It is a kind of logo, with the outer rings made up of dots with P at the top and S at the foot, the initials of the Priory of Sion. The second ring is wider with an equal-armed cross at the top and the inscription *Rosa Crux 1099–1188*. The inner ring has a letter S curled through what appears to be a thigh bone beneath a curved letter M. According to Sion:

> 'Like the cult of Osiris, the Sufic Freemasonry of the final era of
> the Crusades also adopted the thigh bone, later to be employed by
> the early privateers and later Moorish Dancers, etc. Traditionally,
> the crossed thigh bones are the primary symbol of the "Slain
> Osiris".'

A similar device can be found in the church at Rennes-le-Château, high on an arch. The stylized M is a variation on the monogram of the Virgin Mary and is likely to denote Mary Magdalene, to whom the church is dedicated.

Possibly a later addition or specific to my photocopy is what appears to be a library reference: 'DL 20 March 1967. 04927.'

When Vazart later circulated the booklet with a bound cover, the back cover explained the apparent deaths of the authors and the inside back cover contained a news report of the decapitation of a courier, Fakhar ul-Islam on a train from Paris to Geneva. The decapitation and hangings may have been intended to warn the reader that they were handling material that was bound by Masonic oath. Fakhar ul-Islam's death was a real event and he was said by Sion to be in possession of a state secret and possibly also alchemical documents and genealogies that were stolen.

On the second page is the figure of a seated woman with three dice at her feet. She is wearing a scallop shell, the pilgrim's badge for the route to Santiago

Asmodeus statue at
Rennes-le-Château

Father Béranger Saunière's
cassock

St Anthony and St Paul in the Desert – painting by David Teniers the Younger

Et in Arcadia Ego (The Shepherds of Arcadia) – painting by Nicolas Poussin

Altar at Rennes–le–Château with landscape

Left to right: The hills of Coustaussa (with ruin), Pech Cardou and Blanchefort

Splendor Solis: 'Deliver me out of the mire…'

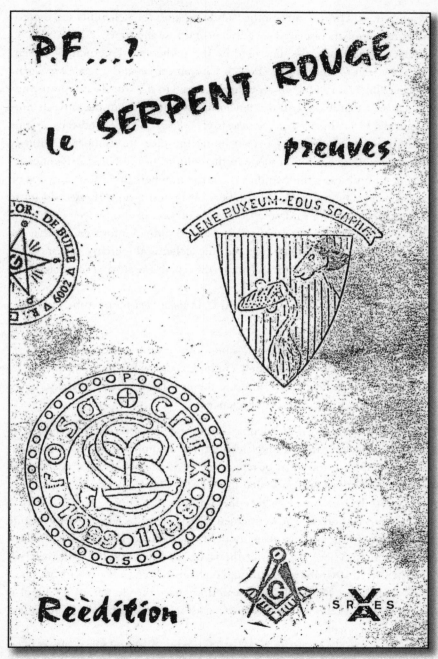

The cover of *Le Serpent Rouge*

de Compostela. The dice are another subtle signpost for alchemists and esoteri-
cists, as the numbers displayed on adjacent sides are incorrect.

This also occurs in the dice used by the soldiers in the crucifixion scene
painted by Jean Cocteau in the French Church off London's Leicester Square
(*see* page 256). Henry Lincoln brought this mural to the world's attention when
he discovered that it was constructed around a pentagram in the same manner
as Poussin's *Et in Arcadia Ego (Shepherds of Arcadia)* and the landscape around
Rennes-le-Château. In the Cocteau mural the dice are numbered wrongly,
as they are in the crucifixion scene in the Stations of the Cross at Rennes-le-
Château. In both cases the two dice show the numbers three, four and five on
adjacent sides. On real dice the numbers on opposite sides always add up to
seven, so three and four cannot be adjacent and this can also be seen in the Jean
Cocteau mural in London mentioned earlier. Sion had informed me that the
three dice in *Le Serpent Rouge* represent the alchemical mercury and are taken
from a 15th-century alchemical manuscript called *The Book of the Holy Trinity*
(which I will cover later).

Also on this page is a quotation from *L'Alchimie Moderne* by Abbé Théophile
Moreux (1867–1954):

> 'After a long sleep, the same assumptions resurface, undoubt-
> edly returned to us with new clothing and a richer person, but
> the foundations are the same and the new mask which they wear
> could not mislead a man of science.'

Note that the term 'man of science' can be used to describe alchemists. The
notion of awakening from a long sleep returns a number of times throughout
Le Serpent Rouge in the form of references to *Sleeping Beauty* (*La Belle au bois
dormant*), the famous tale published in 1697 by Charles Perrault (*see* page 50)
and may also be a reference to 'race memory'.

The general contents that were added to the core of *Le Serpent Rouge* include
a smattering of histories and plans about St.-Germain-des-Prés and its Parisian
district in 1615. There is a plan of the layout of Saint-Sulpice with the Paris
Meridian, dated 1966 and a few cuttings on Saint-Sulpice in Paris with attention
drawn to the artist N Signol, whose paintings grace the church walls. 'Signol' is
written around a reversed N, which the artist uses to sign his work and is said
to be a sign of adepts.

Other material present includes a Merovingian genealogical chart, maps
of France at the time of the Visigoths and Merovingians, and an image of

Childebert, the Merovingian king. These have links to the idea of a bloodline surviving to the present day and will be covered in a later chapter.

The copy forwarded to me had also been stamped with a number of devices. These include stamps from Grand Lodge Alpina, Memphis–Misraim and a Priory of Sion 'Crux Rosa' design. It also has a sample of Arabic handwriting on the back that includes the date 1956 in Arabic numerals.

The core of the booklet is undoubtedly the 13 stanzas following an expanded zodiac that includes Ophiuchus, the Serpent Bearer. Ophiuchus occupies a gap between Scorpio and Sagittarius and it is interesting to note that it was only officially accepted into the astronomical zodiac as recently as 1995. The sun is in Ophiuchus from November 30 to December 16.

What follows is the original French text of the 13 astrological stanzas that describe the journey, taken from a copy released to me by the Priory of Sion.

Note: the rows of 'x's appear in the original text and are used to overprint typographical errors. The numbered headings given here are represented in the actual text by small icons of the astrological signs that contain numbers.

1. Aquarius

Comme ils sont étranges les manuscrits de cet Ami, grand voyageur de l'inconnu, ils me sont parvenus séparément, pourtant ils forment un tout pour lui qui sait que les couleurs de l'arc-en-ciel donnent l'unité blanche, ou pour l'Artiste qui sous son pinceau fait, des six teintes de sa palette magique, jaillir le noir.

2. Pisces

Cet Ami, comment vous le présenter? Son nom demeura un mystère, mais son nombre est celui d'un sceau célèbre. Comment vous le décrire? Peut-être comme le nautonnier de l'arche impérissable, impassible comme une colonne sur son roc blanc, scrutant vers le midi, au-delà du roc noir.

3. Aries

Dans mon pèlerinage éprouvant, je tentais de me frayer à l'épée une voie à travers la végétation inextricable des bois, je voulais parvenir à la demeure de la BELLE endormie en qui certains poètes voient la REINE d'un royaume disparu. Au désespoir de retrouver le chemin, les parchemins de cet Ami furent pour moi le fil d'Ariane.

4. Taurus

Grâce à lui, désormais à pas mesurés et d'un oeil sûr, je puis decouvrir les soix-ante-quatre pierres dispersées du cube parfait que les Frères de la BELLE du bois noir, échappant à la poursuite des usurpateurs, avaient semées en route quant ils s'enfuirent du Fort blanc.

5. Gemini

Rassembler les pierres éparses, oeuvrer de l'équerre et du compas pour les remettre en ordre régulier, chercher la ligne du méridien en allant de l'Orient à l'Occident, puis regardant du Midi au Nord, enfin en tous sens pour obtenir la solution cherchée, faisant station devant les quatorze pierres marquées d'une croix. Le cercle étant l'anneau et couronne, et lui le diadème de cette REINE du Castel.

6. Cancer

Les dalles du pavé mosaïque du lieu sacré pouvaient être alternativement blanches ou noires, et JESUS, comme ASMODEE, observer leurs alignements; ma vue semblait incapable de voir le sommet où demeurait cachée la merveilleuse endormie. N'étant pas HERCULE à la puissance magique, comment déchiffrer les mystérieux symboles gravés par les observateurs du passé? Dans le sanctuaire pourtant le bénitier, fontaine d'amour des croyants, redonne mémoire de ces mots: PAR CE SIGNE TU le VAINCRAS.

7. Leo

De celle que je désirais libérer, montaient vers moi les effluves du parfum qui imprégnèrent le sépulcre. Jadis les uns l'avaient nommée: ISIS, reine des sources bienfaisantes, VENEZ A MOI VOUS TOUS QUI SOUFFREZ ET QUI ETES ACCABLES ET JE VOUS SOULAGERAI, d'autres: MADELAINE, au célèbre vase plein d'un baume guérisseur. Les initiés savent son nom véritable: NOTRE DAME DES CROSS.

8. Virgo

J'étais comme les bergers du célèbre peintre POUSSIN, perplexe devant l'énigme: "ET IN ARCADIA EGO..."! La voix du sang allait-elle me rendre l'image d'un passé ancestral. Oui, l'éclair du génie traversa ma pensée. Je revoyais, je comprenais! Je savais maintenant ce secret fabuleux. Et merveille, lors des sauts des quatre cavaliers, les sabots d'un cheval avaient laissé quatre empreintes sur la pierre, voilà le signe que DELACROIX avait donné dans l'un des trois tableaux de la

chapelle des Anges. Voilà la septième sentence qu'une main avait tracée: RETIRE
MOI DE LA BOUE, QUE JE N'Y RESTE PAS ENFONCE. Deux fois IS,
embaumeuse et embaumée, vase miracle de l'éternelle Dame Blanche des Légendes.

9. Libra

Commencé dans les ténèbres, mon voyage ne pouvait s'achever qu'en Lumière.
A la fenêtre de la maison ruinée, je contemplais à travers les arbres dépouillés par
l'automne le sommet de la montagne. La croix de crête se détachait sous le soleil
du midi, elle était la quatorzième et la plus grande de toutes avec ses 35 centimè-
tres! Me voici donc à mon tour cavalier sur le coursier divin chevauchant l'abîme.

10. Scorpio

Vision céleste pour celui qui me souvient des quatres oeuvres de Em. SIGNOL
autour de la ligne du Méridien, au choeur même du sanctuaire d'où rayonne
cette source d'amour des uns pour les autres, je pivote sur moi-même passant
du regard la rose du P à celle de l'S, puis de l'S au P ... et la spirale dans
mon esprit devenant comme un poulpe monstrueux expulsant son encre, les
ténèbres absorbent la lumière, j'ai le vertige et je porte ma main à ma bouche,
mordant instinctivement ma paume, peut-être comme OLIER dans son cerceuil.
Malédiction, je comprends la vérité, IL EST PASSE, mais lui aussi en faisant
LE BIEN, ainsi que xxxxxxxx CELUI de la tombe fleurie. Mais combien
ont saccagé la MAISON, ne laissant que des cadavres embaumés et nombres
de métaux qu'ils n'avaient pu emporter. Quel étrange mystère recèle le nouveau
temple de SALOMON édifié par les enfants de Saint-VINCENT.

11. Ophiuchus/Serpent

Maudissant les profanateurs dans leurs cendres et ceux qui vivent sur leurs traces,
sortant de l'abîme où j'étais plongé en accomplissant le geste d'horreur: "Voici la
preuve que du sceau de SALOMON je connais le secret, que xxxxxxxxxxx
de cette REINE j'ai visité les demeures cachées." A ceci, Ami Lecteur, garde toi
d'ajouter ou de retrancher un iota ... médite, Médite encore, le vil plomb de mon
écrit xxxx contient peut-être l'or le plus pur.

12. Sagittarius

Revenant alors à la blanche colline, le ciel ayant ouvert ses vannes, il me sembla près
de moi sentir une présence, les pieds dans l'eau comme celui qui vient de recevoir la
marque du baptême, me retournant vers l'est, face à moi je vis déroulant sans fin ses

anneaux, l'énorme SERPENT ROUGE cité dans les parchemins, salée et amère, l'énorme bête déchainée devint au pied de ce mont blanc, rouge en colère.

13. Capricorn

Mon émotion fut grande, "RETIRE MOI DE LA BOUE" disais-je, et mon réveil fut immédiat. J'ai omis de vous dire en effet que c'était un songe que j'avais fait ce 17 JANVIER, fête de Saint-SULPICE. Par la suite, mon trouble persistant, j'ai voulu après réflexions d'usage vous le relater un conte de PERRAULT. Voici donc Ami Lecteur, dans les pages qui suivent le résultat d'un rêve m'ayant bercé dans le monde de l'étrange à l'inconnu. A celui qui PASSE de FAIRE LE BIEN.

TRANSLATION AND COMMENTARY

There are a number of translations available but I have chosen Nicole Dawe's as the mainstay. She is a professional translator and an academic researcher who spent many years in the region and her input, as always, was invaluable in navigating the nuances of French wordplay. My only additions to this were for the purposes of flow or where the direct translation of a quotation differed from a recognizable source such as the Bible.

Various authors, including David Wood and Elizabeth Van Buren, published their own translations in the 1980s and since then other versions have been appearing online and in publications. Each author tends to have their own distinct take on the text and because it is so diverse and symbolic in content it lends itself to completely different readings. Depending on your level of interest you can interpret this text in many ways.

The structure of *Le Serpent Rouge* is astrological. Seeing an array of Greek mythological figures transcribed in dot-to-dot form in a sky of randomly scattered stars may now seem bizarre to us, but it is worth remembering that the Greek civilization's understanding of archetypal influences in psychology was incredibly advanced.

In terms of archetypes and influence, Renaissance philosopher and astrologer Marsillio Ficino also tells us that the planets are within us, and therefore very much in the realm of psychology. The constellations are a projection of our inner psyche to be identified and re-integrated. A student of Jung, Marie Louise von Franz, concurs, stating that the planets within are to be, and their influences realigned (rectified).

We also do well to remember that long before Jung began to explore the unconscious, alchemy had a process of discerning the layers of influence, like the application of heat to distil impurities from substances.

From what I can glean, Sion is interested in all levels of astrology. With an alchemist's eye they view every phenomenon from all sides. They have an interest in 'mundane' astrology – the astrology of locations such as Rennes-le-Château and other important locations around the world. There is also the early work of Franz Mesmer (1734–1815), whom Sion has mentioned a number of times. He was known to have drawn on the work of an English astrologer, Richard Meade, to explore the notion that the tidal effects of the sun and the moon would also affect the human body.

It is also interesting to note that the addition of an astrological sign creates a shift from twelve to thirteen, which would be the true number of disciples were Mary Magdalene's role to be acknowledged and accepted by Church.

Let us now begin our journey. My commentary follows a translation of each stanza with additional guidance from the Priory of Sion. My interpretation is in no way definitive but it might serve as a starting point for others who intend to walk this path.

1. Aquarius

How strange they are, the manuscripts of this Friend, great traveller through the unknown, they came to me individually, although together they make up a whole for him who knows that the colours of the rainbow form white unity, or for the Artist who with his paintbrush makes the colour black spring from the six colours of his magic palette.

The directions included in *Le Serpent Rouge* may at first appear confusing. This is due to the dual nature of the text. Often what is being described is both the route across the landscape and the interior of the church at Rennes-le-Château. The latter is a guide to the former. The church mirrors the landscape and the pilgrim is to keep this in mind as they walk the path. It is interesting that the zodiac begins with Aquarius, as Sion notes:

'[This version of the zodiac] commences with Aquarius – closer to [January] 17 than the bulk of Capricorn. Traditionally, as you are aware, the zodiac (in all its forms) commences at 0 degrees Aries.'

The 17 here is another reference to January 17, with its many correspondences. This explains why *Le Serpent Rouge* neglects to begin in Aries and also indicates that the degrees of the zodiac are important to this undertaking.

We begin our journey under the sign of Aquarius with unknown manuscripts from an unknown guide. The Egyptian god Amen-Ra first comes to mind as a candidate for 'the great traveller through the unknown', which along with the later references to Isis would give these paragraphs an Egyptian slant. The term might indicate the path that Amen-Ra, as the sun, took in his boat across the heavens. It might also allude to a *Nautonnier*, the sailor or helmsman of the Priory of Sion, a term shared with Royal Arch Freemasonry. But this is not conclusive. The 'great traveller' might also be an alchemist, such as Nicolas Flamel, journeying into the unknown regions of science and mysticism.

The 'manuscripts' could also refer to the fabricated parchments of the Rennes-le-Château mystery (*see* page 70). Nicole Dawe has commented that it may be the separate sheets that make up the *Dossiers Secrets*. Another possibility is an early version of the 18th (Rose+Croix) Degree recognizable to Freemasons. It seems that the candidate who would understand these manuscripts is being described as knowing the inner nature of both black and white from the arts and sciences. This is another Masonic allusion, indicating the chessboard floor that appears in the Rennes-le-Château church and all Masonic temples (*see* page 93). An obvious interpretation of the black and white would be good and evil, their interlinked nature implying that these opposites are dependent. There is an idea that good and evil are not separate, and opposites, but merely different aspects of the same thing.

'The colours of the rainbow that make up a single white light' take us in a slightly broader direction. The great mathematician, Freemason and alchemist Isaac Newton was credited with the discovery of the colour spectrum. He was also claimed by Sion through his inclusion in Plantard's version of the Grand Master list (*see* page 44). This supports the Masonic view but may also indicate that we are following the route followed by alchemists through the ages. The 'peacock' stage in alchemy, also entitled 'Iris or the Rainbow' (Nicolas Flamel) is a state where all aspects of nature are visible.

Sion also informed me that the references to the colours of the rainbow are linked to the origins of humankind and can be found in ancient Chinese alchemical texts. Chinese alchemy underpins what is now referred to as Taoism but originally encompassed chemistry, metallurgy, herbalism and the quest for immortality. In Chinese alchemy there is a stage called 'the place of the red dragon' and this is alluded to as 'the red serpent' to inform the reader that Western alchemy also has its roots in ancient China.

The rainbow would have been assigned magical properties by many early civilizations because it was outside their sphere of control and understanding, but the influence of Chinese alchemy can perhaps also be seen in the Vedic texts of India as the god Indra carries a rainbow bow that fires bolts of lightning to kill the primordial serpent. Also, the Indian creation myth tells of how the gods created an ocean of milk from which an elephant was formed whose name means 'rainbow'.

The seven colours are also synonymous with the teachings of tantra as the journey can also be interpreted as the rising of *kundalini* (serpent) energy through the seven *chakras*, or energy centres of the body.

The artist who mixes six tints to make black could be Nicolas Poussin, who apparently limited his palette to only six colours. The landscape in his *Et in Arcadia Ego* arguably includes the peaks of Pech Cardou, Blanchefort and Rennes-le-Château in the background. The painting depicts a tomb that has been identified as one that stands close to these sites.

In terms of location, the colours may allude to the 'River of Colours' that runs beneath the Grotto of Mary Magdalene to the south of Rennes-le-Château.

My main Sion contact, Nic Haywood, elaborated on the alchemical aspect by explaining that the Grotto of Mary Magdalene was a place of initiation, parallel to the first stage of the alchemical process (the nigredo stage) and the first stanza of *Le Serpent Rouge*. In the previous chapter, on pilgrimage, we saw how the 'secret diversion' into the region begins in the Grotto of Mary Magdalene and then follows the River of Colours as the peacock stage.

The use of the grotto mirrors that of the room of contemplation located behind the false cupboard in the church (*see* page 101). The grotto would be used as the preparatory room for the 18th Rose+Croix Degree, which is itself a ritual form of the *nigredo*, or 'blackening' stage of alchemical transformation. Father Saunière's fresco on the altar depicts Mary Magdalene in the grotto with a skull and a cross. These are two of the items to be contemplated during the initiate's time in isolation. The *nigredo* is the clearing out of the unconscious in preparation for the initiation and leads to the 'peacock' stage symbolized by the rainbow.

Near the grotto exists an underground pool that may also have been used but it is on private land and access to it is now sealed.

2. Pisces

This Friend, how can I introduce him to you? His name will remain a mystery, but his number is that of a famous seal. How can I describe him to you? Perhaps as the commander of the imperishable ark, impassive as a column on his white rock, scrutinizing the south, beyond the black rock.

The mystery of the name could also be a reference to the Egyptian god Amen-Ra. According to the myth of Isis she placed in his path a scorpion, which stung his foot so that she could demand his secret name before administering a cure. Traditionally, to know the secret name of a god or demon is to be able to control them and this allowed Isis to breathe life back into her husband Osiris. The story of Hiram Abiff in Freemasonry is an updating of the Osiris myth and there are also parallels in the resurrection of Jesus.

The 'commander of the imperishable ark' again invokes the idea of the helmsman in both Sion and Royal Arch Freemasonry. The ark reference and the hidden name are true to Amen-Ra, who piloted his boat across the sky. Amen-Ra is also said to have a numeric value of 7, which would make the 'famous seal' the 'Seventh Seal' in the Book of Revelation.

The identity of the 'Friend' remains inconclusive because there is a figure behind much of what we are looking at. The most famous 'seal' associated with Masonic mysteries is the seal of Solomon: a pentagram (or hexagram in later interpretations). The hexagram is of interest as a symbol because it is the Hermetic seal and a simplified version of the fleur-de-lys or heraldic lily. In alchemical and Rosicrucian diagrams it represents the joining of fire and water. Water can be used to bind the demon Asmodeus to one's bidding, just as Solomon used a ring to force him to build the Temple in silence. The church of Rennes-le-Château, of course, contains Asmodeus and is designed to reflect Solomon's Temple (*see* page 119). The Sermon on the Mount fresco in the church also includes flowers that grow locally and are commonly known as 'Seal of Solomon'.

As to the secret name, the more esoteric Freemasons break 'Solomon' down into SOL-OM-ON meaning 'light', 'glory' and 'truth', though I have also heard of 'ON' representing Osiris.

Pisces contains another clear reference to a known location. The text mentions the 'white rock' looking south beyond the 'black rock' which places us at Blanchefort, to the east of Rennes-le-Château. Blanchefort is a ruined castle that stands on a white pillar of rock. We are looking south past a pillar of dark rock called Roc Nègre, the Black Rock, in the direction of the Devil's Armchair, the circle and the Dead Man. On the southern horizon is Le Château des Templiers (Castle of the Templars) up on Le Bézu. It is claimed by Sion that this was indeed, as the name suggests, a Templar castle. On the same ridge as the Château des Templiers is Roque Rouge, the Red Rock. As mentioned previously the black, white and red (*nigredo*, *albedo* and *rubedo*) are the three principal stages of the alchemical process.

In spite of this reference there is some confusion as to where we are placed on this stage of the journey. Various statements from Sion indicate that the initiation route near Rennes-le-Château is circular and begins and ends at the Devil's Armchair (Fauteuil du Diable) just south of Blanchefort. This feature is inscribed with the alpha and omega and a triangle. The triangle is symbolic of a mountain but may also be a reference to the 'eye in the triangle' seen in the nearby artificial pool amid a small copse of trees (*see* page 112). The alpha and omega represent the beginning and end of both the *Serpent Rouge* journey and the Great Work of the alchemists. Both Blanchefort and the Devil's Armchair are on the same range of hills but it is a stretch to consider them the same location.

Later in the text we discover that the journey was begun 'in the shadows', so perhaps the view south from Blanchefort relates to the stars. There is another possibility in that the full moon should be present to illuminate various aspects of the landscape, such as the River Sals snaking its way south (*see* page 177). In recent years, even with a full moon, the abundant trees and the light pollution from the houses in the valley below mean that nothing can be seen of the River Sals. I can only imagine that at one time it looked like a stream of mercury weaving its way through the valley below. However, the ruins of the Templar castle at Le Bézu can still clearly be seen in the distance directly south.

3. Aries

In my arduous pilgrimage, I tried with my sword to cut my way through the inextricable vegetation of the woods, I wanted to reach the abode of the sleeping BEAUTY, who some poets believe is the QUEEN of a vanished kingdom. When I despaired of finding my way, this Friend's parchments were my Ariadne's thread.

The use of the word 'pilgrimage' indicates the nature of our journey, in that we are heading toward a location of religious importance. A sword to cut a path through the vegetation would certainly be useful in some areas of this landscape, but the author is also alluding to Charles Perrault's famous tale *Sleeping Beauty* (*La Belle au bois dormant*).

The term 'sword' is often a masculine symbol of wisdom as it cleaves and breaks apart that which it encounters. It is tempered by the Grail, a feminine receptacle that represents healing and understanding. Earlier versions of *Le Serpent Rouge* were said to refer to this as a 'magic sword'. A magic sword appears in many myths, usually in the hands of a king or hero. There is also a complex alchemical reference related to this, as Sion confirms:

> 'Note: "We draw our steel or compass from the belly of the ram" is a familiar, old alchemical aphorism. It alludes to crucial infor- mation concerning "celestial agriculture" – another term for a specific application of alchemical science.'

The 'steel' here is another term for sword. In the chemical application of alchemy is a process that involves the use of ammonium chloride, a salt of ammonia. Ammonia derives its name from Amen-Ra (or Amun-Ra), the Egyptian god who was symbolized by the ram, as was Hermes.

Sleeping Beauty is said by some to be Perrault's most alchemical work. The Beauty of the title is easier to grasp in psychological terms, as the child of the toxic mother who by failing to be conscious of her own destructive nature passes this on to her daughter in the form of an unconscious life. Sleeping Beauty is re-awakened to life by love, but it is worth noting that the awakening of the feminine aspect is important for both men and women. The alchemical stance is to seek the perfection hidden within nature and to bring this to life. Both the Perrault brothers were among the names of Sion members supplied by Nic Haywood (*see* page 47).

The 'queen of a vanished kingdom' is likely to be Isis, who is mentioned further on in the text. It is worth noting that during the 19th century Freemasonry became particularly obsessed with ancient Egypt, so it is possible that we are reading this through a Masonic filter that traces everything back to Egypt. But this female archetype is the same as any other liberated feminine force. The archetype – be it Sleeping Beauty, Mary Magdalene or Isis – reflects the dual nature of the quest. The recovery of the lost feminine archetype is also central to the mystery plays of Freemasonry, regaining the balance of masculine and feminine within the individual. The aspirant is attempting to discover their own feminine nature, a path of intuition and wisdom that may lead them to gnosis, an experience of the divine.

We also learn that the journey is taking us to the 'abode' of Sleeping Beauty.

On the physical pilgrimage the meaning conveyed here is that we are also in search of a real location, a final resting place of this lost feminine. It is likely that we are seeking a 'sleeping beauty' in the form of a corpse. A number of saints are said to have remained uncorrupted after death and I was informed by Sion that if Mary Magdalene's body existed it too would be in such a condition.

Finally there is the mention of Ariadne's thread. In Greek myth, Ariadne gave the hero Theseus a ball of twine so that he could find his way out of the Labyrinth after slaying the Minotaur that dwelt within. The Ariadne reference may be to the 'labyrinth', a local term for a series of caves and mines beneath the landscape near the Devils' Armchair. But the reference also works on a number of other levels. The labyrinth is a rose expressed through geometry.

> 'Labyrinth: a term of multiple usage, referring to the correct-
> but-fraught path of the Great Work, and likened to the maze of
> antiquity at Knosos (Gnosis?) called Ab-sol-om.'

There is an important distinction to be made between the maze and the labyrinth. The maze can be solved by logic, trial and error, and it calls upon the right side of the brain to deduct a solution. The labyrinth is a path of contemplation and transformation that evokes the left side of the brain. It focuses the enquirer on ever-decreasing turns to a point at the centre. Continuing on the path then unwinds back to the outer edge. This is a form of walking meditation, an active and intuitive journey to the divine source of your being and back. There is nothing for logic to solve.

The Gothic cathedral labyrinths are sometimes referred to as 'Solomon's maze', and Freemasons are initiated by being led blindfold around a lodge and to an altar where they kneel and ask for light.

The thread of Ariadne in this context refers to the signposting that all alchemists are obliged to leave for those that follow in their footsteps:

> 'To the few who successfully traverse Ariadne's web is revealed a
> wholly new and largely unsuspected universal reality, in which
> even ancient myths, legends and timeless folk and fairytales –
> themselves a likely vestige of a race-memory – acquire an entirely
> new and all too obvious meaning.'

This is linked to both alchemy and the tradition of preserving knowledge by encrypting it as symbols for later generations. It is a duty placed on all who achieve the Great Work and many, such as Fulcanelli, leave an encrypted manuscript before disappearing from public life.

4. Taurus

Thanks to him, and now with measured steps and a reliable eye, I was able to discover the sixty-four dispersed stones of a perfect cube, which the Brothers of BEAUTY of the dark wood, escaping from the pursuit of the usurpers, had scattered on their way as they fled the white Fort.

Taurus begins with the aspirant locating 64 stones. Sixty-four is the number of squares on a chessboard. The floor of the church at Rennes-le-Château has a chessboard, as does every Masonic lodge, but here they are described as 'dispersed'.

The 'Brothers of Beauty' fleeing the white fort alludes to either the Templars or the Cathars, 'brotherhood' being a term used by secret societies or a religious order to describe their members. The 'white Fort' is Blanchefort and a Templar garrison is said by Sion to have been stationed there and forced to flee when the order was rounded up by the 'usurpers', the agents of the French king, who technically did not rule this area. In this context 'usurpers' might also be a pointed reference to the Knights of Malta, who were given lands and possessions that had belonged to the Templars.

The escapees and their 'treasure' is also very reminiscent of the story of the three Cathar heretics who escaped Montségur with an unknown 'treasure' prior to the sect's demise at the hands of the Albigensian Crusade of 1209–29 (though the last Cathar outposts held out till 1244 or later). From this we can surmise that part of the secret is something that the Templars or Cathars were in possession of, and which they hid just prior to their arrest on October 13, 1307. This may have taken the form of objects or documents, or both.

The 'perfect cube' is another Masonic reference. Masons use the symbol of the roughly hewn stone, or ashlar, to denote an unfinished man. They give a small ashlar to initiates as a symbolic representation of the work that they still need to do on themselves. With hard work and the right tools this stone is to be turned into a perfect cube – symbolically, a perfected man.

The key to the Taurus stanza is the phrase 'measured steps and sure eye'. From the peak of Blanchefort running south of the ruins there is a clear line of sight to the hilltop village of Rennes-le-Château, where Saunière's Tour Magdala can be seen as establishing a line of sight.

5. Gemini

*Collect up the scattered stones, work with the set square and compasses to put
them back into a regular order, search for the meridian by going from East to West,
then look from South to North, and then in every direction to obtain the solution
you seek, stopping in front of the 14 stones marked with a cross. The circle is the
ring and the crown and is the diadem of this QUEEN of the Castle.*

We are instructed to collect the scattered stones and put them back in regular
order. The 64 stones, as we know, represent the Masonic tiled floor in the church
at Rennes-le-Château and the term 'regular order' is used within Masonic
lodges when conducting what is termed the 'regular order of business'. The
'square and compass' are the classic symbols of Freemasonry but could also be
used to align points on the landscape. I am not aware of 'scattered stones' as a
Masonic reference but it echoes the many parts of the god Osiris, who was dismembered by his brother Seth. The scattered parts of Osiris had to be gathered
and reconstructed by Isis, his consort.

The Paris Meridian is marked in the church of Saint-Sulpice in Paris by a
dolmen and this location is referenced directly later in the text. The meridian
was based upon an earlier line that runs between Blanchefort and Arques called
the Rose Line (*Ligne Rose*). This passes through the site of the tomb in Poussin's
Et in Arcadia Ego.

We are then to look 'in every direction', which may mean either within the
church or on the landscape. This might be a reference to both the constellations in view and the symbols within the church. The '14 stones with a cross'
is a reference to the 14 Stations of the Cross within the church and also, surprisingly, to a feature on the landscape. Gérard Thome kindly guided me to this
location where, due south of the Devil's Armchair, there are stones with crosses
carved into them. They lead to a single large rock that once acted as a base for
a tall iron cross but this has long since been removed, leaving only a hole in the
stone. Thome's understanding of the crosses is that they were carved and placed
by Saunière's friend and mentor, Father Henri Boudet.

This location is also close to a 'circle'. There are actually two circles in the
area. One is the small spring beside the Devil's Armchair and the other an actual
circle of trees in a field further south, with a standing stone at the centre. As far
as I can tell, this is on private land but can be viewed from the north hillside
of Château des Templiers even further to the south. If this circle is the 'ring' to
accompany a crown, does this mean a wedding band? If so, our Sleeping Beauty

is married, of royal blood and of the castle. The name Magdalene literally means 'of the tower' (Magdala, or Migdal, in Galilee translates as 'tower') so the castle, ring and crown could all allude to Mary's heretical status as bride of Jesus. Another option is that it refers to another Mary, Countess Marie de Negri d'Ables of Blanchefort castle, a local noble who may have been responsible for the protection and continuation of the secret heresy that was hidden by the Templars, and is perhaps alluded to in the previous stanza.

6. Cancer

The slabs on the mosaic floor of the holy site could be alternately white or black, and JESUS, like ASMODEUS, watch over their alignments, my vision seemed incapable of seeing the summit where the wonderful sleeping woman remained hidden. Not being HERCULES with his magical power, how should I decipher the mysterious symbols engraved by the observers of the past? In the sanctuary however, the font, the fountain of love of the believers, reminds us of these words: BY THIS SIGN YOU WILL CONQUER him.

The Jesus and Asmodeus reference locates us firmly back at Rennes-le-Château, where the chessboard floor is watched over by Jesus and Asmodeus (*see* page 88). There is an almost dualist/Cathar aspect to the mirroring present in this scene. The chessboard was placed diagonally to the church so that its alignments are roughly northeast, northwest, southeast and southwest. It is interesting that above Asmodeus one of the four angels is not touching his forehead in benediction but shielding his eyes as if looking into the distance due east. This is the direction of Blanchefort, Pech Cardou and beyond to Arques.

If, as Nic Haywood told me, the name 'Arques' is derived from the Arabic for chessboard, we are once again seeing the interior of the church mirroring the landscape:

> '*Ru-at, arq-at*, etc. is the root of Arque and means variously 'chessboard' (as in *arq-a-leen* or *aral-kheen*), 'plaid', 'great doorway', and 'secret or sacred language'. It is one of ancient Arabic's more ambiguous and esoteric words, much-used in alchemical and Sufi teaching.'

The hero Hercules undertakes a great series of 'labours' or trials that can be read as an alchemical quest. For example, the androgyny that he experiences in the service of Queen Omphale represents a phase that appears in many alchemical illustrations. Hercules' fifth trial, the challenge of having to clean out the huge and dung-filled Augean stables in one day, can be interpreted as purifying the unconscious or the alchemical *nigredo* stage. The hero's own 'chamber of reflection' was the cave of a hermit in which he pacified a lion. Nicolas Flamel also makes reference to 'King Hercules his Book, which entreateth of the colors of the stone, entitled Iris or the Rainbow.'

We see here again a reference to the importance of the rainbow, as explored earlier. Another alchemical aspect to the stanza is hinted at by the inscription 'By this sign you will conquer him [or it]' (*Par ce signe tu le vaincras*). The inscription can be found on the statue of Asmodeus and the angels in the church and is taken from Emperor Constantine's vision of a cross, with the addition of the word *le* ('him' or 'it'). Interestingly, the phrase appears in the alchemical tree of life of the *Codex Rosae-Crucis* and other alchemical manuscripts.

As Sion says, the mention of Hercules is also an allusion to 'the two pillars' and 'the eagle'. The 'two pillars' is a Masonic reference to Jachin and Boaz, the two pillars of the Temple of Solomon, which are represented in every Masonic temple. The eagle reference refers to the biblical Book of Job, where God tells Job that wherever there is a corpse the eagle is there. The gospels of Mathew and Luke also contain a similar reference. 'Eagle' (also translated 'vulture') seems to be a generic term used for all carrion birds in the Bible, but they are also equated with the highest possible viewpoint. My understanding of this is that the eagle can see the tomb which we seek. According to Sion:

> 'John Dee also made profound allusions to the eagle in reference
> to the disclosure of a body in his hieroglyphical Monad. In
> one sense it could be said that the eagle's eye equates with the
> all-seeing eye — we must not forget that this bird has strong con-
> nections with Zeus and is also a symbol for the oft-cited third eye
> or the eye of the Cyclops, the eye of Argo.'

This may also mean that we are to use the astronomical constellation of Aquila, the Eagle, to get a bearing on the location. This brings us back to the astrological aspect of *Le Serpent Rouge*. In the night sky Aquila is adjacent to Hercules, Ophiuchus (the 13th sign) and the Serpent. How these relate to the landscape is not clear. I have considered the link between the pool in the triangular field and the Eye of Providence (*see* page 112) but mapping these astronomical signs on to the landscape is far from satisfactory or specific in its directions.

The reference to the eagle may also mean that the tomb is visible from a high point such as one of the peaks. But importantly it reiterates that we are searching for a corpse.

7. Leo

From her whom I wanted to liberate rose the emanations of perfume that permeated the tomb. Some had once named her ISIS, queen of the benevolent springs, COME TO ME ALL YOU WHO ARE HEAVILY LADEN AND I WILL GIVE YOU REST, others MADELAINE, with the famous jar full of healing balm. The initiated know her real name: NOTRE DAME DES CROSS.

This stanza is said by Nic Haywood to be heavily influenced by Nicolas Flamel's unpublished diary. We return to the allusion to releasing an archetypal 'feminine' energy in the intended 'liberation' of a Sleeping Beauty. The discovering of the inner feminine appears in many esoteric teachings, such as Freemasonry, but there is a lesson for all in this as the search for our own intuition, that inner voice of insight and personal truth. 'Queen of the benevolent springs' is not a title that I recognize but it may refer to the statue of Our Lady of Lourdes situated in the small garden outside the church at Rennes-le-Château.

In physical terms the perfumed smell would be the odour of an uncorrupted body seeping from the tomb. This would be the smell of the rose, telling us that the physical remains of a female saint are buried in the vicinity. As the name 'Madelaine' is used later in the text it is likely this refers to Mary Magdalene. The idea of the uncorrupted corpse is a tradition of the relics of the saints. St Catherine Laboure's body, for example, was exhumed after nearly 60 years and discovered to be in perfect condition. When the tomb was opened there was said to be the odour of roses.

The use of 'rose' is also a pun on both the Rose Line and St Roseline who is linked to this mystery by the Teniers painting mentioned in the shorter fabricated parchment from the 1970s (*see* pages 247, 249). We will revisit Teniers later (*see* Chapter 16) but for now suffice to say that it also has Masonic/alchemical connotations. Alchemy also has reference to the odour, what Sion calls 'The all-pervading fragrance created at the moment of the *rubedo*.' The *rubedo* or 'reddening' is an alchemical stage that is sometimes shown as taking place in a rose garden.

'Come to me all you who are heavily laden' is from the Sermon on the Mount, as featured in the church, although here it is attributed to Isis. This is supported by the earliest known use of the phrase, which can be seen inscribed over a temple of Isis in Egypt (see Hancock, *The Sign and the Seal*).

During later discussions on this stanza, Nic Haywood sent me the following:

> 'There is an all-important line in *Le Serpent Rouge* which says:
> "*The initiated know her true name: OUR LADY OF THE CROSS.*"
> It should read: "*Les initiés savent son nom véritable, NOTRE DAME DES CROISE[T].*" ("*The initiates know her true/sacred name, OUR LADY OF THE CRESCENT[S]*").'

The term '*croiset*' is a variation on cross that I think is a veiled reference, along with the mention of the rose, to members of the Rose Cross.

The alteration of 'crescent' to 'cross' in the final line may have been an attempt to Christianize the text but the female archetype is here stated as 'Our Lady of the Crescent'. The goddess Artemis was known as 'Lady of the Crescent', a virgin huntress and ruler of the moon and patron of pagan Byzantium, later Constantinople. The banner of the city, and of the later (Christian) Byzantine empire, was a crescent moon, which was retained by the Muslim Ottomans who conquered the city in 1492. There are many images in alchemical manuscripts of the sublimation of the feminine illustrated by the queen standing upon a crescent moon. Even Christian imagery has incorporated this feminine device such as El Greco's *Assumption of the Virgin Mary* and countless others depicting the Virgin Mary standing upon a crescent moon. An interesting example of this is the Louis Niño painting of the Virgin Mary from the 1730s as it also depicts Mary as having a triangular shape, in keeping with the 'Black Madonna' statuettes and paintings of the Virgin Mary. Black Madonna figures are often seated and holding a child which is identical to Isis figures from Ancient Egypt. Isis can also be described as 'Queen of the Fertile Crescent', the 'Fertile Crescent' being the agricultural region formed by the valleys of the Nile, Euphrates and Tigris. The identification of the Black Madonna with Isis is made clear by Sion:

> 'As for the Black Virgin, Isis before conception is the *Virgo Partiturae*, that is to say the earth before its fertilization, which the rays of the sun are soon going to bring to life. She is the mother of all gods as is attested by the inscription: "To Isis, or to the Virgin from whom the son/sun will be born."'

The 'black' of 'Black Madonna' is also said to mean 'wise'. It identifies the archetypal mother, the true creator, as a triangle. In this we also see that the eye in the triangle of Freemasonry is feminine and therefore so too is the 'All-Seeing Eye' of the Grand Architect – God. The feminine nature of God is an ancient wisdom drawn in part on the ability of women, in their role as creator, to produce new life through birth. The tradition of virgin birth stems from the idea of a sole feminine creator.

8. Virgo

I was like the shepherds of the famous painter POUSSIN, perplexed when faced with the enigma: "ET IN ARCADIA EGO...!" Would the voice of blood restore to me the image of an ancestral past? Yes, the flash of genius traversed my thoughts. I could see it again, I understood! I now knew this fabulous secret. And wonder of wonder, when the four horsemen leapt, the shoes of one horse had left four imprints on the stone, this was the sign that DELACROIX had left in one of the three paintings in the Chapelle des Anges. Here was the seventh sentence that a hand had traced: PULL ME OUT OF THE MIRE SO THAT I DO NOT REMAIN STUCK THERE. IS twice, embalmer and embalmed, miracle jar of the Eternal White Lady of the Legends.

We begin with a reference to Nicolas Poussin, the artist responsible for the painting *Et in Arcadia Ego*, or *The Shepherds of Arcadia*. The shepherds are seen deciphering the Latin inscription 'Et in Arcadia Ego' (literally 'I too [am or was] in Arcadia') on an old tomb. There was a tomb on the road between Arques and Blanchefort that was considered by many to be the one in this painting. The debate still rages as to whether they are related, but clearly Sion intends us to make that connection. In the background of the painting three peaks can be seen that match Pech Cardou, Blanchefort and Rennes-le-Château. The painting is discussed at length later (*see* Chapter 16) but the inscription has been brought to our attention so we must briefly consider its meaning.

There is certainly an enigma around the inscription, and the many interpretations of this are covered in later chapters. The next line includes the term 'voice of blood'. The origin of this term is likely to be 'the voice of thy brother's blood crieth unto me from the ground' (Genesis 4.10). In this verse God is accusing Cain of murdering his brother. The murder is not unlike the Egyptian myth of Osiris, who was also murdered by his jealous brother Seth. The shifting through Greek, Egyptian and Christian mythology makes it difficult to determine which is the more important here, but perhaps we are learning that all three myths are essentially the same. Either way, following the references to the tomb and death it reminds us again that there is a corpse involved in the Rennes-le-Château mystery.

There is also the possibility that the 'voice of blood' is race or cultural memory. A possible aspect of the members of the bloodline is that there is something to be 'awakened in the blood'. Perhaps genetic memory is the cause of the sudden realization seen in the line 'would the voice of blood restore to me the image of an ancestral past'. Sion tells us that this point 'is indeed apposite and there are methods for forcing the resurfacing of what you rightly call race memory'.

Professional translator Nicole Dawe, a former resident of the region, also informed me that she feels certain that 'voice of blood' (*la voix du sang*) is a play on words, a reference to *la voie du sang* ('the route of blood', or bloodline) and that once the initiate understood this they understood everything, as conveyed in 'I now knew this fabulous secret.'

We come now to the 'four imprints' in stone left by the four horsemen. The mark left by a hoof is an arch shape, so I initially sought four arches in the region. I found nothing satisfactory, except for the tendency for graveyards and crypts in the area to be gated with an arch. There are a number of rocks in the region with indentations of all kinds so it may be that I have yet to discover an actual example in the rock. The 'four horsemen' may also allude to the Four Horsemen of the Apocalypse, but in this context they are more likely to be a reference to the four knights of the chessboard.

The painter Eugène Delacroix (1798–1863) was responsible for many of the paintings in Saint-Sulpice. Some believe that these paintings represent the landscape of Rennes-le-Château and its environs. Delacroix certainly painted landscapes in the Pyrenees, as he was resident there for a number of years. There is a shape on a pillar of his depiction of *Heliodorus Expelled from the Temple* that looks familiar. It is formed of two circles joined by a square in the middle. A variation on this image appears in the form of the sandal ties worn by the seated woman on the second page of *Le Serpent Rouge* booklet. The same design effect is on the side panel of the Visigothic pillar in Father Saunière's garden beneath the statue of Our Lady of Lourdes. The three Delacroix paintings are complex, so selecting this 'sign' from the wealth of imagery is not conclusive. However, Sion has also alluded to the fact that the geometry of these paintings is important.

The 'seventh sentence' is tantalizing as it leads us at once to search for the other six. The quotation exists in the church of Rennes-le-Château but this might not be the only reference. 'Deliver me out of the mire that I may not sink' is another quote from Christ's Sermon on the Mount. It is also a reference to a plate in the 16th-century alchemical document, *Splendor Solis*. It is no coincidence that both this stanza and the plate are both numbered eight. The *Splendor Solis* plate depicts a red youth rising from mire, raised by the queen. We can interpret this as psychic matter rejected and submerged into the unconscious, just as any aspect of a child's personality that is deemed unacceptable is 'split off' and purposely hidden. This aspect of personality remains stuck in a juvenile state until it is recovered (brought into consciousness) and redeemed. Here we see it rediscovered and lifted out of the unconscious by the Higher Self, an internalized 'mother' or great nurturer who welcomes and accepts this lost aspect.

In alchemy, the captured fumes of the alchemical operation are reintegrated to produce a new substance, and the red sphere of the skull foreshadows the completion of the Great Work. The figure of the queen is pregnant (symbolizing the potential for rebirth) and in all cases the male youth and white queen must unite to become the Hermaphrodite, symbolizing the integration of all opposites and duality. The integration of all fragments of the personality completes the psychological process.

'IS twice' simply means 'ISIS', but this duplication also directs us to a geometric form of the double cube used in Freemasonry. The 'embalmer and embalmed, miracle jar' would be another reference to Mary Magdalene, known for anointing Jesus, and links her to Isis, who had the parts of Osiris embalmed to create the first mummy. The 'embalmed' part of the line reiterates that her body is thought to be buried in the vicinity. The description of 'white lady' puts her in contrast to the Black Madonna, which is thought to represent Isis or perhaps Sarah, who according to legend travelled with Mary Magdalene on the boat to France.

The grouping of these names reminds us that we are also seeking an underlying experience of the feminine aspect. Those who try to walk the route of *Le Serpent Rouge* should bear in mind that the journey serves as both ritual and pilgrimage.

9. Libra

Begun in the shadows, my journey could only end in the Light. At the window of the ruined house, I contemplated the summit of the mountain through the naked autumn trees. The cross on the peak stood out under the midday sun, it was the 14th and the largest of them all at 35 centimetres! So here I was in my turn, horseman on the divine steed straddling the abyss.

The timing here is a kind of reversal of Masonic ritual, in that all lodge workings begin, albeit symbolically, at noon. Here we began in the dark, making our way into the light and arriving at noon. 'Noon' also appears in Nicolas Flamel's account as the time that he achieved the Magnum Opus (Great Work) of alchemy on a January 17; and it is pointedly referenced in Sion's fabricated parchments from the 1970s (*see* page 289). The night aspect takes place in the moonlight to indicate the feminine principle symbolized by the Magdalene.

There is a ruined house to the south of the Devil's Armchair, but I have found no features that make it especially identifiable and there are plenty of other ruins in the vicinity. However, it does offer a view of more than one summit, the peak of Le Bézu with its ruins of Château des Templiers directly to the south, and Pech Cardou to the north.

As for 'the cross on the peak', the Château des Templiers is the likely location as this was represented by a Templar cross on some hand-drawn maps of the region. There are short stone crosses scattered around the landscape in the area, but these serve as old boundary markers. The size of the cross would make it impossible to see across the valley, so it may be a reference to the 14th Station of the Cross in the church. This depicts Jesus being placed in a tomb and the intention could be to give us the impression that the tomb depicted in the church and the location on the landscape are one and the same. Also in view of the Templar ruin is the area of land called L'Homme Mort – 'the Dead Man'.

An enigmatic statement from Sion may also relate to this matter:

> 'I am reminded of the following extract: "and suddenly I realize.
> How beautifully sweet is this pollen, kept safe at the centre of this
> rose of majesty; hanging as it does upon the navigator's cross but
> with the divine ability to invert horizons."'

The 'navigators cross' is a latitude-finding tool in the form of a staff with degrees marked upon it and a movable crossbeam. By aligning the top of the staff with the Pole Star and moving the cross beam up or down until it matches the horizon, you are able to ascertain your latitude. This might be a tool for identifying a specific location on the land using the view from the ruined house. Sion has certainly shown some interest in the dimensions of the staffs held by various figures in the Rennes-le-Château church, most notably the staff that was once held by Asmodeus. This is now missing and to my knowledge no record of its length exists. Other staffs include the cross on the altar painting, the staff held by John the Baptist and another on the statue of St Anthony. It is an idea that warrants further exploration.

As mentioned in relation to Gemini there are also a number of crosses carved into rocks to the south of the Devil's Armchair and the ruined house.

10. Scorpio

Celestial vision for him who reminds me of the four works of Em. SIGNOL around the line of the Meridian, at the very heart of the sanctuary where this source of love of one for the other shines out. I turn on the spot looking at the rose of the P and then that of the S, then from the S to the P… and the spiral in my mind becomes like a monstrous octopus, expelling its ink, the darkness absorbing the light, I am dizzy and I put my hand to my mouth instinctively biting my palm, perhaps like OLIER in his coffin. Curses, I understand the truth, HE PASSED, BUT HE TOO, DOING good AS WELL AS xxxxxxxxx He of the flowery tomb. But how many have pillaged the HOUSE, leaving only embalmed corpses and many metals that they had not been able to take with them. What a strange mystery the new temple of SALOMON, which was built by the children of Saint VINCENT, conceals.

Much of this paragraph refers to the church of Saint-Sulpice in Paris, which Father Saunière may have visited to have the parchments that he discovered in his church decoded (*see* page 70). Saint-Sulpice is named for St Sulpitius (or Sulpicius), the 7th-century bishop of Bourges, who was known for defending his people against the Merovingian rulers of the day. His feast day is celebrated on January 17.

The 'four works of M [for Monsieur] SIGNOL' are paintings at the centre of the church by Emile Signol (1804–92). They are signed in capital letters and depict biblical scenes. Figures in the paintings point either forward or diagonally. If you follow the pointing fingers they lead you in an 'N' shape across the church. The signatures of two of the paintings have the N of SIGNOL reversed. As we have seen, his reflected/reversed theme is a constant in the Rennes-le-Château church and is said to be the sign of an adept.

To the left of one painting is a marble obelisk that is the marker for the Paris Meridian. It has a brass line that runs down the centre of the obelisk and across the floor diagonally through the 'N' route indicated by the Signol paintings. The Paris Meridian continues south through France and passes near to Rennes-les-Bains, close to the Blanchefort mountain. It runs in parallel with the 'Rose

Line' or 'Line of Secrets', which passes through the graveyard at Rennes-les-Bains (*see* page 249).

'Source of love of one for the other' might be a reference to the spiritual legacy left by Jean-Jacques Olier (1608–57), who reconstructed Saint-Sulpice and established its seminary, in the form of organizations such as the Sisters of Charity (*see* Chapter 3). Olier's attempt to elevate the position of women in the Church reflects the love that Jesus would have had for Mary Magdalene had they been married. He also influenced St Vincent de Paul in the creation of the Daughters of Charity. Nic Haywood had this to say about Olier and his work:

> 'Bearing in mind that Olier's mentor was an adept of the
> alchemical process (having gleaned his 'clues' from the distilled
> material which had been well guarded by our old friends the
> Templars), he set about a synthesis which was known in eccle-
> siastical circles as a form of heresy, but which could not be
> suppressed.'

Nic followed this with a further statement:

> 'St Vincent's Daughters of Charity were formed on January 17,
> 1681, 300 years to the day from when Nicolas Flamel achieved
> his Great Work. Its purpose was to care for destitute women and
> orphans, something Flamel had funded with the wealth he had
> attained, in the form of orphanages. It was institutions such as
> these that symbolically upheld the tradition of caring for Mary
> Magdalene and any attendant children that accompanied her to
> France after the crucifixion. It is in a way the response to the
> perennial Masonic question of "who will take care of the Widow's
> Son?" The physical wellbeing of Mary was but one concern;
> in taking care of her tradition it was ensured that her teachings
> would also survive.'

There is another link between St Vincent's Daughters of Charity and Rennes-le-Château in that Elizabeth of Rennes, a local dignitary, was in the care of the Daughters of Charity

In Saint-Sulpice there are two round windows above the north and south aspects of the Meridian. In the center of these there is a P in the north and an S to the south. Sion intimated back in the 1970s that these stand for the 'Priory of Sion', but this could have been an attempt to attach themselves to the mythology of the church or simply to bring themselves to the public's attention. We are instructed to turn from the P to the S and vice-versa.

As we discovered in Chapter 9, a spiral can be experienced as a route to the source but also as the dormant serpent. The octopus is a primordial image but may also indicate the spiralling arms of the labyrinth, both beneath the ground and within the mind. At the centre is the source, the origin, and this is identified in *La Source*, the small natural spring beside the Devil's Armchair. The black ink absorbing light might be a reference to the alchemical Hermaphrodite (*see* the preceding stanza), a merging of the black and white.

According to Sion, 'the reference to the octopus – familiar metaphysical symbolism apart – is likely a direct reference to the Throne of St Peter: Rome itself.' This indicates that the hiding of the light is in part seen as the fault of the Catholic Church; this entire stanza would then be moving us toward a search for a more balanced form of Christianity.

I visited Saint-Sulpice many years ago in the company of Sarah Hurst and together we examined the church using *Le Serpent Rouge* as a guide. There is a plaque on the wall with a profile of Olier, but he is not holding his hand to his mouth so I suspected that another portrait of Olier existed. As mentioned earlier, we discovered that the mural in the chapel of St.-Jean Evangéliste (St John the Evangelist) has a figure who clearly resembles Olier. This figure has one hand to his mouth and beneath his arm are three large scrolls and a book. At the time I drew no conclusions about the possible content of these documents, but I noted the similarity between the painting's notion of hidden texts and this aspect of the Rennes-le-Château story. I will return to these scrolls in the next section as there is more to be learned about them (*see* Chapter 15).

In the next part of this stanza the narrator then instinctively bites his palm. This is a Masonic gesture of horror but also of completing the Great Work. Nic Haywood tells us:

> 'As to the "gesture of horror", this is a known term and relates, in the main, to the moment of discovery of the [Philosopher's] Stone or rather to the fact that to discover the Stone is in fact "to become the Stone":
>
> *"When that joyful moment appeared and God granted me, by his eternal grace, this most precious of gifts; this 'Divine Quintessence,' this Stone of the Wise. When that fateful hour struck I accomplished the gesture of horror and retired, fleeing from the sight of the world."'*

The latter quote is most likely Nicolas Flamel's unpublished journal, which is in Sion's possession. The term 'doing good' is often used to describe Rosicrucians (see Jean Markale, *The Church of Mary Magdalene*) and is also a quotation from one of the gravestones at Rennes-les-Bains. It is inscribed on the tomb of Paul Urbain Vincent de Fleury – 'he of the flowery tomb'. He was the grandson of Marie de Negri d'Ables, countess of Blanchefort. Of interest is the fact that de Fleury has two tombs in the same graveyard bearing different dates of death. One of these tombs is known to be empty but presumably served another purpose at some point in history.

The de Fleury family owned lands around Rennes-le-Château, including Blanchefort. The landscape in the Sermon on the Mount mural in the church of Rennes-le-Château is based on the region and includes a rose-covered tract of land owned by de Fleury.

The 'pillaged house' tells us that there is a tomb there, but all that remains are the embalmed corpses and metal objects too heavy to carry. There are a number of options for this location. It could refer to one of the crypts beneath the Rennes-le-Château church that were sealed by Saunière (see page 72). It seems likely from his behaviour that Saunière was pillaging treasure from somewhere close to home. We know that Olier was buried at Saint-Sulpice but the reference is unlikely to be to him because 'bodies' is plural. The plural also indicates that it is the tomb of a couple or a family.

The de Fleury lands are a possible location for such a tomb, as is the cave shown on the Rennes-le-Château altar painting, with Mary Magdalene beside a grave. But as we are physically south of the Devil's Armchair, somewhere between Blanchefort and Château des Templiers to the east of Rennes-le-Château we are far from both. The area of land called L'Homme Mort, the Dead Man, is here, and I discovered from Sion that this was once a way into the local tunnel system that would lead to a sacred site. More of this is covered in the following chapter.

As mentioned earlier, Olier was an associate of Sion and oversaw the reconstruction of Saint-Sulpice. The design of this church, like that of the church at Rennes-le-Château and all other Masonic/Rose+Croix temples, is based upon Solomon's Temple. There is a broader interpretation to this, in that the new Temple of Solomon is not just the microcosm (the church at Rennes-le-Château) it is also the macrocosm of the surrounding landscape. This too is further explored in the following chapter.

St Vincent de Paul, Olier's contemporary and fellow Sion associate, is also mentioned. A statue of St Vincent surrounded by children is on display in Saint-Sulpice. But this also hides another level of intrigue. In the Middle Ages St.-Vincent was the name of a suburb of Carcassonne, the walled city 30km (18 miles) north of Rennes-le-Château. This was part of the Jewish quarter and located outside the walls of the main city. The Jewish communities in the region are said to date back to before the time of Christ, hence the region would have provided a safe haven for Mary Magdalene fleeing the Holy Land. If she had a child this Jewish settlement would have cared for the child just as St Vincent himself became renowned for embracing the children of God.

11. Ophiuchus

Cursing the ashes of the profaners and those who live in their tracks, emerging from the abyss where I was plunged making the sign of horror. "Here is the proof that I know the secret of SALOMON'S seal, that XXXXXXXXXXX of this QUEEN, I visited the hidden residences." Friendly Reader, be careful not to add or remove one iota from this... think, think again, the base lead of my writing XXXX perhaps contains the purest gold.

Ophiuchus is illustrated by a man holding a serpent. He is the 'Golden Serpent-Bearer', reminiscent of Freemasonry's 25th (Knight of the Brazen Serpent) Degree. The existence of the 13th sign is problematic for astrologers in that it was recognized by the celebrated astrologer Ptolemy at the time of the Romans, but he chose to ignore it because it upset the balance of sun signs in the zodiac. The sun passes through the sign during late November and early December but to this day astrologers in both Vedic and Western astrology choose to ignore the constellation.

The name is also connected directly with 'Ophir', the secret land whence Middle Kingdom ancient Egyptian priests were said to have obtained their vast quantities of gold. Author and Egyptologist E A Wallis Budge suggests that they maintained a supply of the precious yellow metal at the same place. Furthermore, these journeys to obtain large quantities of gold involved a voyage by sea, and not in the direction of southern Egypt.

The use of Ophiuchus in *Le Serpent Rouge* is interesting as it seems entirely absent from Freemasonry, alchemy and other traditions that appear here. Perhaps it has been included to support the idea of the alchemical 'red serpent'. Sion has maintained that it was added in part to facilitate a shift to a more alchemical experience of the journey.

The stanza begins with the narrator cursing and emerging from the abyss. It seems that he has managed to visit the underground location that has been the goal of the quest so far after making the Masonic 'gesture of horror'. Caves exist in abundance in the area, especially around and beneath Blanchefort, and the region has been mined since Roman times.

As for 'Solomon's seal' we recall that there is a flower called the Seal of Solomon, which appears on the Sermon on the Mount mural at Rennes-le-Château along with the de Fleury lands mentioned in the previous stanza. Perhaps by understanding this the seeker has found the hidden location of the 'queen'. But then the text takes a turn and we are told to 'Think, and think again', requiring the reader to meditate on what has come before. It tells us that through contemplation we can discover the secret of this text. We are then informed that we have been instructed in alchemy and must not add or remove anything at this stage.

12. Sagittarius

Returning then to the white hill, the sky having opened its gates, I seemed to feel close to me a presence, feet in the water like him who has just received the mark of baptism, turning myself to the east, opposite me I saw his rings unravelling endlessly, the enormous RED SNAKE mentioned in the parchments, salty and bitter, the enormous unchained beast became red in anger, at the foot of this white mountain.

In this stanza we have returned to the hill of Blanchefort and are positioned at the Devil's Armchair, where the alpha and omega carvings denote the beginning and end of not only the journey but of the alchemical process.

The journey ends with an act of washing the feet in the pool beside the Devil's Armchair. This originated with Jesus washing the feet of the disciples after the Last Supper and was practised as a ritual among various Christian orders, including the Cathars.

The 'Balneum Mariae' (Bath of Mary) is a warm-water bath used by the alchemists and there are many natural hot springs at Rennes-les-Bains that are used to this day.

From the Devil's Armchair, through the trees, we have a limited view of the 'serpent' of the River Sals that runs through Rennes-les-Bains. Appearing silver in the moonlight, when we began our journey, it is now visible in the daylight. As Nicolas Flamel wrote:

'He which is washed is the Serpent Python, which, having taken
his being from the corruption of the slime of the Earth gathered
together by the waters of the deluge, when all the confections
were water, must be killed and overcome by the arrows of the
God Apollo, by the yellow Sun, that is to say, by our fire, equal to
that of the Sun.'

At the culmination of the alchemical Work the mercurial serpent becomes
red as it enters the stage of *rubedo*. As Lyndy Abraham puts it in *A Dictionary of
Alchemy*: 'The river serpent is transmuted into the celebrated goal of the work,
the elixir or stone.'

The red serpent also appears in many cultures associated with the orphic
egg from which the universe was thought to have emerged. In psychological
terms it represents the conscious that must be fused with the unconscious. In
alchemical terms it is the red man that marries the white queen (as in Plate 7
of the *Splendor Solis*). In terms of actual geography the River Sals ('Salt') runs
through Rennes-les-Bains and joins the River Blanc ('White'). The Sals turns
red during heavy downpours owing to the high iron oxide content of the soil
that is washed into it.

The 'presence' close to the narrator might be a reference to the corpse he
has just witnessed below ground or something more divine.

13. Capricorn

*My emotion was great, "DELIVER ME FROM THE MIRE" I said, and I
awoke immediately. In effect, I omitted to tell you that this was a dream which
I had on this JANUARY 17, on the feast day of Saint SULPITIUS. After
this, my worry persisting, I wanted, after the usual reflection, to tell you one of
PERRAULT'S stories. Hence, Friendly Reader, in the following pages here is
the result of a dream that rocked me in the world of the strange and the unknown.
That he who passes might do good!*

Having witnessed the inscription, and the meaning of it, the narrator enacts it
himself and is immediately awakened as if enlightened.

'Deliver me from the mire', as mentioned before, is the *Splendor Solis* plate
showing the white queen lifting the black and red 'Ethiopian' from the waters,
receiving him in his partially transmuted state between *nigredo* and *rubedo*. There
is another interpretation of this sentence, in that Adam was created from dust or

clay and brought to life by the breath of God (or Goddess, in the form of Isis). The woman who raises the boy is Sophia (Divine Wisdom), the wisdom and the spirit transferred by the breath of God.

Perrault is referred to again and his tale *Sleeping Beauty* provides a good analogy for both the alchemical journey and the physical attempt to visit the tomb of the lost queen. On another level there is the aspect of the divine feminine, the 'sleeping beauty' within us all. Therefore perhaps it is not Sleeping Beauty herself who awakes but the narrator, who revives this aspect of himself and is awakened from his own dream state after requesting help from this archetype.

The date January 17 makes another appearance and although the many meanings of this date were covered in the chapter on Rennes-le-Château, we are reminded that on Flamel's *Exposition of the Hieroglyphical Figures* he claims to have achieved his first use of the 'powders of projection' by converting mercury into silver on the January 17 at noon. It signifies the completion of this stage of the *Magnum Opus*.

The phrase 'do good', as we have seen, is both a reference to the Rosicrucians and also the de Fleury tombstone as explored in Scorpio. It is also a final call to fellow Rosicrucian adepts to undertake this journey.

A CONCLUSION – OF SORTS

No doubt there are a few who will find *Le Serpent Rouge* as easy to read as a Perrault fairy tale. But for the rest of us we must continue to peel back the layers of meaning and peek into the unknown.

Outright conclusions regarding *Le Serpent Rouge* are a hard-fought battle and clearly I have only scratched the surface of this enigmatic document. I think there is more to be gained by walking the land, the 'path of the *el diablo*' as Nic Haywood once phrased it, than by only reading it remotely. It is worthy of serious contemplation.

We know that one of the driving goals behind Sion's public surfacing in the 1950s was the identification and gathering of the adepts who had become scattered after the Second World War. This document also acts as another signpost, to be read and recognized by those who know Flamel's alchemy and the mysteries of the Rosicrucian and Masonic lodges. It emphasizes the feminine archetypes and the link to Saint-Sulpice in the time of Olier.

With Sion we often get the feeling that they are directing us toward something of great importance but without exactly telling us why. They are drawing us to the region of Rennes-le-Château and hinting at a tomb and a heresy that exist there. There are numerous connections for us to consider as we pick up the threads of what Olier was attempting at Saint-Sulpice and what Father Saunière communicated through his church.

Alchemy is a means to transformation at all levels of existence, from the purely material (as in the familiar image of the alchemist transforming lead into gold) to the more profound quest for spiritual enlightenment and gnosis: in other words, the transformation of the soul.

Rennes-le-Château is the perfect environment to illustrate this. A truly Hermetic aspect of the journey is that the red river called 'Salt' flows into the river called 'White' in exactly the same way that the 'Ethiopian' of the *Splendor Solis* joins and merges with the white queen. The names of the region's hills, valleys, rivers, springs and caves and so on are seemingly inspired by the Great Work of alchemy, and once this is understood it makes perfect sense that the Priory of Sion should direct us to this area when we ask what secrets they hold.

As with life, things have moved or changed and landscapes around Rennes-le-Château have altered over time. Some land is now in private hands and inaccessible, some significant objects or sites have been removed or destroyed, and tree-planting programmes have obscured many of the views. This makes our journey difficult but not impossible, although I caution those who set out at midnight and expect to undertake the journey with ease. The landscape after dark is dangerous and unforgiving.

I must also warn you that the route can lead to a number of entrances to an underground passage, part of which passes under rivers. I was given a clear instruction not to attempt this passage before May as it is prone to flash floods in the winter months and is a death trap. I waited until the weather cleared but on the route I took I found that the underground passage had collapsed. More will be said on this in later chapters.

I think the idea of awakening from a long sleep, as mentioned in the final stanza and visited throughout the text with references to Sleeping Beauty, hints at a link between alchemy and the bloodline. The search for the lost queen continues but there are other gateways to the glory of the perfumed rose. For now we must leave behind the ever-uncoiling serpent to consider the final resting place of our Lady of the Crescents. I leave you with this passage from FitzGerald's translation of *The Rubaiyat of Omar Khayyam*:

'Up from Earth's Centre through the Seventh Gate
I rose, and on the Throne of Saturn sate,
And many Knots unravel'd by the Road;
But not the Knot of Human Death and Fate.'

CHAPTER 11

TEMPLES
AND TOMBS

THE GOAL OF THE QUEST

Our quest led us off the broad road of the pilgrimage to Santiago and along the 'diversion' of *Le Serpent Rouge*. On this diversion, part Via Dolorosa, where the Stations of the Cross had at one time been symbolically added to the landscape, and part initiation, we searched for the secret place of the 'lost queen'. *Le Serpent Rouge* points to a specific location in the hills around Blanchefort to find the 'hidden rose'. It is time to consider this location, the goal of our journey.

Guided by the art and architecture of the churches of Saint-Sulpice in Paris and Sainte-Marie-Madeleine (Mary Magdalene) at Rennes-le-Château, we undertook a pilgrimage through the landscape. The theme that underlies both churches is that they are based on Solomon's Temple, the first Temple of Jerusalem and the blueprint for all Masonic temples. The tradition of building in this manner is attributed to the Templars, who were once headquartered on the Temple Mount, where Solomon's temple once stood, and had excavated beneath it for a number of years.

The wider landscape of Rennes-le-Château takes us through a recreation of Jerusalem, with place names such as 'Jaffus' and 'Cardou' representing the Jaffa Gate and the Cardo, Jerusalem's main street in Roman times. Along this route we encounter the 'Via Dolorosa', locations matching those on the final route of Jesus, as seen in the Stations of the Cross and enacted in the Rose+Croix degrees of Freemasonry.

The journey along this route is contained within the grander scheme of a new and invisible Temple of Solomon, an area above ground that I refer to as the 'invisible cathedral', and this is where we shall begin. I have omitted some of the precise details to prevent vandalism or the unscrupulous exploitation of these sacred locations.

THE INVISIBLE CATHEDRAL

Solomon's Temple returns us for a moment to our old friends the Templars, whose legacy can be seen across the region in the form of ruined Templar fortifications. They were known to have actively sought both learning and relics in Jerusalem and they are likely to have encountered both through physical excavation and exposure to Arabic knowledge. Expelled from Jerusalem following the end of Crusader rule, they gathered together the knowledge and material wealth that they had accrued and returned to the west, with many settling in the Languedoc, an area outside the kingdom of France and once known as Septimania. They were wealthy, powerful and secretive and the treasure they discovered on the Temple Mount is the stuff of legend. According to Sion,

> 'Septimania, still independent, was to be the New Jerusalem set up
> by the Templars, who could not keep the Holy Land. The placing
> of the Temple loot here, including menorahs, stone tablets and
> bodies, is mirrored in an overground 'Temple' on the land.'

This hidden Temple and its mirror-image above ground would need to be in a location that the Templars could protect. They had secured the fortification at Le Bézu to the south of Blanchefort and Sion maintains they had other properties in Arques to the east. Interestingly, Sion also states that

> 'The Templar preceptory was, for a time, located at the Château
> d'Hautpoul. The inner sanctum, the Rose+Croix Veritas, was
> located at Arques before it moved to a purpose-built structure
> overlooking the plateau and Le Cercle.'

Château d'Hautpoul is the old castle at Rennes-le-Château, from which the village is named. Arques lies to the east, beyond the tomb reputedly featured in Poussin's *Et in Arcadia Ego*. The 'purpose-built structure' is the Château des Templiers, which stands on the hill to the south of Rennes-les-Bains. It affords a view northward of the entire valley of Rennes-les-Bains, Valdieu (the Valley of God) and Rennes-le-Château.

If we were to step back and view the landscape from the hillside on Le Bézu at a specific point marked by a stone below the Château des Templiers itself, the greater 'groundplan' becomes apparent. We realize that our path in *Le Serpent Rouge*, both overground and underground, led us through an 'invisible cathedral'.

The invisible cathedral is a recreation of the first Temple of Jerusalem and runs from east to west across the landscape. Part of Rennes-le-Château is the 'doorway', Blanchefort and Rennes-les-Bains are the gateway to the 'inner sanctum', while the *Fauteuil du Diable* (Devil's Armchair) is the throne of Solomon and the nearby spring the baptismal font.

Standing in the shadow of the Templar ruin on Le Bézu and looking north it becomes obvious that the land has been rendered to convey the existence of this giant structure. The features and details can be located with the assistance of a map because some, such as the Devil's Armchair, are now obscured by forestry.

According to Sion, the landscape Temple perceptible from Le Bézu 'is mirrored in a Temple beneath the land'. As mentioned in the chapter on Landscape (Chapter 7), Henry Lincoln's work explores the geometry of the landscape and includes a vast pentagram laid out across the mountain peaks. The pentagram was also identified with Poussin's painting, which uses the shape in its structure. This painting was first associated with the Rennes-le-Château mystery through coded parchments that first appeared in Gérard de Sède's *The Accursed Treasure*, and were then decoded for *The Holy Blood and the Holy Grail*. One parchment contains the line: 'Shepherdess, no temptation, Poussin and Teniers hold the key.'

While 'Shepherdess' points to Poussin's work (also titled *The Shepherds of Arcadia*), the 'no temptation' surely refers to Teniers' *St Anthony and St Paul in the Desert*, his sole depiction of St Anthony the Great, in which the hermit saint is depicted resisting temptation. This will be covered at length in Chapter 15, but in short it is a landscape painting with St Paul and St Anthony in the foreground in the respective roles of teacher and pupil, and a shepherdess in the background.

Sion provided me with the only accurate copy of this painting, the original of which has been in private hands since the 1920s. Two aspects of the painting relate to the hidden Temple. One is that the shepherdess in the background represents St Roseline and indicates the 'Rose Line' that runs a close parallel to the Paris Meridian. The second is that it provides a view from one corner of the Temple. The two paintings taken together give two corners of the hidden Temple. Regarding the tomb in the Poussin painting, Nic Haywood states:

> 'The tomb itself, being constructed in accordance with the Golden Rule, may equally be a device indicative of a Temple structure.'

The invisible Temple of Solomon is a signpost toward the secret. At its heart is the inner sanctum or Holy of Holies, the sacred place that originally housed the Ark of the Covenant. I can find no evidence for the Ark being present in the landscape but the Holy of Holies is represented in the form of a mountain: Pech Cardou, opposite Blanchefort, across the River Sals.

Many of the mountains in the region are riddled with caverns and some, like Pech Bugurach, contain vast underground caves so it is likely that our second, subterranean, Temple is within this mountain. If it exists this Temple is the very centre of the mystery, the focus around which all else revolves in terms of the physical aspects of the mysteries of Rennes-le-Château and the Priory of Sion. It is both a place of initiation, and the last resting place of our 'lost queen'. It forms the Holy of Holies in the new Temple of Solomon, at the heart of the New Jerusalem.

With this knowledge the urge might be to rush down to the region and discover all that can be revealed, but we are not dispassionate archaeologists cataloguing and emptying the sacred places of the dead to fill museums with ornaments. These are holy shrines and our quest is worth nothing if it is not truly a search for the sacred. The discovery and revelation of such places and the items within them must be done in a manner that ensures that they remain protected from looters of all kinds by honouring the spiritual importance of where they are located. It is my personal understanding that the objects in these places should not be removed; on the contrary, items taken previously should be returned.

TOMBS

The possibility of various hidden tombs existing in the area is very real. The presence of Templar ruins and the possibility of earlier refugees from the Holy Land fires the imagination with all manner of possibilities. But there seems to be one specific tomb in the area that we are being directed to – one that makes use of the natural caves and tunnels that riddle the valleys and mountains.

I have spoken to various researchers who claim to have located one or more tombs, including David Wood, Gérard Thome and of course Ben Hammott. Hammott's find can be seen in the *Bloodline* movie. He claims to have discovered a tomb in the region and has provided footage of his find, showing a body beneath a Templar flag surrounded by objects and manuscripts.

I have some concerns with Hammott's footage of the tomb in that it looks staged. The manner in which the contents have been laid out for the viewer looks suspicious, and the diversity of contents – from treasure to manuscripts and a Templar flag – are a Rennes-le-Château researcher's wish list of discoveries. Add to this the lack of dust on any of the objects and the fact that the Templar flag has survived underground also make me question the age of the tomb. The Languedoc has a very damp climate, and I am reasonably sure that any cloth left in a tomb would degrade in a matter of decades, not centuries. I would also note that corpses tend to be buried inside a sarcophagus *within* a tomb, not left to rot on top.

There is a possibility that this is an earlier tomb that has been reused at a much later date; or that the body on display rests on an existing rose marble sarcophagus and not just on a rock. A body within the sarcophagus would be far more interesting but we will have to wait for professionals to get access before we can know for sure. In any case this may be one of the lesser 'satellite' tombs that are known to be later additions to an important site. Any great sacred site attracts smaller sites, as devotees seek to be buried near the focus of their devotion, and such is also to be expected of a major tomb at Rennes-le-Château. The original body in Hammott's tomb could be of anyone from local nobility to an exiled Pope. Further burials may have been made here in recent years, accounting for the body on top of the tomb.

As for the principal tomb of which this may be a 'satellite', its whereabouts can be estimated, but without an obvious entrance it is impossible to gain access to it. To narrow our search we must look first at the supporting material.

MAPS AND PARCHMENTS

During the filming of *Bloodline* I encountered a local researcher, Gérard Thome, who has spent many years exploring the region and has amassed a lot of evidence for the existence of a hidden temple in the landscape. He has discovered paintings and decoded some aspects of the church at Rennes-le-Château to support his theory. He is also in possession of a number of parchments that match in style the two parchments that Sion released in the 1970s (*see* page 289). These are likely to be from the same source that produced encoded documents during the 1960s and early 1970s. The parchments, mostly vellum and hide, have various maps of the region and encrypted text in the same biblical style as the others in existence. Thome himself claims to have stumbled across these at various points in his researches or had them left in his name at local shops by an unknown party. He may well be the unwitting benefactor of some of Sion's archive that was stolen in the late 1970s from Paris and that has since surfaced in Spain.

Having briefly viewed some of the parchments I can state that phrases such as 'come to the tomb' are readily discernible, while crude maps of the landscape near Rennes-le-Château are easily identified. On one map a circle has been drawn at an identical location to one on a map published by Patricia Villiers-Stuart in the early 1980s. I recognized it instantly because Sion had provided me with a copy of Villiers-Stuart's work early on in my investigation (*see* page 294). She had found the circle in the Poussin painting and transcribed it onto the landscape in the picture. The Villiers-Stuart design is a circle with twelve divisions representing the rose, as can be seen in the design of rose windows in many cathedrals across Europe.

What also surprised me about the information we were receiving was the potential scale of what was hidden beneath the mountains.

Based on his research, Thome has drawn up quite a detailed mythology of the hidden temple. He claims that there was a two-storey subterranean structure with two levels of crypts. He called it a 'necropolis' and gave detailed descriptions of its design based upon evidence he had found both in the parchments and local churches. However, Sion refused to acknowledge the structure as a necropolis, preferring to use the term 'temple'. To me it resembled a temple of Mithras, a Persian god popular in the Roman Empire, and whose temples were typically underground.

At one point Thome produced a painting of the Crucifixion scene and indicated to us the landscape behind Jesus. In the centre of the landscape is a cutaway mountain with a temple hidden inside, although upon closer inspection the temple resembles the Islamic Dome of the Rock more than a Mithraic structure.

At the time Sion seemed willing to support Thome's claims but, as I have said, they upheld the idea of a temple rather than a necropolis.

Sion also said that 'the notion of a subterranean temple is by no means a new one'. The possibility of a structure existing inside a mountain is not unlikely. The landscape has limestone and granite in vast quantities. Over time water erodes the soft limestone, creating caverns and tunnels among the much harder granite. At least two of the mountains in the region have underground lakes, one of which is large enough to warrant having a rowing boat moored to its bank. Even the modest hill of Rennes-le-Château has a reservoir beneath the summit. This source of fresh water was used until relatively recently by those who lived here, and in prehistoric times both this and a good elevated defensive position overlooking the surrounding plains supported the thriving community that inhabited the plateau.

APPROACHING THE TEMPLE

During my researches into the temple I discovered three entrances to the underground system and a further possible entrance that is now too small to pass through but affords a view of an underground tunnel wide enough to drive a car in. These are all situated in locations that fit crude maps of the tunnel system that were shown to me by Gérard Thome. I asked Sion if they intended someone to locate the temple as the entrances are sealed and require excavation.

> '[Father] Boudet [of neighbouring Rennes-les-Bains] did not
> do any of the digging himself, that is how things work. It is
> damp, wet, and not without pitfalls, there is one fast-flowing
> underground river to cross and a downward climb that is quite
> considerable. Very few would undertake that climb down in the
> dark.'

Toward the end of *Le Serpent Rouge* the narrator emerges from the underground 'abyss' (*see* page 168). His journey into the underworld resulted in him understanding the final truth, the existence of a real temple, and the real tomb of the 'Sleeping Beauty'. Within the temple is the answer, the secret of the Priory of Sion and physical proof of the greatest lie in Western history. At this point in *Le Serpent Rouge* we are south of Rennes-les-Bains, beyond the Devil's Armchair and near an area of land known as the Dead Man (L'Homme Mort). I found a route into the mountain close by but was unable to proceed very far as the cave I was in had become partially blocked. Visible beyond the collapse was a cave wide enough to drive a car through. As Sion confirmed,

> 'There *is* an entrance very close to L'Homme Mort and likely the
> cave to which you refer. It is partially collapsed? It is an area well
> worth a visit in the spring when rainfall has minimized and the
> water table is less high. During the period 1992–5 this arm, this
> entrance, was a one-way ticket to certain death due to the terrible
> deluge of the time.'

As the exploration progressed I confirmed that there is a tunnel system beneath the mountain of Blanchefort. It runs north/south and originally had two entrances. The entrance in the area of L'Homme Mort was furthest from the site. The second entrance was a vertical shaft at the ruins of Blanchefort.

Sion provided very specific directions on where to excavate, but the route to the final resting place can no longer be navigated from this mountain. The entrances at Blanchefort and the Dead Man all lead to a single tunnel that takes you beneath the river, but in recent years a long section of this tunnel has completely collapsed. The route, formerly open, is now closed forever. I believe it to form a part of a larger underground complex of tunnels that radiate out from a central location. An obvious symbol for this would be the spider that appears on some of the Priory of Sion documents.

There were likely to be other entrances so I enquired further. The following is taken from an unofficial conversation I had with a French member of the Priory of Sion who chose to remain anonymous. I have since confirmed their membership through other Sion members. The clipped form of the sentences is due to my limited grasp of conversational French:

> 'There are 12 tunnels. Only one is open at any time. The journey
> is an initiation. The road underground goes under a river. The
> ways in are seasonally open – in winter some are under snow and
> ice, some flood at certain times of the year.'

This account was supported by a later communication from Nic Haywood:

> 'The "legend" of such a temple with its 12 gates, each opened –
> usually – by Mother Nature herself was extant a time long before
> Boudet appeared in the locale.'

Unfortunately, the three possible entrances that I initially identified are all now closed, two purposely by man and one by nature in the form of a collapsed tunnel. As two are accessed from churches in the area it is better not to reveal anything specific about their location, as vandalism and illegal excavations are rife in the region. This is not an attempt to appear obscure but simply to protect sacred places. One further location is said to exist beneath a private house and another is on private land, though I have only scant ideas about where it surfaces.

Nic Haywood told me that there were 12 entrances, which were intended to open in accordance with signs of the zodiac, and that beneath the ground the shape of a triangle is significant and linked to the tradition of 'Black Madonnas' in Christian art, so called from their typical dark hues. In past times the sites of three Black Madonnas forming a triangle pattern were a guide to an important location. The Black Madonnas themselves are thought to have first been introduced to France at the time of the Crusades and generally follow the form of a triangle. The idea being presented here is that there are *three* locations below ground, in the centre of which is the shrine that we are seeking.

THE INNER TEMPLE

According to Sion the temple itself once served as a place of initiation. The journey into the underworld has many alchemical and psychological interpretations and appears in many forms in literature, most notably Dante's *Inferno*. One thinks of this as a journey of self-discovery into the depths of being.

The maze of tunnels may also replicate the use of the underground labyrinth, another well-known initiatory tool dating back at least as far as ancient Egypt. As a continuation of *Le Serpent Rouge* the tunnel labyrinth would serve as the final rite of initiation on the pilgrimage to the hidden temple.

The site itself is said to be of vast historical and religious importance and to have been in use as a temple since Celtic times. Many additional secrets and items are said to have been buried there over the centuries.

The use of the cave could well date back to the vast, thriving prehistoric community that once inhabited the area, and early pagan religions may have adopted it as a sacred place. There are said to be other caves in the area that have rough stone altars carved into them that date back to prehistory.

The tendency to rebuild structures on the foundations of a previous holy site dates back to Sumerian times, where the ruins of a temple would be built upon in the belief that the new temple would take on the spiritual energy previously imbued in the site. It is a tradition that underpins the choice of sites for many of today's Christian churches and cathedrals.

As I understand it, knowledge of the location of this great sanctuary remained within the noble families descended from the Templars, such as the de Blancheforts, up until the French Revolution. At the time of the Revolution the threat of destruction forced the old families to entrust the secret to a predecessor of Saunière. Other heretical French priests at Rennes-le-Château also knew of its existence and it was rediscovered at the time of Saunière and Boudet. The latter was a well-placed member of one of Sion's affiliate groups at this time and was responsible for disseminating the secret in a manner that future initiates could decode. Boudet published *The True Language of the Celts and the Stone Circle of Rennes-les-Bains* (*see* page 82) but this failed to have the desired effect so instead he oversaw the refurbishment of the church at Rennes-le-Château.

Sadly, Saunière's own involvement seems to have been less than pious and we can only wonder at what priceless artefacts Saunière spirited away in order to fund his ostentatious lifestyle.

The main temple was most likely looted in part and it is possible that parts of any corpses there were removed and distributed as relics. Other items found their way into museums and private collections but I was also given the impression that wherever possible, removed items were acquired and returned by the Priory of Sion. As to the complete nature of what might be present in the temple, this will be considered in the next chapter on relics.

The opinion of Sion is that the Templars fashioned the landscape according to Solomon's Temple and renamed some locations after places in Old Jerusalem. In doing so they had created an inverse or reflection of the city of Jerusalem with the concealed Temple at its heart. Here they stored the spoils of the Crusades but it also served as something far more important. They were recreating what they considered to be a New Jerusalem in the south of France.

This links to the apocalyptic aspect of the temple, a theme further considered later in this book, but for now it is worth remembering that this is the New Jerusalem of the Templars, with an invisible Temple above ground mirroring the hidden Temple below.

CONCLUSION

The idea of the hidden Temple is very attractive to researchers because it answers so many questions about Rennes-le-Château and the Priory of Sion. It would explain the source of Saunière's wealth; provide a tomb that supports the bloodline theory, the legacy of the Templars' treasure and the destination of the hidden pilgrimage. A temple, with bodies, treasure and so on is a fitting resolution to all these mysteries and in a way it is the only possible answer to all the threads of the Rennes-le-Château mystery apart from alchemy – but even that is present in the form of symbolic pilgrimage.

Also, it is not difficult to imagine why such a temple would be so important that it has been kept a secret throughout history.

If we are to believe the Priory of Sion they, and their numerous incarnations, are the guardians of the temple. They have used it as a place of initiation and ritual, seeding the degrees of Freemasonry and influencing other secret societies to ensure that the secret survives. There is an uneasy alliance with the Vatican to ensure that the evidence – the content of the tombs in this sacred place – are protected from the general public and defended from the profane until the time is right for release. When society is deemed capable of accepting the shock of what is enshrined there, and it will come as no great surprise, only then does the Catholic Church believe that it can withstand the revelation. Then will be the time for light to enter the sanctuary and for the truth to find its mirror.

What remains unclear is the exact identity of those who are buried in the temple. *Le Serpent Rouge* makes reference to Mary Magdalene, bodies (in the plural), and various accompanying objects. Some researchers, such as Gérard Thome, consider the temple to be the family tomb of Jesus, Mary Magdalene and their two sons. The Priory of Sion refused to corroborate this claim directly but have referred to a 'body of evidence' on numerous occasions and its potential to upset the Vatican. In the light of this the *Et in Arcadia Ego* (*Shepherds of Arcadia*) painting may well depict that family, the bearded father in the foreground, his wife by his side and their two sons, now safely entombed in the Arcadia of the Languedoc. A perfect resting place kept secret through the ages.

The bodies, we are told, are mummified, protected over time from decomposition while radiating the perfume of the rose. These are possibly the greatest relics of all time. But can we trust them? Are they authentic or some random find by the Templars, pillaged a thousand years after the fact from a misidentified grave in the Holy Land?

Before we can even consider the identity of those in the tomb and the possible attendant objects we must look at the bigger picture of a medieval landscape littered with the remnants of the holy persons – from splinters of the True Cross to the four corpses of St Peter. We turn now to the problem of relics.

CHAPTER 12

THE AGE OF RELICS

INTRODUCTION

Many authors and researchers have reached the inevitable conclusion that there is something of great importance buried in the vicinity of Rennes-le-Château. Should such an item exist it is likely to be of a religious nature as we are clearly dealing with a secret linked to the local priesthood. At this point we must err on the side of caution. There are plenty of ideas about what might be buried there, but with the exception of Ben Hammott's questionable discoveries (*see* page 183) little or no actual finds have come to light.

On the ground an unspoken battle for religious artefacts is taking place. On the one side, the Vatican has a history of gathering anything relating to the Bible and the saints, including relics, alternative scripture and occult material. In the late 1990s a Vatican-funded team of Italian archaeologists used ground radar to survey the church at Rennes-le-Château. The Israeli secret service, MOSSAD, has also taken an interest in Rennes-le-Château, and have been quite openly exploring the area and questioning local inhabitants. Author David Wood recounts how he was approached to survey the area for an individual who, when challenged, claimed to be working on behalf of MOSSAD. I have also encountered a modern Templar order looking to recover something from the area. Local residents are reluctant to speak of the mystery but some are known to have used metal detectors, bulldozers and even dynamite in their own ongoing searches.

Having located if not the temple itself, then the idea that such a temple exists, we are faced with the issue of what it might contain. This may seem simple, but any location of real importance may have become a repository for more than one item of veneration. Relics bring with them all manner of issues and often have notoriously suspect origins. This chapter is intended to explore relics in their many contexts.

The word *relic* comes from the Latin *reliquiae* which means 'remains' and was already in use long before Christianity adopted it in its modern sense. The *Catholic Encyclopaedia* describes a relic as 'some object, notably part of the body or clothes, remaining as a memorial of a departed saint'.

During the Middle Ages, when pilgrimage became a huge industry, priests would beg, borrow, buy or steal anything that could genuinely be − or at least passed off as − a holy relic for their church. Priests petitioned Rome to disturb and desecrate the tombs of the holy fathers for body parts. Where possible, Rome delivered.

An early Christian example of a relic is to be found in a letter written c156CE by the inhabitants of Smyrna, describing the death of St Polycarp:

> 'We took up his bones, which are more valuable than precious
> stones and finer than refined gold, and laid them in a suitable
> place, where the Lord will permit us to gather ourselves together,
> as we are able, in gladness and joy, and to celebrate the anniversary
> of his martyrdom.'

There is a morbid fascination for the remains of the dead. It is as if collecting and owning these objects somehow puts us in a direct relationship with the source. I suspect that the veneration of relics is a primitive instinct, like the keeping of mementoes and trophies from dead animals as tokens of power. Even with regard to saints, it is clear in some cases that the objects as much as the individual were being venerated, creating a kind of idolatrous 'cult of the dead'.

For over a thousand years pilgrimage has drawn the devout to behold in awe some fairly gruesome remains. For example, the 800-year-old tongue of St Anthony of Padua, who was renowned for his eloquence, is kept in a jar that is often kissed by the pilgrims who line up to see it. If the jar were removed one wonders if they would kiss the shrivelled tongue instead.

There are other approaches to venerating relics. They may be seen as simply representative of the saint, divorced from any supernatural power themselves.

Some are given a symbolic meaning, such as St Clare of Montefalco's (1268–1308) three gallstones, which are said to represent the Holy Trinity. However, the majority of relics are regularly credited with divine or indeed frankly magical qualities. At shrines where long lines form and the afflicted petition for a cure, there is an assumption that the relic possesses some power that is in some way transferable to the visitor.

As the veneration of relics became more prevalent, there was a matching growth in their supposed powers to heal and revive. In Europe, stories circulated of miracles experienced by those lucky enough to come into contact with relics. In some cases, as when St Helena (*see* below) identified the 'True Cross', a dead or dying person was used to prove the authenticity of the relic. Contact with relics was believed to be a source of healing and has remained so ever since.

> 'The blind and cripples are restored to health, the dead recalled to life, and demons expelled from the bodies of men.'
>
> *The Roman Catechism* (1566)

The veneration of relics is not limited to the bodies and body parts of saints. A variety of objects from the Bible have also attracted attention over the years. The remains of Noah's Ark, for example, are claimed by some to be visible on Mount Ararat in present-day Turkey.

RELICS FROM THE LIFE OF JESUS

Naturally, items said to be linked directly to Jesus enjoy special recognition and popularity. For example, among his reputed garments is the 'Holy Coat of Trier' which, when first put on display in the 16th century, attracted 100,000 pilgrims in 15 days. It would seem from the list of items currently treated as 'authentic' that everywhere Jesus went, his followers removed anything he touched for later veneration.

The first surge of interest in Christian relics began with St Helena, the mother of Emperor Constantine the Great. At the age of almost 80, and almost 300 years after the death of Jesus, she travelled to the Holy Land with the aim of discovering sites and artefacts from Jesus' life. She was shown a tomb and told that it contained, among other items, the cross of the Crucifixion. She then took it upon herself to have this cross broken into three pieces and distributed across the Roman Empire. Fragments would later be enclosed in small gold crosses to be worn around the neck – a fashion that endures to this day in the wearing of crucifixes.

Aside from obvious issues of authenticating the relics, St Helena's location of the tomb does not fit well with the description in the gospels. It is highly likely that she was looking on the wrong hill. But before anyone could question the authenticity of the discovery, the race to secure the relics of the saints had begun in earnest.

Seven centuries after St Helena claimed to have found the tomb of Jesus, an identical collection of relics was discovered during the Crusades. Amalric I, one of the Crusader kings of Jerusalem (1162–74), wrote of the Crusader finds in the Holy Land:

'The relics included the most precious evidence of the Passion of Our Lord, namely the cross, nails, lance, sponge, reed, crown of thorns, shroud and the sandals.'

If the last item on that list seems familiar it is probably due to it being parodied in Monty Python's film *The Life of Brian*. Added to these, the following items exist in various churches across Europe, all of which are considered authentic relics by many within the Church:

- The Swaddling Cloth of the Infant Christ.
- Christ's Seamless Garments.
- The Holy Stairs which Christ climbed to Pilate's office.
- The Scourging Post on which Christ was whipped.
- The Crown of Thorns (a remnant of which remains in Notre Dame, Paris).
- The Holy Sponge from which Christ drank (also broken up and distributed to various churches).
- The Holy Lance that pierced Christ's side (a few examples).

If the unlikelihood of any of these items being genuine may seem glaringly obvious, there are even more bizarre relics in the form of breastmilk from the Virgin Mary and no fewer than 14 foreskins of Christ, three of which are thought to be in the Vatican.

TEMPLARS AND THE AGE OF RELICS

Tasked with protecting pilgrims in the Holy Land, the original nine Templar knights set up camp on the Temple Mount and spent eight years excavating it. While seemingly misguided in the short term, this act may have had a long-term positive effect for pilgrims, in that it potentially produced relics that could be relocated to relatively safer sites in Western Europe and therefore save many of the faithful the long and arduous journey. When the Holy Land eventually fell back into the hands of Muslim rulers, Christians in the West perhaps took some comfort from having access to what they believed were authentic biblical finds.

The Order of the Knights Templar could well have removed items from their excavations of the Temple Mount and other sacred sites. Stories come down to us of how the Templars were in possession of many sacred relics that they had discovered during the Crusades, such as yet another True Cross. (By this time, it has been remarked, there were already enough True Crosses and Crucifixion nails in existence to build a small wooden church.)

The notion that the Templars discovered the True Cross over a thousand years after the event seems very unlikely, as do the various stories of the relic's demise. My favourite account is that the Templar cross was buried by a Templar soldier who feared it would be lost to the opposing army in an impending battle. Later the victorious soldier was unable to remember exactly where he had buried the relic and after three days gave up trying.

What is beyond doubt is that the excavations of the Templars did take place, so perhaps they did find something. According to Nic Haywood,

> 'of the Temple of Jerusalem [discoveries], part was hidden at
> Rennes-le-Château, part was located at Toulouse but later melted
> down and dispersed. The rest is in the Vatican under the control of
> the Italian Priory of Sion members.'

With the landscape around Rennes-le-Château modified to represent the Temple of Solomon (*see* Chapter 11) it is likely that the Templars would have placed any finds from the ancient Temple in this area.

The original Temple of Solomon was destroyed by the Babylonians in 586 BCE and rebuilt around 80 years later after the return of the Judean exiles. This Second Temple was sacked and desecrated by the Greek kings of Syria. According to the biblical First Book of the Maccabees, the Temple's 'hidden treasures' were taken (Maccabees 1.21.3). Some of the treasure was also used as bribes to fend off threatening foreign armies.

Under Herod the Great, Roman client king of Judea (37–4 BCE), the Second Temple was renovated in a magnificent 'Herodian-Classical' style. The rebuilt Second Temple was the one that Jesus knew.

The Second Temple was sacked and demolished in 70CE during the First Jewish War by the Roman general Titus, son of the emperor Vespasian. A great menorah is known to be among the loot taken back to Rome, where it is depicted on the triumphal arch of Titus. There were originally ten menorahs in the Temple, seven-branched solid gold candelabra estimated to be at least four feet (1.2m) high. The menorahs were said to be based upon an original that stood in the Tabernacle of the Hebrews in the wilderness after Moses led them from Egypt. The menorah is a symbol of Judaism and at least one Jewish leader has asked the Vatican to return the Temple menorah. But there is no confirmation that the object, if it still exists at all, remains in Rome.

It may have been taken by the Visigoths who plundered Rome in 410CE and are thought to have subsequently headed for Spain and southwest France, possibly near Rennes-le-Château. This raises the possibility of the Temple menorah being in the vicinity, although it does not bode well for the survival of other items from the Temple.

Nic Haywood had mentioned the menorah on a number of occasions as being part of the Temple furnishings that had originated in the Temple of Jerusalem and were later secreted in the Languedoc by the Templars. With sufficient gold, a new menorah could have been produced as part of an attempt to build a New Jerusalem. But there had definitely been an ancient Temple menorah in Rome, and the Visigoths had looted Rome before moving into the region; furthermore, the Templars themselves had excavated the Temple Mount. It becomes increasingly possible, therefore, that the Templars acquired an original Temple menorah at some point in their history.

BEN HAMMOTT'S FINDS

There are claims of other relics having been found near Rennes-le-Château.

During the making of the *Bloodline* documentary, co-producer Bruce Burgess joined researcher Ben Hammott on his quest to locate a wooden chest based on a series of clues buried in glass bottles. He recovered the chest and found it to contain items including an ointment jar, a stone cup and some Templar coins. The cup and jar were authenticated as being contemporary with the time of Jesus by archaeologist Dr Gabriel Barkay of Bar-Ilan University in Israel. The cup, we are told by Sion, is possibly the one used at the wedding of Jesus and Mary Magdalene. But why anyone would keep a piece of wedding crockery is questionable because at the time they would have had no idea that this wedding would one day become a heretical secret.

The inclusion of Templar coins is also suspicious in that it is the equivalent of keeping loose change in a chest with a priceless antique. These were not valuable coins in their day so may have been a later addition. But I think the chest is contrived in order to link together two periods in history and for the latter to give credibility to the former.

Sion had hinted at such a possibility many months prior to the discovery. When we reported that one of its members had been seen in the area they voiced concern not that the member would be 'removing objects,' but at 'what they may be leaving there for you to find'. I decided that Sion was not being entirely honest about what they knew. Nic Haywood's response:

> 'The points that you make are entirely valid. There is a difficulty here, and you're correct about the concerns re [name of Sion member removed by author] and the likelihood of him *placing* objects in the area.'

The purpose of the chest is to reignite the Rennes-le-Château debate and bring attention back to the mysteries that Sion seeks to publicize. In spite of this, Sion continued to maintain that the cup is the actual wedding chalice of Jesus and Mary Magdalene. It is impossible to say for sure that the items are *not* real, but their authenticity remains unproven. However, this does not detract from their value as *representative* of the original items – the Cross in any church is an example of the symbolic power at work here.

Perhaps the most famous relic from the life of Jesus is the Holy Grail. Stripped of its mystical properties and removed from the Arthurian romances, the Holy Grail is simply the cup used by Jesus at the Last Supper. There are a number of contenders for this relic, including the Chalice of Antioch, which resides in the Metropolitan Museum of Art, New York, and was found in Syria in 1910. The Cup of Valencia, on display in Valencia cathedral, Spain, is said to have been passed down by the early popes. There is also the Marian Chalice, which comes to us courtesy of St Helena and was believed to have been the one used by Mary Magdalene to collect Christ's blood. There are various other 'Grails' in existence.

The idea, proposed by some researchers, that the 'Grail' is not a physical object but a symbol of the bloodline of Jesus, seems both an opportunity and an obstacle. The bloodline might be one facet of the Grail story, but if this becomes its entirety I suspect that something is lost.

In symbolism the Grail takes on a very different nature. The archetypal symbol appears in therapy sessions as the unconscious image of the mother. Its shape is a vessel for holding and nurturing, endlessly nourishing like a mother to her newborn baby. This shows how the object has transcended function to become imbued with meaning. I have taken part in psychology groups where candidates from different religious and cultural backgrounds have meditated on the idea of the 'feminine' and almost all have arrived at the image of a cup. The Grail is the feminine receptacle, healing and making whole, representing under-standing, whereas the sword/spear is male and cleaving, the act of separation signifying wisdom and the ability to break apart and examine.

In Grail legends, the Grail as feminine aspect is lost to the world and must be recovered and restored. In the Arthurian Grail romances it is often described as accompanying a spear or sword during displays and rituals (*Parzival* and so on). This illustrates how the balance of masculine and feminine must be maintained, and the spear and the Grail are the perfect archetypal images of this relationship.

The return of the Grail is sometimes heralded by the arrival of an apparition often referred to as 'the Lady of the Cup'. Others in the vicinity who witness the apparition mistake the figure for the Virgin Mary, but often she is interpreted as Mary Magdalene. This is the emancipated woman but also the feminine aspect of manhood that must be rediscovered.

DOCUMENTS

In many ways, documents are more important than relics. They occupy a slightly different position than standard relics in that they have the potential to carry information down the ages. In theological terms discoveries of ancient documents have the potential to undermine accepted religious texts if, like the Dead Sea Scrolls, they pre-date the gospels or, like the Nag Hammadi Library of Gnostic texts, they have escaped editing or censorship over the centuries. Biblical scholars believe that three of the New Testament gospel accounts of Jesus may draw upon a now lost earlier source known as 'Q' (from German *Quelle*, 'source'), a collection of Jesus' sayings perhaps taken down verbatim by an early follower. Should a complete manuscript of 'Q' ever be discovered (or revealed) it has the potential to completely transform our under-standing of the life of Jesus. Some scholars think that Q, if it physically existed (as opposed to being an oral collection) may have been very similar in form to the Gnostic *Gospel of Thomas*.

Like many of the documents related to the Rennes-le-Château mystery, those that appear in the *Bloodline* film could be entirely recent in their creation but, as in the case of the *Le Serpent Rouge*, they may still hold vital information. It is believed that Father Saunière also found documents at Rennes-le-Château, early versions of the fabricated parchments in circulation today. Until Saunière's discoveries are revealed we can assume they contained genealogies and alternatives to accepted doctrines, or perhaps a map leading to a hidden location. Of course genealogies, like any other document, can be contrived.

THE BODY OF MARY MAGDALENE?

A recurring idea in this mystery is that Mary Magdalene is buried near Rennes-le-Château. Sion has referred to a 'body' being present a number of times. The problem with the body just being that of Mary is that this changes nothing. There is also a 'body of Mary Magdalene' at Vézelay in Burgundy and another at Saint-Maximin-la-Sainte-Baume in SE France. The latter was not discovered until 1279 and so is unlikely to be genuine, in any case, its existence has had no noticeable impact on Christianity.

For there to be any real impact on Christianity, the body at Rennes-le-Château would have to be that of Jesus. Nothing else justifies the amount of mystique and religious interest that the area attracts.

THE BODY OF JESUS

As we discovered in the chapters on pilgrimage and *Le Serpent Rouge*, Sion maintains that a body of great importance is buried in the region. Along with the pilgrim's badge depicting the head of Jesus, this statement would indicate that the intended destination of medieval alchemical pilgrims was a body they believed to be none other than that of Jesus Christ.

The likelihood of Jesus having ascended to Heaven, as the New Testament recounts, will be covered in a later chapter, but a recurring theme of the Rennes-le-Château mystery is that the body of Jesus might be somewhere in the vicinity. If this is true, then we are searching for what would be the most important and most controversial relic to exist in Christendom.

Imagine for one moment that the relic of relics – the corpse of Jesus – was discovered. Would it be instantly recognizable, an uncorrupted body, charismatic even in death? What strange worship would grow up around it? Would the Catholic Church and other Christian denominations clamour for Christ's body, claiming right of ownership? Or would they continue to deny its existence? Would they loot the tomb of Jesus and scatter its contents to fill the collection plates of churches, cathedrals or, God forbid, museums?

But like all relics, any finds would require a lot of supporting material that could be verified to establish any degree of credibility. This brings us to the core of the entire problem of relics: authenticity.

THE PROBLEM OF RELICS

Even the merest consideration of relics throws up a number of issues. It seems to me to be disrespectful for a corpse to be dug up, dismembered and scattered. For example, St Luke's reputed body is in the basilica of St Justina in Padua while his head is thought to be in the Vatican. It difficult to believe that this desecration is what Luke would have wanted (assuming the corpse in question is actually his).

Even today relics are much sought after. On eBay 'an old relic of the True Cross' recently sold for $1,100. This is frowned upon by some Christians and an organization called the International Crusade for Holy Relics is attempting to have the online trafficking of relics banned.

But this traffic is nothing new. As early as the end of the fourth century, St Augustine denounced impostors who dressed as monks and made a profit by the sale of spurious relics. Any thriving business is prone to unscrupulous traders and in the relics trade forgery and misidentification were rife. As Bart Brewer comments in his book *Pilgrimage from Rome:*

> 'Even Martin Luther wondered how there could be 26 apostles
> buried in Germany, when they were only 12 in the entire Bible.
> … It is clear that most "relics" are frauds.'

One amusing anecdote relates how, during the Middle Ages, a travelling monk once encountered a merchant who offered to sell him the skull of John the Baptist. The monk was dumbfounded. Hadn't he just seen the skull of St John in a church during a recent visit to France? 'That was the skull of St John when he was a *child,*' explained the merchant. 'This is his skull when he was an adult.'

By the Middle Ages it had become fashionable for churches to contain at least a part of a saint. This would guarantee them a flow of pilgrims and thus a steady income, so they seem to have been happy to accept anything as authentic.

The Catholic Church made various attempts to combat the proliferation of spurious artefacts and in the 16th century the Council of Trent decreed:

> 'No new miracles are to be acknowledged or new relics
> recognized unless the bishop of the diocese has taken cognizance
> and approved thereof.'

In recent years science has supplied us with perhaps a better way of testing relics in the form of radiocarbon dating. For example, a recent radiocarbon dating of the remains of St Luke in Padua found that the body belonged to a person who died 150 years after the time of Luke. Even allowing for the margin of error involved in radiocarbon dating the body is unlikely to be the real thing. The Church itself has profound misgivings on the actual authenticity of many relics, as the *Catholic Encyclopaedia* states:

> 'It remains true that many of the more ancient relics duly exhibited
> for veneration in the great sanctuaries of Christendom or even
> at Rome itself must now be pronounced to be either certainly
> spurious or open to grave suspicion.'

There are ethical considerations as well. The saints were often committed to poverty and chastity, surrendering their wealth to the poor during their lifetimes, only for the Catholic Church to enshrine their remains in gold- and jewel-encrusted reliquaries and to display them for the purpose of eliciting donations from the poor believers whom the saints had tried to help.

A case in point would be St Elizabeth, a Hungarian princess who gave away all her possessions and wealth to the poor and was reduced literally to living in a pigsty. She refused to wear her crown in compassion for Jesus' suffering the Crown of Thorns and she devoted her life to helping the poor and the sick. Years after her death she was canonized. Her tomb was ransacked and her body dismembered for use by the Church. A gold shrine was built for her body and her skull was put on display with a gold crown placed upon it.

In many cases it may be that the authenticity of the relic is no longer an issue. Should any item be venerated for centuries, such as the famous "Turin Shroud" (recently revealed by radiocarbon dating to be medieval), it may take on a certain power as a symbolic trigger to inspire devotion and to change consciousness. To touch something that one believes in strongly enough can have the same effect as touching the real thing.

CONCLUSION

In spite of all the evidence against the majority of relics, some are undoubtedly authentic, some have been treated with the utmost respect, and some, no doubt, have been kept hidden from the world. This brings us back to the idea of the temple in the landscape around Rennes-le-Château and the possible treasures that lie within.

In the case of Ben Hammott's chest and Gérard Thome's parchments, they may not be authentically ancient but could be considered legitimate from their intended effect. It should be noted that they have been made public in a manner that can easily be dismissed by the staunchly religious, who may find their implications unacceptable. If Sion is behind this, we are witnessing an elaborate game of 'show-and-tell' between them and the Vatican. It would be simple enough for Sion to publish the original parchments and to present conclusive evidence, but things are moving at a certain pace. This pace is a point of contention, with the Catholic branch of Sion wishing to prolong the status quo indefinitely while other members see the current world situation as an opportunity to move matters forward.

As these relics come into circulation the Vatican cannot help but recognize them and understand the subtle goading that is taking place. The question is: where is this leading?

In the first instance I think that there will be further discoveries, with more relics emerging and perhaps the ultimate relic: the body of Jesus or at least Mary Magdalene. Sion has often spoken of the 'body' as the trump card in the game that they are playing with the Vatican.

Sion informed us that there are heretical clergy within the Catholic Church who would 'down tools' should the actual body of Christ come to light and the 'great lie' be overturned. The others, faced with the truth, would have no choice but to concede and adjust their theology accordingly.

This would lay the groundwork for a more important shift away from the dogma of the Church and back to a more personal experience of spirituality. There is evidence that this is happening naturally, as seen in the current upsurge of alternative spiritual practices. But ultimately, it needs to be directed towards gnosis – the direct relationship between an individual and God. There may be enough fragments of the 'True Cross' to build a real bridge, but no amount can build a bridge to the divine.

So now we must take the next logical step and explore the importance of redressing the balance. The physical search for Mary Magdalene's body is mirrored by the search for an understanding of what she means to us. The blood that cries from the ground can no longer be ignored and we are inevitably drawn toward the bloodline of Jesus and Mary Magdalene. This and many other ideas surrounding the mystery throw into question what we know about the life of Jesus and of Mary Magdalene. But it is not for the sake of Christianity that we rake this soil, but for the sake of the search for truth.

PART 3

THE
BLOODLINE

CHAPTER 13

MARY MAGDALENE

I came a across a wedding that old families had contrived,
Bethlehem the bridegroom and Babylon the bride.

Leonard Cohen, *Last Year's Man.*

In the garden I committed no crime.

Tori Amos, *Raspberry Swirl*

INTRODUCTION

When Pierre Plantard was charged in the 1950s with circulating the idea that Jesus and Mary Magdalene had been married, he made public the game of chess that was taking place between Sion and the Vatican. The discovery of what Sion claims to be a 'Cup of Matrimony', placed by Sion in the path of Ben Hammott (*see* Chapter 12), is another gambit on their part to try to accelerate the release of knowledge and evidence. As a relic the cup points to a greater prize and is part of the supporting material for a wider secret to which Sion is alluding. Books such as *The Holy Blood and the Holy Grail* and *The Da Vinci Code* have helped to seed public awareness of heretical ideas, and now the evidence to support these ideas is being released in a safe and controlled manner. A great 'heresy' is now coming to light as truth. But what is this heresy, and why does it need to be revealed?

The answer seems to lie at the feet of Mary Magdalene. She truly is *Notre Dame*, Our Lady, our 'lost queen' of *Le Serpent Rouge*. She impacts upon our quest in more than one way. The idea that she was married to Jesus has generated the most controversy in recent years, but this is not the most important factor of her story. With that in mind, the aim of this chapter is to explore the life and work of Mary Magdalene on a number of different levels.

ANCESTRY

Our story of Mary Magdalene really begins with her ancestors, as these provide a context for her position in the Bible. Authors such as Margaret Starbird in her book *The Woman with the Alabaster Jar* make a case for Mary having been descended from the Israelite tribe of Benjamin. The tribe of Benjamin takes its name and its origin from Benjamin, the son of Jacob in the Bible. The Benjaminites were said to be great warriors and feature prominently in the Old Testament. They were the founders and first rulers of Jerusalem.

The tribe is relevant to our mystery in a number of ways. For example, the Freemasons refer to themselves as Benjaminites in some of their rituals, seemingly holding the tribe of Mary Magdalene in high esteem. As the authors of *The Holy Blood and the Holy Grail* point out, the Benjaminites included a clan called 'Ahiram' and one of the children of this clan was named Benoni. Central to Freemasonry is the tale of Hiram, the master builder of Solomon's Temple. In this tale Benoni is Hiram's disciple.

Having founded and first ruled Jerusalem, the Benjaminites were entitled to consider the city and Solomon's Temple as theirs to govern by birthright. But, like the Templars, they were dispossessed of their lands and exiled for what was described as the 'Benjaminitic crime'.

The Bible (Judges 19–20) records that a mob of Benjaminites gang-raped the concubine of a Levite while he was staying in Gibeah, a Benjaminite town. The concubine died, and for this murder – and the equally sinful crime against tribal hospitality – a council of the tribes demanded that the perpetrators be handed over for execution. But the Benjaminite leaders took up arms to protect the culprits and war ensued. During the conflict the Benjaminites were nearly wiped out at the battle of Gibeah and their lands were seized. (Here we also find echoes of the Templar trial and seizure of their lands.) The other Israelite tribes then forbade their women to marry into the tribe, threatening it with extinction. The effect of this was that many of the Benjaminites went into exile and married into non-Israelite families.

After a period the Benjaminites were accepted again among the Israelites, and even produced their first king, Saul. But the crime was long remembered as an example of wickedness and some Benjaminites remained in exile, having migrated to the region of southern Greece called Arcadia. As we have already seen, the theme of Arcadia returns many times in our mystery. For example, it was said to be the birthplace of the Merovingian kings.

THE MAGDALENE IN SCRIPTURE

A number of individuals in the Bible are associated with Mary Magdalene. Many think of Mary as a reformed prostitute, but this term is never actually used in the Bible to describe her. The idea that she was a prostitute was misconstrued from a statement by Pope Gregory (540–604) when he referred to Mary as a sinful person whom Jesus forgave. This was in fact a reference to the woman accused of adultery, who was saved by Jesus from being stoned to death (John 7.53–8.11). (There is an important painting of this episode by Poussin that is covered in Chapter 16.)

Mary Magdalene's appearances in the New Testament are few but they give clues to her role and relationship to Jesus. The first chronological appearance of Mary Magdalene occurs when Jesus casts seven demons out of her (Mark 16.9; compare Luke 8.1–3):

> 'Now when Jesus was risen early the first day of the week, he
> appeared first to Mary Magdalene, out of whom he had cast
> seven devils.'

The casting out of demons can be interpreted on a number of levels. In ancient Babylon demons were seen as the cause of illness but in the Bible we find King Solomon summoning and binding the demon Asmodeus to do his bidding. The Zoroastrian interpretation sees demons as false or fallen gods so a less supernatural interpretation might be that Jesus converted her from being a follower of pagan gods, either Greek ones or older regional deities still worshipped in those times.

Demonic possession can also be a misinterpretation of a number of psychological disorders such as the rare Multiple Personality Disorder, or the more common Subpersonalities Disorder as described by psychologists such as John Rowan.

Other passages of the gospels describe how 'Mary of Bethany' (presumed by ancient tradition to be Mary Magdalene) anointed Jesus (John 12.3):

> 'Then took Mary a pound of ointment of spikenard, very costly,
> and anointed the feet of Jesus, and wiped his feet with her hair:
> and the house was filled with the odour of the ointment.'

The washing of the feet is an intimate and devotional act. In this passage the use of expensive ointment is derided by the other disciples, but it is an act of anointing befitting someone of royal standing. Anointing a king would have been acceptable practice and through this we are beginning to see hints that both the relation of Jesus and Mary and the status of Jesus are perhaps being underplayed by the Church.

Mary Magdalene's presence at the crucifixion is recorded by Matthew, Mark and John. While the other disciples hide and deny knowing Jesus, Mary stands in full view of the Roman soldiers beneath the cross (John 19.25):

> 'Now there stood by the cross of Jesus his mother, and his mother's sister Mary, the wife of Cleophas, and Mary Magdalene.'

After the crucifixion Jesus is removed from the cross and sealed inside a tomb on private land belonging to Joseph of Arimathea. The following day Mary visits the garden and finds the tomb open (John 20.1):

> 'The first day of the week cometh Mary Magdalene early, when it was yet dark, unto the sepulchre, and seeth the stone taken away from the sepulchre.'

The body of Jesus is missing. A man speaks to her, whom she assumes to be the gardener before recognizing him as Jesus. He subsequently reveals himself to the remaining disciples. 'Doubting' Thomas tests his existence in flesh and blood by touching the wound in his side.

Putting aside the magical elements in this account, we are being shown here that Jesus survived the ordeal of crucifixion.

From this point onward the story of Mary Magdalene is picked up in a number of non-canonical gospels, notably the *Gospel of Mary*, which not only describes her as being closer to Jesus than the other disciples but also the recipient of his innermost teachings. The 'Mary' of the title is not named, but is generally assumed to be Mary Magdalene from other sources.

Other texts, such as the medieval *The Golden Legend* attempt to describe the life of Mary based upon the stories in circulation at that time. They are scant pieces but as a whole they begin to paint an interesting portrait of the woman who walked beside Jesus.

The Golden Legend also tells us that Mary was born of noble lineage. Her parents were said to have been born of kings and they owned the castle Magdala whence the name Magdalene comes. She is described as wealthy, which would account for her use of expensive oil to anoint Jesus.

THE FLIGHT TO GAUL

A short time after the crucifixion, Mary Magdalene is said to have been transported to the south of Gaul (France) by boat. Joseph of Arimathea, who according to Sion was a wealthy trader, is also said to have travelled on the boat with Mary Magdalene making it likely that the boat was more than a small affair. As a merchant he would probably have commanded a number of long-distance vessels. Others on the boat are said to have included an Egyptian girl called Sarah. Sarah means 'princess' so if this was a title rather than a name it is perhaps unlikely that she would have travelled in the contemporary equivalent of economy class. Heading west via Greece they would have followed the Mediterranean coastline for safety. The journey is described in detail in *The Golden Legend*, which is not unlike Butler's *Lives of the Saints*. Written in the late 13th century by the archbishop of Genoa, Jacobus de Voragine, it details the lives of hundreds of saints and is interesting to us as the primary source for a detailed account of Mary Magdalene's flight to Gaul. It was widely read at the time and was said to have drawn upon works of earlier authors and other existing documents. Jacobus also wrote extensively on the Virgin Mary, and attempted to raise her status to that of a necessary part of the path to God through Jesus.

The arrival of Mary in Greece entirely depends on the flight to Gaul as having happened and this forms the next part of our journey. Nic Haywood sent me the following:

> 'The legend of Our Lady [Mary Magdalene] taking refuge in
> France is fact. The order possess substantial evidence for this, but
> we ask that for the moment you concede that our 'proof' is the
> ultimate. To demonstrate this – to offer the actual proof – would
> be to present our trump card prematurely.'

The 'proof' as mentioned above would seem to be that the body of Mary Magdalene is located in the south of France.

Having arrived in southern Gaul, Mary begins her ministry, teaching the faith as told to her by Jesus. She converted many of the inhabitants to the teachings of Jesus and is said to have appeared in dreams to local nobles, instructing them to 'comfort the poor and needy'. During this time she gained many followers, but eventually her ministry in Gaul came to an end and she retired to a cave where she lived out her remaining days devoted to God.

MARY AND THE TRUE TEACHINGS OF JESUS

Mary could not have known at the time whether this new religion would take hold, but she would have been compelled to communicate as truth what she knew. Since Mary had received teachings directly from Jesus and had travelled away from the influence of the other main apostles, especially Peter and Paul, what she taught was potentially a very different strand of Christianity to that which would become the orthodox view.

In the *Gospel of Mary*, Peter acknowledges that Jesus had spoken privately to Mary and questions her accordingly (*Gospel of Mary* 5.6):

> 'Tell us the words of the Saviour which you remember, which you know but we do not, nor have we heard them.'

Only a partial account of Mary's response has survived and takes the form of a vision describing the soul rising and being challenged by the 'powers'. The soul overcomes these powers in an inner dialogue and then ascends through a number of mystical states. The extant text also refers to the 'aeons' and other metaphysical ideas commonly found in Gnostic teachings. The disciples are incredulous at Mary's account and respond that Jesus would not have used such 'strange words', and nor would he have said them to Mary in preference to the other disciples.

The *Gospel of Mary* speaks of higher realms, what psychologists describe as the 'transpersonal'. The inclusion of this material shows Jesus to be more of a mystic than the New Testament allows for. Even more of a threat to the Church is that these teachings have entirely Gnostic leanings, in that they advocate direct contact with God through an internal dialogue.

The influence of Mary and other Gnostic writers remained a potent force within Christianity until the Council of Nicaea in 325CE selected the final texts for inclusion in a Christian Bible. Until then, many documents were in circulation that told a different story from those in the four gospels and Acts. In these Mary Magdalene was not only accepted as an important figure among the disciples, but she was also recognized as one who continued the true teachings of Jesus.

Unfortunately we can see from the direction that Rome took that the Gnostic influence was entirely removed from the teachings of Christianity. Yet here they form the secret, inner teachings of mysticism.

Mary has since been used to symbolize these hidden teachings of Christ, passed down through the ages in her name. The Council of Nicaea was called by Emperor Constantine I with the goal of imposing Roman-style order on the

Church's teachings throughout the empire. As a result the canon of acceptable works compiled by the Council, while certainly ancient were incomplete, as it was decided not to reveal the truth for fear of relinquishing control of spirituality to the individual. As a result orthodox Christianity was a shallower entity than it could have been.

The external teachings of Jesus have been used to maintain control, to govern individuals and entire countries in order to carry out the earthly will of the various churches and the various secular regimes that have supported them. But there is no true spiritual path in these teachings.

I believe that Mary Magdalene held, for a moment, a pure Christianity – the closest form to the Jesus archetype. I will return later to the purity of spirit and the power of identifying with archetypes in the chapter entitled Gnosis. This places the kingdom of heaven not in space, or after death, but as an internal experience attainable in life, as stated in Luke 17.21: 'Behold, the kingdom of God is within you.'

THE MAGDALENE TRADITION

There is a second aspect to the mysteries of Mary Magdalene that could potentially have the most impact on modern society: her gender.

There might be a reason why Jesus told Mary his 'inner teachings', aside from any intimate relationship he had with her. Among Jesus' female disciples Mary is the most prominent, and the feminine aspect is important as it is already aligned with the intuitive path to God. In Gnostic teachings the Holy Spirit is feminine and appears in the form of Sophia, Divine Wisdom, personified as a female figure. To commune with Sophia, the feminine, intuitive side, gives an individual access to a higher wisdom and potentially to God. While the marriage of Mary and Jesus is a threat to the status of the Church, the idea that individuals can find God directly within themselves entirely undermines the whole construct of priests and Popes dictating faith to the masses.

The gender aspect also caused resistance from the other leading disciples, whose intolerance of Mary is all too apparent. In the *Gospel of Thomas* (verse 114), Peter goes so far as to say to the disciples: 'Make Mary leave us, for females do not deserve life.'

There are other telling admissions of misogyny. In the *Gospel of Mary* both Andrew and Peter, while admitting that Mary knew Jesus better than any other woman, dismiss her claim that Jesus spoke to her about matters that he did not share with the other (male) disciples. Eventually Peter becomes angry and states (*Gospel of Mary* 9.4):

> 'Did He really speak privately with a woman and not openly to
> us? Are we to turn about and all listen to her? Did He prefer her
> to us?'

The arrival of Mary Magdalene in Gaul brought an alternative form of Christianity that was balanced in terms of gender, and she was said to have converted many to Jesus' true teachings. However, it would seem that the more esoteric aspects of the teachings survived mainly among the few noble families who took up Mary's cause.

Preserved in ritual and oral tradition, these esoteric teachings were communicated only to an elect few not only because they were deemed heresy but also because they bestowed certain powers and knowledge of certain locations. As the teachings became the domain of a few powerful families, they were also upheld by a few wise patrons among the clergy. The teachings surface from time to time and influenced such groups as the Cathars in the Middle Ages and Jean-Jacques Olier at Saint-Sulpice in the 17th century. Together with St Vincent de Paul and St Louise de Marillac, Olier created the Daughters of Charity order with the express intention of acknowledging and continuing the work Mary Magdalene had begun. Sion comments:

> 'Surely it did not escape notice that the very existence of the
> Daughters of St Vincent, fashioning themselves (as was claimed)
> after the role of the benevolent Magdalene, ultimately speeded up
> the notion of females within the institution of the Church.'

This charitable organization managed by women was created to emulate the Magdalene's maternal role by protecting orphaned children. The 'widow's son' of Masonic legend had finally found a home.

During the 17th century, European Freemasonry was taking shape and rituals began to include references about belonging to the tribe of Benjamin. The development of Co-Freemasonry, distinguished by its acceptance of women into the craft, in the 18th century makes it is clear that the addition of women to the Craft mirrors the attempt by Olier, at much the same point in history, to create a role for women within the Church.

A subtle matriarchal revolution had begun. By the end of the 19th century in all areas of culture and society women were moving toward a position of equality.

Le Serpent Rouge (*see* Chapter 10) is unusual in its description of Mary Magdalene. It is the only text I have seen that treats her as an archetype by naming her as another form of Isis and 'Our Lady of the Crescents'. This is an expression of Mary's potential influence in Christian thought. She has an energy that can be connected to even today. The lost aspect of the wise and loving feminine can be summoned and expressed, for she resides in the psyche of all men and women.

In the light of this any concealed 'body' is elevated from a small secret, the humble corpse of a biblical figure, to a symbol of the lost, repressed feminine principle, and a key to the source – gnosis.

FINDING MEANING IN THE MAGDALENE

An opportunity is emerging to find meaning in a redeemed image of Mary Magdalene. The 'repentant sinner' of a thousand paintings is in need of redemption. She was not a prostitute; even the Vatican has conceded that this lie was attached to her name centuries after her life. She is described in the *Gospel of Mary* as 'the chosen one', the woman whom Jesus loved more than all the other disciples. It also states that she was party to the secret teachings of Jesus. She is, in my view, the most important feminine role model in Christian history yet she was resented by her fellow (male) disciples and denigrated by the male bastion that was the early Catholic Church. The reason the Catholic Church fears Mary is also the reason why it is so important to redeem her.

Entirely lacking from the Christian mindset of the past two millennia is the archetype of the sexually empowered feminine as a positive force. From Eve through to Mary Magdalene, this has created a vacuum in the Western psyche. As Christian archetypes we have virgins, whores and crones. The objectification of women would not be possible if the strong, sexually active female were restored and respected. With the repression of the feminine come the inequality, objectification and denigration of women and the loss of the feminine aspects of man, such as intuition.

Pure intuition is a means to hear our inner voice that connects us to the divine. It brings direct knowledge of spiritual matters and as such avoids the need for a Church. In short intuition is a tool for gnosis and that is why the Church fears it so much. To fully experience gnosis is to communicate directly with God.

We can now re-evaluate Mary's depiction in biblical, apocryphal and Gnostic texts. In the *Gospel of Philip,* when the disciples challenge Jesus and ask him why he loves Mary more than them, Jesus replies: 'Why do I not love you as much as I love her?'

And so we come full circle. The woman who was closer to Jesus than all his other disciples, and who for centuries bore the stigma of being labelled a prostitute, can now be redeemed. It is up to us now to drive the seven demons from her, just as Jesus did. The term 'prostitute' has its roots in the word 'priestess', and this is a role befitting Mary. Her rightful place in the Christian Bible and in the Church should be that of a high priestess and I cannot stress enough how important it would be to reinstate such a role in all Christian churches. Without this aspect of the divine feminine, the Christian churches will always be out of balance.

The role of Mary in our story is threefold. She is wife and mother, the feminine principle, sexually active and emancipated; she is a vehicle for the inner path of Jesus and true Christianity, as recorded in the *Gospel of Mary* and other Gnostic texts; and she is herself an embodiment of that truth as she emerges to take the role of a high priestess of Christianity.

While we can re-evaluate Mary Magdalene's historical status and relationship to Jesus, it is the meaning that these hold for both Christians and those of us in an environment shaped by Christianity that is important. By 'shaped' I mean that although organized Christianity is declining in the West, its influence on the psychological make-up of all Westerners cannot be underestimated. Patriarchal structures exist at all levels of society. The role and equality of women is a battle far from being resolved in a fair and balanced manner. Issues such as the ordination of female priests may seem to outsiders to be trivial disputes among the ever-declining body of churchgoers, but they are indicative of a wider negative mindset about the value of women in society as a whole.

This issue of equality might be why so many people found that *The Da Vinci Code* resonated with them. In Catholicism the representation of women in senior positions within the Church is almost entirely lacking whereas the Gnostics made Mary Magdalene a more central and important figure to Christianity as a whole. However, the reestablishment of the 'lost feminine' is more important to people in the 21st century than any religious implications.

AT REST

There is a sadness about the fate of Mary Magdalene's reputation. As she sank into the mire of misogynistic history, something was lost that belonged to each and every one of us. Her body, lost and lamented, should be venerated not as a relic but as a symbol of the path of intuition, which in turn leads to union with the divine.

Mary's skeleton is incomplete, so we are told: some of the bones having been removed to be used as relics elsewhere. According to Gérard Thome, his parchments inform him that Mary resides in a family tomb, which is highly possible. In which case this 'body of evidence', as Sion refers to it, will risk being overshadowed by that of her husband, Jesus, although the presence of the 'King of Kings' would certainly confirm her position as a queen.

According to Nic Haywood,

> 'The body of evidence is incontrovertible. Whether or not it will be headline-making depends on when it is revealed. As Church influence lessens and science goes round in circles, it might not be found until it is probably expected. If revealed today it would have an impact on science and religion as much as Darwin's *[Origin of Species]*.'

The history of Mary Magdalene certainly challenges traditional Church orthodoxy but it should not be seen as a challenge to the Church's very existence. On the contrary, it has the power to redress the balance and breathe new life into the old religion.

However, there is another force at work that is even stronger than the truth about Mary Magdalene, and this force *is* beginning to undermine the Church. It is the truth about Jesus.

CHAPTER 14

HERESY AND HISTORY

*The antiquity and genealogy have been preserved in greater
entirety than no others, except those of the Messiah, of which
I do not speak, for it is not my business.*

François Rabelais, *Gargantua*

INTRODUCTION

Through the previous chapters we arrived at the idea of a 'body of evidence',
in both senses, buried in the region of Rennes-le-Château. This body,
according to the signs we have followed, is likely to be that of Mary Magdalene.
The importance of this is heightened by a renewed understanding of what Mary
was and what she means today, as set out in the previous chapter. Researchers
are beginning to re-evaluate her place in New Testament history and what is
emerging has the potential to instigate a fundamental shift in Christian belief.
But there is a problem; the body of Mary Magdalene alone is not a sufficiently
unique item to underpin the heresy that has grown up in this little region of
France. Relics of Mary can be found in the basilica of Mary Magdalene in
Vézelay and elsewhere, and so far these have failed to have any great impact
on the world.

The body of evidence may certainly include Mary Magdalene's corpse but
there would need to be something even more convincing to trigger such a
powerful change in belief. The only body that would undeniably challenge the
dogma of the church would be that of Jesus himself. The corpse would need
to be readily identifiable (from the scars or marks of the crucifixion), possibly
mummified or uncorrupted. However, the body of Jesus should not exist at all

in an earthly form as this would contradict the New Testament reports that he died on the cross, was resurrected on the third day, and ascended to heaven soon after (40 days later according to Acts 1.3).

Jesus' death by crucifixion and his subsequent return to life are the two most important events in the gospel story and the cross is the prime Christian symbol of Christ's sacrifice and resurrection. The problem is: they may not have happened.

JESUS SURVIVES THE CROSS

While researching *The Holy Blood and the Holy Grail*, Henry Lincoln received a letter from an English priest, a Reverend Bartlett. He claimed to have received information directly from his mentor, the theologian Canon Alfred Lilley, who had made a discovery at Saint-Sulpice in Paris. This is the same church that features heavily in *Le Serpent Rouge*. The letter informed the authors that, according to Canon Lilley, the secret of Rennes-le-Château was that Jesus had survived the crucifixion and that there was 'incontrovertible proof that Jesus was alive in 45AD'. Lilley claimed that the documents he had examined were later relocated to the Vatican. Lincoln's co-author, Michael Baigent, explores this letter extensively in his book *The Jesus Papers*. The Priory of Sion confirms that they believe this information to be correct.

The idea that Jesus survived the crucifixion is nothing new. An account of this can be found in the writings of early Christianity such as the *Pistis Sophia* and in other sacred texts. The *Qur'an* states:

'Surely we have killed the Messiah, Isa [Jesus] son of Mariam, the apostle of Allah; and they did not kill him nor did they crucify him, but it appeared to them so and most surely those who differ therein are only in a doubt about it; they have no knowledge respecting it, but only follow a conjecture, and they killed him not for sure.'

(*Surah* 4, 'The Woman', 157)

Of course, if this was the case and either Jesus did survive the crucifixion or a substitution was made, this would have been recorded in the gospels. Here is what the gospels report:

'And as they came out, they found a man of Cyrene, Simon by name: him they compelled to bear his cross.' (Matthew 27.32)

'And they compel one Simon, a Cyrenian, who passed by, coming out of the country, the father of Alexander and Rufus, to bear his cross.. And they bring him unto the place Golgotha, which is, being interpreted, The place of a skull. And they gave him to drink wine mingled with myrrh: but he received it not. And when they had crucified him, they parted his garments, casting lots upon them, what every man should take. And it was the third hour, and they crucified him.' (Mark 15.21–25)

'And as they led him away, they laid hold upon one Simon, a Cyrenian, coming out of the country, and on him they laid the cross, that he might bear it after Jesus.' (Luke 23.26)

It is worth noting that none of these descriptions mention the cross actually being returned to Jesus. The replacement of Jesus is but one possibility. There is also the issue that the man on the cross was not there long enough to die. To speed this process the Roman soldiers would break the legs and, unsupported, the prisoner would swiftly suffocate. But the Roman soldier chooses not to break the legs of Jesus, believing him to be already dead (John 19.33). If Jesus had been merely unconscious, this would have ensured that he survived. The gospels also tell us that Joseph of Arimathea 'went in boldly unto Pilate and craved the body of Jesus', pleading to bury it before sunset, the start of the Sabbath, as Jewish law required. Pilate is surprised that Jesus should be 'already dead' until a centurion confirms what Joseph says (Mark 15.42–45). Joseph ensures that the 'body' is taken to an empty tomb on his own private property.

Then there is the curious fact that the three women (Mary Magdalene, Mary the mother of James, and Salome) went to anoint Jesus on the morning after the Sabbath. This is odd first because they could have gone the previous evening, immediately after sunset, when the Sabbath ended; and also because the anointing of a corpse normally took place *before* burial. But what if the ointment of 'sweet spices' (Mark 16.2) was not funereal but *medicinal*?

The fact of Jesus' death on the cross seemingly went unchallenged until in 1947 a collection of texts were found at Nag Hammadi in Egypt that became known as the Nag Hammadi Library. They consist mainly of early Christian and Gnostic writings including a fascinating scripture called *The Second Treatise of the Great Seth*.

This text appears to be an account of the crucifixion as narrated by Jesus himself. If authentic it affords a radical new insight into the personality of Jesus. The first section is of the most interest to us (the extract is from *The Nag Hammadi Library*, edited James M. Robinson):

> 'It was another, Simon, who bore the cross on his shoulder. It was another upon whom they placed the crown of thorns. But I was rejoicing in the height over all the wealth of the archons and the offspring of their error, of their empty glory. And I was laughing at their ignorance.'

Although the evidence above would point to the crucifixion as not having happened there were a number of reasons for maintaining that the crucifixion itself was a fact.

If Jesus survived the crucifixion he would not have been able to stay in Judea. He had been condemned by the Roman authorities, others were beginning to recognize him, and rumours would have spread that he was still at large. What is seen now as a miracle, the moment when 'Doubting' Thomas the apostle touches the physical wound in the side of Jesus, can simply be seen as further evidence that Jesus survived the crucifixion. The flesh and blood still walked and talked, but naturally still bore the injuries of his ordeal. Stripped of its fantastic elements, it would seem that Jesus not so much ascended as absconded.

Following the reappearance of Jesus, Mary Magdalene also had to flee Judea in the company of Joseph of Arimathea. At the time of the crucifixion she stood at the foot of the cross in full view of the Roman soldiers while the other disciples hid and denied knowing Jesus.

The New Testament tells us that Jesus ascended into heaven to be received by heaven but it is more likely that he was smuggled out of Judea by Mary Magdalene and Joseph of Arimathea in order to avoid rearrest and re-execution – and the Romans would have made certain he did not survive a second time.

So did Jesus accompany Mary to a remote part of Gaul, to live out his last days and be buried near what is now Rennes-le-Château in the Languedoc? The altar painting at Rennes-le-Château church suggests that this was the case, with its depiction of Mary kneeling beside a grave in a setting that includes numerous local landmarks.

The tradition of crucifixion

To discover that Jesus did not die on the cross does not detract from the importance of crucifixion as an image of self-sacrifice and liberation. Just as the seasonal death of nature in winter allows for the new life of spring, all the cycles of life, death and rebirth can be seen in the image of the crucified saviour and Jesus was by no means the first figure to illustrate this. The self-sacrifice of the priest-king for the good of the people is an important image in many mythologies, from Quetzalcoatl in Mesoamerica to Osiris in ancient Egypt. There are also numerous gods who were sacrificed and resurrected. Mithras, Tammuz, Baal and Orpheus feature in the cultures of Jesus' time and region, and other examples include Odin in Norse myth and Vishnu in Hinduism.

The tradition of the crucified saviour is lodged in the collective unconscious as both a fundamental experience of nature and an archetype of psychological progression. It enacts the sacrifice of the individual ego to allow for a more spiritual way of life. Once it is understood as a symbolic act there is no need for Jesus actually to die in the drama that unfolded on Golgotha.

Another version of this ritual appears earlier in the life of Jesus in the 'miracle of the raising of Lazarus'. In the gospels Jesus, the Son of God, raises Lazarus from the dead in the town of Bethany. This is a Christianized version of an old Egyptian initiation ritual in which Horus, son of the Egyptian god Ra, raises Osiris from the dead in the Beth of Anu. 'Beth' means house. The raising is re-enacted by the Freemasons in their third degree, which symbolizes the archetypal death and revival of nature as the Masonic candidate is laid out upon a tomb, blindfolded in symbolic death and raised by the hand to see the light of the world again and enter a 'new life'.

If the death and resurrection of Jesus are seen to be mythological other stages of his life must also be reconsidered. Notable among these is the idea of the virgin birth.

THE VIRGIN BIRTH

Like the crucifixion, the virgin birth has its roots in many other traditions and may not have actually taken place. The Gnostic *Gospel of Philip* denies it:

> 'Some say Mary conceived by the Holy Spirit. They are in error,
> when did a woman ever conceive by another woman?'

The *Gospel of Philip*, along with the *Gospel of Mary* and the *Gospel of Thomas* were among the Nag Hammadi Library. These documents have transformed scholarly understanding of the depth of meaning that Christianity had at its inception.

The beginning, like the end of the life of Jesus, can also be read in a different historic context. The story of how he was conceived by a divinity and born to a virgin is in no way unique to him. These traditions also predate Christianity and are attributed to numerous 'chosen ones' and heroes throughout the pagan world. It is likely that this attribute was grafted on to the story of Jesus to increase his appeal to pagan Gentiles, especially Greeks. Greek myth has many examples of gods fathering children on mortal women, and most of the great heroes were conceived in this way. Thus Perseus was the son of Zeus by Danaë, and Herakles was the son of Zeus by Alkmene. There are Babylonian precursors and the Persian Zoroaster was also described as being born of a virgin birth with semidivine origins some two thousand years prior to Jesus. Zoroastrianism is particularly interesting as some of its tenets found their way, via contemporary Judaism, into Christianity, such as the strands of dualism and the angelic hierarchy. Figures with divine parentage also abound in other cultures, such as the Buddha and Krishna.

The tradition of the coupling, and sometimes marriage, of a human with a God is termed the *hieros gamos* or holy marriage. This term is described in detail by Margaret Starbird in her books beginning with *The Woman with the Alabaster Jar*.

Arguments are sometimes raised that although these figures are divinely conceived only a few are described as 'virgin births' (or rather, virgin conceptions). It has long since been understood that the term 'virgin', translated from the Greek *parthenos* actually means 'young woman of marriageable age' so Mary was not necessarily also a virgin. However, the gospels are pretty clear that this was the intended sense (*see* page 219).

If Jesus was conceived by the Holy Spirit descending into Mary, as the gospels of Matthew and Luke state, then without a natural father he had only a matriarchal lineage. This fact was only accepted as doctrine by the Roman Church as late as 325CE at the Council of Nicaea, nearly 300 years after Jesus lived. The Church also subscribed to the view that Jesus' royal line ended with his death (he died, as far as they were concerned, childless). This served to remove Jesus from the political milieu he was born into. By discounting his royal heritage the Roman Church was free to choose who ruled the Church instead of acknowledging the succession of priest-kings that had come before.

In the psychology of archetypes this relationship can be interpreted as the joining of sexuality and spirituality, intertwined like the two serpents on the staff of Hermes. Tantra is the Eastern manifestation of this phenomenon.

We are beginning to see a pattern here. Was the life of Jesus a collection of anecdotes distilled from earlier sources to make him look more important than he was? The more that the words, actions and events of the life of Jesus are found to be symbolic or to have their origins or precedents in earlier stories the less he becomes a person and the more an idea. But stripped of divinity and the virgin birth Jesus takes his proper historical place among his tribe. He becomes an heir to the throne of Israel.

KING JESUS

If we dispense with the supernatural embellishments when considering a true historical background for Jesus we are left with the humble possibility that Joseph, the husband of Mary, actually fathered Jesus. Evidence of this exists in the New Testament in the form of genealogies:

> 'Now Jesus himself was about thirty years old when he began his ministry. He was the son, so it was thought, of Joseph.'
> (Luke 3.23)

> 'We have found the one Moses wrote about in the Law, and about whom the prophets also wrote: Jesus of Nazareth, the son of Joseph.' (John 1.45)

Other passages establish Joseph's position in society at that time.

> 'A virgin pledged to be married to a man named Joseph, a descendant of David. The virgin's name was Mary.' (Luke 1.27)

> 'So Joseph also went up from the town of Nazareth in Galilee to Judea, to Bethlehem the town of David, because he belonged to the house and line of David.' (Luke 2.4)

While the first two are explicit about the natural fathering of Jesus (if we accept the words 'so it was thought' as a later interpolation), the latter two establish Joseph as a descendent of the royal line of David. Joseph's son would have been eligible to claim the title of 'King of Israel' were it not for the fact that the land was under Roman occupation at the time.

The gospel of Matthew has a complete genealogy that traces Jesus back through Joseph to Abraham (Matt.1.1–17). The gospel of Luke has a complete genealogy back to Adam. Both Noah and Enoch are also included in this list (Luke 3.23–37):

'Now Jesus himself was about thirty years old when he began his
ministry. He was the son, so it was thought, of Joseph,
the son of Heli, the son of Matthat,
the son of Levi, the son of Melki,
the son of Jannai, the son of Joseph,
the son of Mattathias, the son of Amos,
the son of Nahum, the son of Esli,
the son of Naggai, the son of Maath,
the son of Mattathias, the son of Semein,
the son of Josech, the son of Joda,
the son of Joanan, the son of Rhesa,
the son of Zerubbabel, the son of Shealtiel,
the son of Neri, the son of Melki,
the son of Addi, the son of Cosam,
the son of Elmadam, the son of Er,
the son of Joshua, the son of Eliezer,
the son of Jorim, the son of Matthat,
the son of Levi, the son of Simeon,
the son of Judah, the son of Joseph,
the son of Jonam, the son of Eliakim,
the son of Melea, the son of Menna,
the son of Mattatha, the son of Nathan,
the son of David, the son of Jesse,
the son of Obed, the son of Boaz,
the son of Salmon, the son of Nahshon,
the son of Amminadab, the son of Ram,
the son of Hezron, the son of Perez,
the son of Judah, the son of Jacob,
the son of Isaac, the son of Abraham,
the son of Terah, the son of Nahor,
the son of Serug, the son of Reu,
the son of Peleg, the son of Eber,

the son of Shelah, the son of Cainan,
the son of Arphaxad, the son of Shem,
the son of Noah, the son of Lamech,
the son of Methuselah, the son of Enoch,
the son of Jared, the son of Mahalalel,
the son of Kenan, the son of Enosh,
the son of Seth, the son of Adam,
the son of God.'

Note that Adam is described as the Son of God, a title that Jesus inherits through his lineage. With an established genealogy going back to King David and beyond Jesus becomes a very important political figure for his time. As rightful king he is in a position to instigate an uprising against Roman rule by claiming the throne of Israel. Later, it would be necessary for the Roman Church to maintain that the Davidic line had ended with Jesus' death in order to protect the position of the emerging papacy.

By viewing the virgin birth, the crucifixion, miracles and the divinity of Jesus as symbolic we are left with a Jesus who was still an important political and spiritual figure during his time, but one who was entirely human, and an example of how to lead a good spiritual life that is attainable by anyone. However, there is one final falsehood to be removed. No longer beholden to a Church that claims to act in Jesus' name, we can discard its final layer of mystification.

MARRIAGE

The New Testament provides some evidence that Jesus was married. For example, Mary Magdalene addresses Jesus as 'rabbi' (teacher) after the crucifixion. According to Jewish law at the time 'rabbi' was a title that could only be conferred upon married men.

There are also references in historical texts and in apocryphal scripture such as the *Gospel of Mary* and *Gospel of Philip* that identify Mary as having an intimate relationship with Jesus. Even *The Golden Legend* says:

'And this is she, that same Mary Magdalene to whom our
Lord gave so many great gifts. And showed so great signs of
love, that he took from her seven devils. He embraced her

all in his love, and made her right familiar with him.'

According to the *Gospel of Philip*,

'The companion of the Son is Miriam of Magdala. The Teacher loved her more than all the disciples; he often kissed her.'

The Greek word taken to mean 'companion' is *koinonia*, a noun that can also be used to mean 'intercourse'. From this we can ascertain that the companion of Jesus was intimate with him.

The *Gospel of Philip* only came to light in 1947 yet in the Languedoc the belief that Jesus and Mary were married has endured publicly for at least a thousand years and still exists today.

In the church of St Martin in the town of Limoux, just north of Rennes-le-Château, is a stained glass window depicting Jesus and Mary Magdalene standing side by side as a church elder administers the rite of marriage. The interior of this church is said by researcher Gérard Thome to have been funded by Father Henri Boudet from Rennes-les-Bains in the early 20th century. Boudet, as you will recall, was the mentor of Father Saunière in neighbouring Rennes-le-Château.

This is evidence that at least some Catholic priests in the Languedoc believe that Jesus and Mary were married, so while the Vatican may go to great lengths to dismiss any such notions as fabrication, the idea has some support even within the Church's own ranks. This region is home to a heresy and has been so since the Middle Ages. Let us look once again at the Cathars.

THE CATHARS AGAIN

The belief in the marriage of Jesus and Mary Magdalene was held by the Cathars, a heretical Gnostic sect that was so popular in the Languedoc region by the 13th century that Pope Innocent III decreed the Albigensian Crusade in order to destroy them. The Cathar faith had spread from Eastern Europe as far as England, but it was only in this region that its adherents upheld the belief in the marriage.

Evidence of this belief and many other important Cathar texts are collected in *Heresies of the High Middle Ages* by Wakefield and Evans (Columbia Press). They include *An Exposure of the Albigensian and Waldensian Heresies*, an early 13th-century document that contains evidence against the Cathars compiled by the monk Peter of Vaux-de-Cernay. According to Peter, 'they teach in their secret meetings that Mary Magdalene was the wife of Christ.'

The Cathars practised a form a dualism which, as the word suggests, emphasized the struggle between good and evil. They are also notable for their sense of equality, as they allowed women to become priests.

But why has this belief occurred both in the High Middle Ages among the Cathars and in the 20th century in the environs of Rennes-le-Château? What convinced devout Catholics to convert to a heretical belief that included the tenet that Jesus was married? The Priory of Sion has a clear answer: 'The marriage of Jesus and Mary is recorded on stone tablets'.

The idea of stone records of the marriage also fits in with the rumour that the Cathars were, as Sion claims, 'the custodians of a book of tablets or plates' that contained an important teaching and 'were subsequently relocated or hidden'.

These may be part of the underground temple near Rennes-le-Château or it is possible that they were placed in one of the two crypts in the church of Mary Magdalene sealed around the turn of the 20th century by its incumbent, Father Bérenger Saunière.

To convince devout Catholic priests that Jesus was married, the evidence would need to be overwhelming. At least the body of Mary Magdalene, along with stone tablets and relics associated with her wedding to Jesus would build toward an undeniable physical proof that this interpretation of Christianity was the correct one.

CONCLUSION

After the first Council of Nicaea in 325CE had decided that Jesus was God incarnate, links to his royal ancestry would have been suppressed. It was a decision made not by God but by people with a political interest.

It is worth noting that Nicaea did not determine that Jesus was only divine, simply that his divinity was identical with God. This was to counter the belief of Bishop Arius of Alexandria, who claimed that Christ was not fully God but the most exalted of God's creations. Nicaea did not deny Christ's human nature. The Church subsequently came to the view (still orthodox today) that Christ was both fully divine and fully human in the same 'person', a view expressed in the doctrine of the Trinity. The paradox was accepted as a divine 'mystery'. That Christ was fully human was important because this showed that the resurrection of the body was open to all believers.

For Arius, 'Son of God' was a status akin to Enlightened One, a reward for making supreme progress in spiritually advancing toward God. What is of interest here is that Arius was probably influenced by the Gnostics of Egypt, and that the Visigoths – who ended up in the region of Rennes-le-Château – were followers of Arian Christianity, which the Roman Church took a long time to stamp out – if it ever did fully.

For his divinity to be accepted as dogma, any references to Jesus having a family of his own had to be removed from the canon of biblical texts. It is that simple – a few hundred years after he died, a group of men got together and decided that Jesus was fully divine, and over the next 1,600 years he became God incarnate to millions of people via that unquestioning, irrational function called faith.

It is worth remembering that there are people in the Vatican who know the truth. As Pope Pius X said, 'this myth of Jesus has served us well'. But the myth is now under attack from many directions owing to the discovery of alternative scriptures and our ability to research the contradictions of the Bible for ourselves.

The Vatican, and all Christian constructs, can either remain entrenched in trying to uphold the myth, or accept the coming revolution of faith and support the transition of the congregation toward a less encumbered, more genuinely spiritual future.

And somewhere, excluded from the gospels, are the names of those who were said to be descended from Jesus. Since that time, despite the power of Christianity spreading across the globe, the tribe of Judah has continued to crown kings and attract many to its cause.

CHAPTER 15

THE BLOODLINE
AND THE AGE
OF KINGS

INTRODUCTION

The idea that Jesus founded a dynasty first came to public attention with the publication of *The Holy Blood and the Holy Grail* by Baigent, Lincoln and Leigh. This is still the first place to start and a 'rite of passage' for anyone researching these areas.

The Priory of Sion, it seems, was a little bemused by the focus of *The Holy Blood and the Holy Grail* and the attention that it brought to the bloodline aspect of the mystery. As Nic Haywood affirmed:

'I have never stated to you that Sion's primary concern is the bloodline of Christ, merely that there *is* an extant line.'

Other authors have since looked more closely at the idea of the 'Holy Matrimony' of Jesus and Mary Magdalene. Margaret Starbird's books go a long way in exploring the many aspects of the sacred union. Her evidence is drawn from many different historic sources and makes for a compelling argument.

The idea of a bloodline dating from Jesus to the present day is not a modern fabrication. Many of Europe's old noble families, such as the Merovingians and the Hapsburgs, openly claimed such auspicious origins.

BLOODLINE

Apart from a window depicting the marriage of Jesus and Mary Magdalene, a second window in the church of St Martin in Limoux depicts Jesus presenting a boy to Mary Magdalene with the following inscription: 'Woman, I give you a son.'

Mary was born of the tribe of Benjamin, which had at one point been exiled from Israel and prevented from marrying among the other Israelite tribes owing to the 'Benjaminitic Crime' (*see* page 205). By the time of Jesus this ruling had been overturned and if he married Mary Magdalene this would unite the two tribes of Judah and Benjamin as the king and queen of Israel.

The altar painting in the church of St Mary Magdalene in Rennes-le-Château depicts Mary kneeling by a grave marked by a branch that has two live shoots. In the background there are clear references to the local landscape. If we consider that the painting shows Mary at the grave of Jesus, the two live shoots would likely represent their living offspring. This idea that Mary and Jesus had two children forms the basis of the bloodline theory.

While in exile, some of the tribe of Benjamin are said to have migrated to the region of Greece called Arcadia, and the theme of Arcadia returns many times in the mystery. According to *The Golden Legend* the boat on which Mary travelled from Judea to Gaul sailed via Greece so it is possible that she rejoined her tribe briefly and perhaps placed a child in its care to hide it from further persecution.

In this context Poussin's painting of the Arcadian shepherds (*Et in Arcadia Ego*) takes on a new level of meaning. Arcadia also happens to be the reputed place of origin of the Merovingian dynasty of Frankish kings (*see* page 248) and so it is not a great leap to see how a child of Jesus and Mary may have been the source of the new European dynasty. Sion confirms this:

> 'Yes, the Merovingian blood royal is connected directly with the
> Davidic line. More correctly still, it is connected inextricably with
> the true "Benjaminitic Crime".'

The Franks are said to have migrated west and entered Gaul no later than the third century. Their early chieftains rose in power and by the time of the Merovingians in the fifth century, following the collapse of Roman imperial authority, they had become kings of most of present-day France.

According to legend the Merovingians were said to be identifiable by the birthmark of a cross between their shoulders or over their heart, and *The Golden Legend* states that 'Mary Magdalene set the sign of the cross on their shoulders'.

The Merovingian dynasty continued until the eighth century and was responsible for circulating a number of heresies concerning Christ, including that they themselves were descendants of his bloodline. This claim was also taken up by their successors, the Carolingians, and later by the Hapsburgs.

Our attention was brought to the Merovingians by the inclusion of their genealogy in *Le Serpent Rouge* booklet. The Merovingian dynasty is reproduced in an extended form that includes additional names not commonly accepted as part of their ancestry.

History records that the Merovingians died out with the murder of Dagobert II in the seventh century, but the story spread that his son Sigisbert was smuggled away to the Rennes-le-Château region to preserve the royal line that later joined with the Hapsburgs. A reference to this can be seen in the ninth Station of the Cross at Rennes-le-Château, where a Frankish warrior stands behind Jesus and holds aloft a red cape, symbol of the Hapsburgs.

RESTORATION

The restoration of a royal dynasty to power is a myth that is found down the ages in many forms. Like the lost and returning king motif, this also echoes the Masonic story of the widow's son and that of the child of Mary Magdalene and Jesus.

The evidence that Sigisbert survived and that the Merovingian bloodline continued in secret is said to exist in the form of a letter belonging to the families local to Rennes-le-Château. *Le Serpent Rouge* also directs us to the church of Saint-Sulpice in Paris, where there is a portrait of King Dagobert II on his deathbed. There are two boys in the painting, whereas Dagobert is said to have had only one heir. This illustrates the secret continuation of a royal line, hidden from view and protected by organizations such as Sion.

The tradition of removing a bloodline child and placing it in the care of others to protect the lineage is seen in the early lives of both Moses and Joan of Arc. In literature and legend the same happened to King Arthur and was also common practice among the Celts, as seen in numerous Irish myths. Before the painting of Dagobert there is a statue of St Vincent de Paul holding two children and *Le Serpent Rouge* mentions the 'Children of St Vincent' as builders of the new Temple. St Vincent de Paul was responsible for the care and protection of orphans and in its way this too answers the question that echoes back to Mary Magdalene in 'who will take care of the widow's son?', the child who would have instigated this royal lineage.

The bloodline continued as the Merovingians until 751, when they were succeeded as rulers of the Franks by a new dynasty, the Carolingians, named for their first ruler, Charles Martel. Martel's son was Charlemagne, who ruled most of Western Europe and was crowned 'Emperor of the Romans' in 800. From Charlemagne the bloodline spread out into several medieval royal families of Europe, such as the Hapsburgs.

Another clue to this exists in the Rennes-le-Château mystery, for while Father Bérenger Saunière was incumbent priest of the church he opened a number of bank accounts with the Hapsburgs, the ruling imperial family of Austria-Hungary. Many believe that Saunière was paid by the Hapsburgs to pass on the secret documents he had discovered in the region. This would likely include the letter of evidence belonging to Countess Marie de Negri d'Ables and hidden by Saunière's predecessor, Father Antoine Bigou (*see* page 72).

The Château Hautpoul at Rennes-le-Château was occupied by Marie de Negri (or de Nègre) d'Ables from the mid-18th century until her death on January 17, 1781. A decade later many nobles and priests were forced to flee France following the French Revolution of 1789. If the 'secret' of Rennes-le-Château was more than just documents and included an important location in the area, it would make sense that before Bigou himself left for Spain in 1792 he would have hidden any references to it, as well as any associated documents, somewhere within the church.

At this point in history the two strands of the secret are reunited: the heresies of the secret Christian teachings (*see* page 211) and of the bloodline come together. At the time, with the priesthood under threat, the Priory of Sion surfaced under the guise of the Rosicrucians to instigate and influence the array of manuscripts, books, carvings and inscriptions that would ensure the survival of the heresy. From this tradition the mystery of Rennes-le-Château was born.

Sion also brought with it the alchemical slant that permeates the entire mystery. The de Negri are said by Sion to have gained their name ('of the Blacks') by marrying outside their race as a re-enactment of an earlier event. This event is possibly the punishment visited upon the decimated tribe of Benjamin when no other tribes were permitted to provide them with wives (*see* page 205). There is also an alchemical image of the 'White Queen' marrying the 'Ethiopian' but this would seem too primordial, too archetypal an image to have stemmed solely from the French aristocracy.

Following Countess Marie's death, the Marquis Paul-Urbain de Fleury inherited her residence, the Château Hautpoul at Rennes-le-Château, and his presence in the region is visible today in the churchyard at Rennes-les-Bains. He has two tombs with conflicting dates on them, one of which refers to the date January 17 and the other says that '*Il est passé en faisant le bien*' – that is, he was a 'good man', the term used by both the Rosicrucians and by the Freemasons in their 18th (Rose+Croix) Degree, which originated in the region.

Further Masonic connotations are hard to ignore, for example the Seventh (Royal Arch) Degree contains references to lost documents and bloodlines. This ritual is an enactment of the discovery of a secret document beneath Solomon's Temple as if by the Templars. The link here is that the Royal Arch rite would appear to be a vehicle for the idea of the bloodline, with its revelatory exclamation: 'We are of the bloodline of David and princely tribe of Judah'. *Le Serpent Rouge* also refers to Fakhar ul-Islam, who was decapitated, supposedly while in possession of genealogies relating to the bloodline. Decapitation is a threat associated with revealing the secrets of this degree (*see* Walton Hannah's *Darkness Visible: A Christian Appraisal on Freemasonry*).

At the present time it must be considered that bloodlines would seem to run everywhere, as by now any ancient family will have descendants scattered across the globe. Through all the legitimate and illegitimate offspring of Europe's royal and noble families, countless numbers will have a speck of 'blue blood' coursing through their veins. However, in spite of this we are told that the bloodline has a purpose, an outcome caused by the 'two purest bloods of the two tribes' – Jesus and Mary Magdalene – joining to produce an heir.

Sion tells us that according to their timeline a marriage between the Hapsburgs and another noble family, possibly the house of Lorraine, was meant to happen at the end of the 19th century but did not occur. It was further delayed by the two world wars, the first of which was sparked by the assassination of the Hapsburg heir and his wife.

In the case of the Hapsburgs and the house of Lorraine, there was a trend of claiming descent through Jesus and back to Abraham, or even Adam. Historically the Hapsburgs can be traced back to the Frankish kings so that may account for this genealogical tradition being upheld. Descendants of the Hapsburgs and Lorraines are still very much extant today in various parts of Europe.

ROYAL BLOOD

When we look upon a coat of arms we take for granted that the symbols representing the different threads of ancestry somehow confer something of status upon those bearing the arms. The symbols on banners and shields and their attendant names that come down through the ages may have no more glorious an origin than our own. Indeed, many of us may be related to nobility through some long forgotten or illegitimate coupling.

Historically, royalty has attained the highest of power over others but was there ever a king or queen truly worthy of this privileged position, deserving the power they held? A monarch like Solomon perhaps: both wise and spiritual.

The tradition that is being upheld by the idea of the bloodline is that the Israelite dynasties were, as scripture claims, appointed by God and born to be priest-kings and the chosen leaders of nations; the idea that Jesus and the other disciples had families and descendants and that some of these migrated to the West to found the royal families of Europe.

Standing back and considering the issue objectively, we discover that kingship counts for nothing if it is merely a position of ruling and succession. Any despot who seizes power in a tribe and pronounces himself king would be different in title only to the rest of the tribe. The king's descendants would succeed to the throne and eventually adopt the pretence of being somehow elevated in nature above the rest of humanity.

On the face of it, modern European royalty is generally bereft of real political power. It exists primarily owing to tradition, funded by its inherited lands and other wealth and also by taxation. It performs little or no service to humanity and deserves no more respect than you or I.

But before we take to the streets we must look deeper into the notion of kingship. It would be unjust to sacrifice that which we do not fully understand.

The pre-Christian bloodline has been covered previously, quoting the lists of Jesus' descendants in the gospels (*see* Chapter 14). It should be clear from these lists that not everyone was thought to have descended from Adam or we would all be kings. What the bloodline seems to imply is that Adam and his descendants are in some way different.

Before we get too carried away with the romance of such an idea we must be aware that some of the traditions surrounding the bloodline have the potential to be used to justify racism. Modern genetic testing proves that we all include a mix of either African or Middle Eastern ancestry. Anyone who sees the bloodline as some herald of racial purity would be laughed out of any scientific establishment. And any attempt to claim sovereignty on grounds of race or heredity is to be ignorant of all that may be important about the bloodline.

Likewise to entertain the notion that any of the Twelve Tribes of the Old Testament managed to stay 'pure' is counter-evolutionary and actually genetically unsound. In any tribe that remains exclusive the number of hereditary diseases grows exponentially over time. Porphyria, for example, is a hereditary enzyme deficiency present in the British royal family and is believed to have been responsible for the 'madness' of King George III. Limiting the gene pool leads not to a 'purer' species but to an increase in genetic defects that would eventually ensure that group's extinction. Rather more sensibly, the tribal demarcations in place among the Israelites seem to have denoted certain religious roles or practices than actual physical origins. The elitist view of kingship is entirely undone when we understand that the purpose of a king or queen is to be in the service of their people. To be given the honourable power to rule one must administer it not from ego but as service guided by wisdom.

THE RETURNING KING

Sion makes it clear that the esoteric aspects of the bloodline are just as important as any real notion of a family line. There are many traditions of kings and lost bloodlines that mirror this story, but these are more than just a means to keep the story in the public eye.

The bloodline has families but also includes followers, who have subscribed to an ideal throughout history. It carries a body of knowledge down through the ages that works on a number of levels. This is what Sion refers to as the 'underground stream' (*see* Introduction). Before we immerse ourselves entirely in this we must stay for a moment with the bloodline and examine the myth of divine kingship failing and returning to rule again.

That the various strands of the bloodline survived in secret and will one day return to power is a theme we see again and again in history and mythology. There is a tradition in France for 'lost kings' that appears in such accounts as the legend of the possible survival of Louis XVII, who died in prison in 1795, aged ten. The story of his survival was so popular that even today there are those who claim to be his direct descendants and therefore rightful heirs to the French throne. The return of the lost king is a notion that can be found in the Egyptian myth of Osiris, the Second Coming of Christ, and even in that epic of modern mythology, *The Lord of the Rings* trilogy. A particularly famous example is that of

Arthur. The medieval Arthurian legends speak of a 'once and future king' who will return one day to rule again, just as the Holy Grail is lost and periodically rediscovered. These courtly legends of chivalrous Arthurian knights are likely to have been influenced by the troubadours' mythologizing of the crusading Templars. Sion told me that the legends include names of families that still exist in the Languedoc area. Some consider the castle of Montségur, to the west of Rennes-le-Château, to be synonymous with the castle of 'Montsalvaat' in Wolfram von Eschenbach's *Parzival*, where the Holy Grail resides. Montségur was the last major Cathar stronghold to fall during the Albigensian Crusade and the Cathars have long been rumoured to have possessed the Grail in any of its many forms.

The authors of *The Holy Blood and the Holy Grail* interpreted the 'Holy Grail' to be Mary Magdalene, who continues the blood of Jesus through their children. But it also has an important spiritual aspect.

MELCHIZEDEK

At the conclusion of the 19th (Grand Pontiff) Degree in the Ancient and Accepted Scottish Rite of Freemasonry – the Freemasonry alluded to by the boy depicted in tartan in the church at Rennes-le-Château – the candidate is given the title 'Priest after the Order of Melchizedek'. In the Bible, Melchizedek appears in Genesis as the king of Salem prior to the Deluge. He is mentioned again later in Psalms, after the Deluge, which supposedly wiped out all humankind save for Noah and his family. This causes some confusion for those who take Melchizedek to be an individual. This is because Melchizedek is not a name but a title, meaning 'Teacher of Righteousness', a term later used to describe Jesus. It is the title of a priest-king who returns many times to rule.

Priest-kings are believed to be divinely appointed rulers. Like the pharaohs of Egypt, they were seen as an incarnation of divinity in human form and Melchizedek was said to have no earthly parents. But what does this actually mean?

ORIGINS

From the outset Sion has evaded all enquiries about the exact origins of the bloodline. I have attempted in a number of ways to get an answer to these questions: what is in the blood that makes it so important? Is it different from the blood of me and you? If so, how, and where did it come from?

According to the Bible, the first man created was Adam (a word that simply means 'man' in Hebrew). Sion affirms that 'the bloodline existed long before Christ. It is from the house of David, back to Adam.' Adam is seen as the perfect man, originally free from sin and self-consciousness before his fall from ignorance by eating from the tree of knowledge and expulsion from Eden. Eden maps psychologically onto the experience of being in the womb, the only time we live in a perfectly blissful state. The womb offers an attractive but unhealthy retreat from the suffering of being present in the world. Adam is our unborn self, to which some wish to regress. However a healthier intention is not to go back to Eden but to re-imagine a new version of Eden in the future, where bliss is not ignorance but enlightenment.

Even as an idea rather than literally a person, Adam was not a product of the Bible. The earliest known account of a god-made first man is that of Marduk, a god of the Babylonians, putting 'flesh to bone'.

Merovech or Merovius, the legendary founder of the Merovingians, was said to be the son of a human mother and a sea deity. Henry Lincoln is credited with the idea that the half-man, half sea-being Merovech symbolized the offspring of Jesus and Mary Magdalene as the fish was an early symbol – pre-dating the cross – of Jesus, the 'Fisher of Men'. (The Greek for fish, *ichthus* or *ichthys*, was held to stand for *Iesous CHristos THeou Uios Soter* – Jesus Christ, Son of God, Saviour'.) I personally do not hold with this interpretation but the image of the divine-human hybrid is compelling to some for other reasons.

THE NEPHILIM

Genesis 6.1–4 contains a reference to a race of giants called 'Nephilim'. They are described as the result of the 'sons of God' mating with the daughters of men. The Nephilim also appear in a number of non-canonical texts such as the *Book of Enoch* and the *Book of Jubilees*, while the Bible also refers to 'the giants, the sons of Anak, which come of the giants' (Numbers 13.33).

The Babylonian equivalent of the Nephilim are the Ananaki, the fallen gods of royal blood. In Babylonian art these are always depicted as giants. This would imply, as argued by authors such as Zecharia Sitchin and Laurence Gardner, that the origin of the bloodline is extraterrestrial, or at least an as yet unidentified lost race. The claim that these beings are 'giants' is of particular interest. Sion's Nic Haywood raised the idea of giants in conversation a number of times.

Giants are present in the myths and religions of many cultures, including those of the Celts in Europe, who credit them with shaping the landscape, for example. The presence of the Anak giants of the Old Testament seems to decline after the battle between David and Goliath. Indeed this event may have signalled their fall from power, or the episode could be seen as symbolic of a passing from the old blood to the new.

The giants also appear in our story in other ways. There is an old legend from the region of Rennes-le-Château that concerns a cave filled with sleeping giants waiting to be awoken.

Giants may well deserve much further research than is possible in this short space, but their presence in so many myths and cultures makes them difficult to discount completely. And while giants provide a difficult supposition to accept, the idea that they are extraterrestrial in origin requires an even greater suspension of disbelief.

THE PROBLEM OF 'ALIEN INTERVENTION'

The various theories of 'alien intervention' in human development draw on many sources in order to glamorize the humble process of our evolution. Some authors and researchers are willing to put their necks and reputations on the line and state what seems absurd. William Gray in *Sangreal Sodality* claims that the blood of the bloodline is important because it is alien. Laurence Gardner in *Genesis of the Grail Kings* proposes the same notion.

A good starting point for these claims is of course the Bible. As stated above, in Genesis we read that 'the sons of God came down and took the daughters of men to be their wives'. These brides produced strange offspring with 'shining faces'. This has been interpreted by some to mean that the DNA of humanity was hybridized.

The major flaw in this theory is that it is not possible for different species to interbreed, so any genetic influence via breeding would have to come from other humans. The blood need only be of a species that was seen as alien in the broader sense of foreign to the biblical region. The 'shining faces' in Genesis are more likely to indicate the influence of relatively paler-skinned Europeans, who were establishing trade routes with these cultures. These 'sons of God' who came down from the sky did so at a time when mountains were considered by many ancient cultures to be where the gods resided.

Rather than some extraterrestrial input, therefore, it would seem that some other aspect of the blood is being brought to our attention. Perhaps a more symbolic or mythic quality is being communicated.

ROYAL BLOOD – PART II

Looking at the rulers of Europe's principal historical dynasties we rarely find them to be particularly enlightened individuals. So why is the blood in these families so special? As Sion tells us: 'The blood has properties.'

There is a tradition that comes down to us from pre-Christian times that might indicate something of importance in the blood. In c1200 BCE Persian Zoroastrianism was one of the most popular religions in the Middle East. It was a dualist faith with elements (such as the virgin birth of its quasi-mythical founder, Zoroaster) that would clearly influence Christian mythology over a millennium later. In the Zoroastrian sacred book, the Zend Avesta, Zoroaster states that his seed would remain dormant 'in the lake' for 3,000 years and then return in the form of a saviour. This is clearly echoed 1,000 years later by Christ, who promised to return after a further 2,000 years. In addition, Genesis 28.14 states:

'Thy seed shall be as the dust of the earth, and thou shalt spread abroad to the west, and to the east, and to the north, and to the south: and in thee and in thy seed shall all the families of the earth be blessed.'

This 'seed' is important and can be found described in similar fashion in Egyptian mythology. Osiris is murdered by Seth, who dismembers him into 16 parts and scatters them throughout Egypt. Isis, Osiris' wife, travels the land to recover the pieces but according to one version of the myth she only finds 15 of them. The phallus of Osiris is absent, having been thrown into the Nile and lost (or devoured by a fish). Isis rebuilds Osiris, and breathes new life into him, but his phallus remains absent. Here again we have the image of the seed lost in the lake. This was one of the most important aspects of Egyptian mythology, as seen in the proliferation of obelisks. The obelisk represents the phallus of Osiris and it is interesting to note that there are Egyptian obelisks in both Saint-Sulpice and the Vatican.

Obelisks are akin to the pagan standing stones of Europe and both have a common source. The pagan version is a general symbol of masculine fertility, like the maypole with its streamers, around which people would dance to herald the arrival of spring. It is the rebirth stage of the cycle of death and resurrection.

We can see now why the Roman Catholic Church co-opted such an image, knowing that at the same time it was adopting the idea of the returning messiah.

Another biblical version of the 'seed in the lake' story can be seen in the account of the Deluge, when Noah is instructed to build an ark 'to keep their seed alive' (Genesis 7.3). Both this and Egyptian flood myths hark back to the flood myth of Babylonia, where the counterpart of Noah is given this command: 'Bring into the ship the seed of life of everything.' (*Epic of Gilgamesh*, XI.27.)

A further instance of this symbolism can also be found in the Arthurian legends. The 'Lady of the Lake' raises Arthur's sword, Excalibur, from the water to help establish the nobility of the 'once and future king'. King Arthur receives Excalibur and returns it to the lake once the wasteland of his kingdom is healed.

Interestingly, in Wolfram von Eschenbach's *Parzival*, the narrator cites his source as 'Kyot', and claims that he in turn received the story from 'Flegetanis', an astrologer and descendant of King Solomon. Flegetanis, Wolfram claimed, had seen the name of the Grail in the stars.

The tradition of using astrology to predict the coming of the Messiah appears in the gospel of Matthew as the 'wise men from the East' (Matthew 2.1) following a star to the birthplace of Jesus. The gospel calls them *magi*, a Greek term that meant 'magicians' in the sense of skilled practitioners of esoteric arts, especially astrology and divination from dreams. Owing to their supernatural wisdom they understand that the particular star they are following manifests Jesus' royal status (Matthew 2.2).

SLEEPING BEAUTY

The idea of something lying dormant may account for a marked lack of divinity in the actions of those kings and nobles who theoretically descended from Jesus in continuation of the bloodline. Perhaps there is a quality in the blood that must be awakened to achieve the 'return' of the priest-king of the line.

This is where the hypothesis wanders into strange territories. For the blood to have a different quality to normal human blood it must contain some other property. This is not necessarily 'alien' but might be a genetic defect of some kind, which can be triggered under conditions, rather like porphyry, a hereditary disease historically found in many of the British and other royal families which can be triggered by prolonged stress – such as George III underwent over the America war. His first bout of the illness – at the time described simply as 'madness' – was in 1781, when Britain faced defeat. If there is a tool for activating this genetic defect I would imagine it to be alchemy.

Alchemical literature is often illustrated with images of coats of arms and other heraldic devices, seemingly without explanation. Heraldry is central to bloodline symbolism as it can be used to identify family origins without the explicit need for a family tree. The figures on coats of arms act as instant reminders to those who know the source of the imagery they contain. Sion tells us: 'The dove and the bear and our Holy Spirit are the ancient signs of the priestly line.' Certainly the tradition of alchemy takes a great interest in how Isis 'breathes' life into Osiris and 'raises' him from the dead. Perrault's *Sleeping Beauty* mirrors this myth with what appears to be a gender reversal, but resolves in a quest to awaken the feminine aspect of the male hero.

'RACE MEMORY'

There are plenty of modern advocates for the bloodline who seem eager to align themselves with the priest-kings. An illicit trade in titles and fake gene-alogies sprang up in the 1990s, and 'channellers' and mediums began to report links to the bloodline from their 'spirit guides'. It is possible that this urge to be linked to the bloodline is not entirely based on ego but may also have its roots in something termed 'race memory'. Sometimes termed genetic memory, this is the idea that our genetic material contains imprints from previous states of being and that these can somehow seep into our living consciousness. It does seem entirely far-fetched but past- and sometimes future-life memory is a phenomenon accorded plenty of credence in the cultures of India and Tibet.

Race memory does not have to be tied to reincarnation but could also be an impression of consciousness on genetic matter. If this could be triggered in some manner such as through ritual, tantra or alchemy, the path through our genes would lead us, like a labyrinth, back to the source of the 'underground stream.' As *Le Serpent Rouge* puts it: 'Would the voice of blood restore to me the image of an ancestral past?'

CONCLUSION

The 'hidden' quality of the bloodline might be lying dormant, like those giants in a cave beneath the French mountains or the absent aliens that Zechariah Sitchin expects to return to earth, riding his '12th planet'.

Depictions of giant humanoid beings tend to show them to be hairy, like the Sasquatch or the yeti. In Jungian psychology such images represent the primitive form of humans, archetypal images associated with primal feelings such as rage. They can appear in dreams as people covered in hair, and are symbolic of how we fear our own primal urges.

It also comes as no surprise how foetal-looking the image of aliens is in popular culture. The typical large eyes and head on small, underdeveloped and asexual bodies look remarkably like unborn babies. In this context the 'alien abductee's' descriptions of floating sensations may stem from our time in the womb. These are regressive states but also necessary stages of experience in psychological and spiritual integration. The integration can clearly be seen in myths as the archetypal challenges that we all face throughout our lives.

In *An Order Outside Time*, Robert B Clarke argues that the 'royal bloodline' consists of those who have undergone individuation in the Jungian sense. He credits alchemy with influencing this tradition and being the lantern to guide humanity toward higher evolution.

Alchemy forms a central part of the body of knowledge passed down through the ages. Its ideals, and that of the bloodline, were encoded into art, literature, architecture and symbolism that were perfect vehicles for secret societies to disseminate information. Aside from being the highest forms of expression, the physical products of the creative arts are often valued and protected and therefore act as a permanent record, their message often hidden in plain view. These messages take many forms but are known collectively among adepts as the 'underground stream'.

CHAPTER 16

ART AND
SYMBOLISM

*Artists are initiates who teach through their work.
The paintings have a 'higher vibration' that is recognized
by other initiates.*

Anonymous Priory of Sion member

ART

I trust art more than I trust history. Art is capable of providing an alternative way to record information through symbols and images that will survive the bias and censorship suffered by historical accounts.

The arts, especially painting, literature, and to some extent music, are an obvious place to record secrets. They are a platform for encoding symbolic meaning and messages that will endure indefinitely. The arts are generally a protected medium that survives well in private collections and museums, innocuously populating the walls of wealthy abodes.

At many times in history art has been a means to hide ideas in plain view. The symbolism in paintings is a perfect medium for heresy as it can portray political and religious ideas beneath imagery that is seemingly innocent. For example, the works of Hieronymus Bosch were hung in Catholic churches while blatantly depicting Catholic priests as fools. Author Lynda Harris in *The Secret Heresy of Hieronymus Bosch* makes an excellent case for Bosch being a Cathar heretic.

In art all iconography is heresy to some extent. By homogenizing the likeness of God into an image of a man we have set limits to the idea of God. As a man he cannot be the underlying force that connects all life in the universe. The Muslim tradition of not depicting Allah or his creations would serve us well here as it prevents a physical image coming instantly to mind and demands that we actually reach for a sense of knowing the divine.

The mysteries of the Priory of Sion have often manifested in the arts and can be seen in the works of notable figures who are considered to have been aligned to their cause. Leonardo da Vinci, Nicolas Poussin, Jules Verne, and Jean Cocteau all carried on the tradition of the Gothic cathedral-builders and incorporated the Hermetic sciences into their works.

The artists themselves need not be adepts, and many have simply worked to order for their patrons, so in all cases of creativity we would do well to consider where the money came from. However, Leonardo painted according to his own inspired knowledge while others such as Poussin may have benefited from more 'hands-on' direction.

Apart from being used to encode and protect knowledge, art can also have the power to impact upon society by seeding it with ideas both old and new. A good artist is capable of capturing the public imagination, creating and facilitating changes they perceive as coming. Creativity traditionally acts as an expression of the higher self – the divine and true creation that seeks to build upon and update the information that has come before.

To the initiate, the space between the simple urge to create and a contrived concept gives rise to the idea of 'complete art'; that is, art that draws on all sources, not just itself. Like the Renaissance thinker, informed by science, spirituality, politics, history, mythology and psychology, 'complete art' should engage and reflect humanity at every level of being. Examples of meaningful art and architecture can be seen in the occult geometry of the great cathedrals, the Kabbalistic languages and the paintings of many great artists. Hermetic thought has influenced many notable painters from the Renaissance to the Surrealists.

A follower of André Breton (*see Surrealism and the Occult*) wrote that the artist should at all times 'keep their left eye on the telescope and their right eye on the microscope'. Such advice allows the Hermetic axiom of 'as above, so below' to be kept plainly in view.

SYMBOLISM

The symbols used in art can be transformative to the individual who looks upon them with the right understanding. At a time when books were hand-copied and pictures were limited to church windows and the homes of the wealthy, symbolism was recognized as a universal language that had the potential to speak directly to the psyche. Today we are bombarded with visual information in print and electronic media and we are so overwhelmed that our ability to read the depth of a symbol drains from our eyes. We have become unused to having to work at reading and to viewing pictures with our fullest attention and respect. With this our ability to engage with symbols has declined, degrading them to simple icons or signs with no depth of meaning. But symbols have the potential to hold power and can affect us deeply, as a national flag stirs the emotions of a patriot.

Symbolism is a language that functions on three levels: the archetypal, the personal and the intentional. As an *archetype*, a symbol can be used as a psychological tool to communicate often complex ideas by reducing them to simple pictograms, such as a *mandala*. The *intended* level of meaning is that which the author aimed to convey. This is not always apparent and is prone to cultural and historical influence. The *personal* interpretation is the level of meaning that we bring to a symbol when we view it from our own standpoint. In this way a symbol can be adapted to suit the needs of those who use it.

Ultimately we have to strip away the many interpretations and conclude what symbols mean in the context we find them. The encapsulated form of a symbol can be experienced as a 'short cut' to an underlying concept in all its depth and ramifications, but it also acts as a barrier to those who only consider it superficially.

ART AND ARCADIA

Symbols can acquire layers of meaning over time. This is often the case in art, where different artists may reproduce an idea at different times. Hermetic symbolism, psychological imagery and religious subversion can develop in meaning as they are communicated through the ages. These ideas can be as simple as the colour of the clothing on figures portrayed on the canvas. In Poussin's *Et in Arcadia Ego* (*The Shepherds of Arcadia*) the shepherds' robes could represent the influence of different planets, giving the work an astrological meaning (see the plates section for a reproduction of this painting). And at one point in history there was a confusion over Mary Magdalene wearing blue and white – colours traditionally used to depict the mother of Jesus – that eventually prompted a papal decree to prevent this from continuing, lest Mary Magdalene should encroach on the power and influence of the Virgin.

Conversely, in both of Caravaggio's depictions of the *Madonna and Child*, Mary is wearing red, usually the symbolic dress of Mary Magdalene.

NICOLAS POUSSIN

In 1656, the Abbé Fouquet wrote to his brother:

> 'He [Poussin] and I discussed certain things, which I shall with
> ease be able to explain to you in detail – things which will give
> you, through Monsieur Poussin, advantages which even kings
> would have great pains to draw from him, and which, according
> to him, it is possible that nobody else will ever discover in the
> centuries to come. And what is more, these are things so difficult
> to discover that nothing now on this earth can prove of better
> fortune nor be their equal.'

The artist Nicolas Poussin was initially brought to our attention by the
parchments circulated by the Priory of Sion in the 1970s. Henry Lincoln
decoded two parchments back in the 1970s, having discovered them in a French
publication called *The Accursed Treasure* by Gérard de Sède. De Sède claimed
that the parchments were among Father Saunière's discoveries at Rennes-le-
Château and Sion has since supported this, while admitting that the texts have
been modified in more recent times. Once decoded, one of the parchments
revealed a message that begins: 'Shepherdess no temptation, Poussin and Teniers
hold the key'.

Poussin's *Et in Arcadia Ego* was already central to the Rennes-le-Château
mystery since it was claimed that when Saunière visited Paris he purchased a
copy of this painting from the Louvre. Painted during the early 1640s, it shows
three shepherds and a shepherdess contemplating a tomb in a landscape setting.
One of the shepherds is kneeling to indicate a Latin inscription on the tomb
that reads ET IN ARCADIA EGO.

In the early 1980s the authors of *The Holy Blood and the Holy Grail* were
directed to similarities between the tomb in the painting and an actual tomb
at Les Pontils near Rennes-le-Château. The superstructure of the tomb was
destroyed when the local landowner grew weary of trespassers examining it, but
the setting remains intact. There are some questions as to whether this tomb
existed before Poussin's painting but as yet no earlier maps have been published.
I know Sion is in possession of a hand-drawn map of the region that contains
the older place names but as yet they have not released this for examination.

Some also argue that Poussin was never in the region, but Sion maintains that
Poussin undertook several pilgrimages while travelling between France and Italy.
As mentioned in the chapter on pilgrimage it was common practice for artists

and poets of the time to undertake the journey to Santiago de Compostela via the region of Rennes-le-Château.

The shape of the tomb at Les Pontils was certainly identical to the one in the painting but deciding if the tombs are literally one and the same remains a matter of personal judgment. Irrespective of this, we can see that Poussin is still directing us to this area from the striking similarities in the landscape. In the background of his painting are three hills, which match Pech Cardou, Blanchefort and Rennes-le-Château in the distance when seen from the tomb at Les Pontils.

If the visible part of the Les Pontils tomb was destroyed, what lay beneath it remains and is highly intriguing. The position of the tomb is somewhat unusual as it was situated on top of a mound beside a river and a main road, where it would attract attention. The mound itself is more rock than soil so makes little sense to tunnel so far into it, yet when it was opened in the 1970s a shaft of some depth was discovered. I have heard claims that this shaft also leads to another exit from the tomb, and it is odd to have a tomb fitted with a back door. It was also visible in photographs of the uncovered tomb that a small pulley had been installed, which leads us to conclude that the tomb served another function at some point in its history. It may be that the pulley and tunnel are recent additions, for instance the French Resistance could have stored munitions there during the Second World War.

Furthermore, the location of the tomb is exactly on the 'Rose Line' that runs parallel to the Paris Meridian and so may serve as a marker of some kind. Its prominence certainly makes it a useful landmark.

Henry Lincoln studied Poussin's canvas for his book *The Holy Place* published in the 1980s. He concluded that it was constructed around a pentagram and that this pentagram can be outlined on the landscape with points linking Rennes-le-Château, Blanchefort and the Château des Templiers at Le Bézu. Even ardent critics of our mystery have conceded that this vast pentagram is accurate across these peaks. But as I remarked earlier, it is difficult to draw conclusions from this as the hills have been in place since the Pyrenees first rose from the sea (*see* Chapter 7).

A number of other authors and researchers have made use of the geometry found in this painting while some have brought their own designs to bear on the canvas and this has also been covered in the earlier chapter.

The content of Poussin's painting is open to further interpretation. For example, the kneeling shepherd points to the inscription on the tomb and this action can be found in the Masonic 17th (Rose+Croix) Degree when the initiate kneels in front of an altar and points to letters representing faith, hope and charity.

The Latin inscription itself, ET IN ARCADIA EGO, has no single definitive translation but roughly means 'I too was in Arcadia' with the 'I' usually presumed to mean death, owing to the inscription being on a tomb. The sense would be that even in idyllic Arcadia there is death. However, as we have seen from previous chapters, there is some scope for interpreting the 'I' to be a specific historical figure who is actually buried in the region.

Sion claims that the phrase can also be read as ET IN ARCADIA ERGO SUM, ('And in Arcadia therefore I am'), commenting that 'The interchangeable nature of *ego* and *ergo* is a much used form of coded Kabbalah.' I believe that Sion members use this phrase as a form of greeting and response when meeting other members.

Arcadia itself is a specific region of Greece but also symbolizes a place and a time of perfection, a kind of paradise or Eden, and an idea very much in keeping with the French rural idyll. In mythology Arcadia was the birthplace of Pan, the god of shepherds and flocks. The psychology of the mythic land before humankind's 'Fall' from innocence should not be ignored.

The alchemists Paracelsus (1493–1541) and Gerhard Dorn (c1530–1584) used 'Elysium', a term equivalent to 'Arcadia', to refer to an original state of being. Paracelsus describes metals in their purest form as *eleuseria metalla*, 'paradisial metals'. Elysium is the paradise of Greco-Roman antiquity, much the same as Eden or Arcadia. This original state can be applied to metals, to the body and to the unconscious. In the alchemical process, the false structure is dissolved to allow the true nature to emerge. Dorn also made much of the separation of the soul from the blood, and refers to how the alchemist may kill the sick in order to save them. This is reminiscent of how the blood of Jesus, through symbolic self-sacrifice, seeps into the earth and revives Adam to his state prior to the Fall from paradise.

The Arcadia region is often represented in art as containing either a tomb or a fountain, but both mean a place where the subterranean comes to the surface. The fountain is symbolic of the 'underground stream' of knowledge that has been passed down through the ages. The name itself, Arcadia, is also linked etymologically to *arca* and to *arc* and *ark*. The arc motif returns many times in the mystery and through the application of the Hermetic 'green' language (*see* page 82) it can be seen to have many meanings. Importantly the area is close to the

Paris Meridian and the 'Rose Line' and although these are pictured as straight lines, due to the curvature of the earth they are in reality both arcs.

Other levels of interpretation lead to the Pole Star, which is also known as the 'Star of Arcady' because the son of Callisto was called Arcas. The arc theme continues with the word 'ark', meaning a sacred container. The artist Poussin chose for his personal seal the image of a man holding an ark. It is an unusual design, as if he carried the sum of all life on earth. The ark motif has evolved through history from the Egyptian arks paraded to celebrate the annual flooding of the Nile and containing statuettes of the Egyptian gods. This symbol was transformed into the Ark of the Covenant containing the Ten Commandments, the essence of the teachings of Yahweh. Noah's Ark is the same word in the sense of a vessel that carried the essence of all life on earth.

The figures in Poussin's painting are a shepherdess and three shepherds. The hand of the shepherdess rests affectionately on the shoulder of one of the young men. This was pointed out to me by Nic Haywood as being akin to portraits of the Virgin and Child and is intended to indicate a mother and her son.

Jesus was described as the 'Good Shepherd' and if you believe Mary Magdalene to be his bride she then automatically takes on the role of shepherdess, especially with regard to disseminating his teachings. The shepherdess and her lover mentioned in the Bible in the Song of Songs is also thought by some to be about Mary and Jesus (*see* Starbird), although the Song of Songs is much earlier than Jesus' time, being in the Hebrew Old Testament.

Sion affirms that when Mary went to Gaul via Greece, 'she was to be far from alone; other family members would embark on the relatively short journey too'. These relations account for the remaining shepherds.

This is evidenced by St James, the brother of Jesus, whose foot rests on the cornerstone rock. The same figure can also be seen in other paintings by Poussin, for example *Extreme Unction* also shows St James with his foot on the cornerstone. There are two versions and a sketch with the cornerstone present in all three but the version with the shield in the background is the clearest. Jesus' brother headed the early Church in Jerusalem and this could be seen as James standing in opposition to the 'rock' of St Peter and later St Paul, on which the Roman Catholic Church was founded. There was indeed a split between the Jerusalem Church under James, and Paul, who wanted to relax some tenets of the Jewish faith in order to give the teachings of Jesus (as he understood them) a greater appeal to Greeks and other pagans. For example, they would not be required to be circumcised nor to avoid certain foods. Paul won. On the other hand, Jewish sources record that James and others were executed by stoning in 62CE on the orders of the high priest Ananus.

If we take this shepherdess to be Mary it opens up various avenues of interest. She was known to be of the tribe of Benjamin, many of whom were probably exiled to the region of Arcadia in Greece, which was also the legendary place of origin of the Frankish kings. The painting can therefore be seen as a depiction of the bloodlines, showing its progress via the tribe of Benjamin in Arcadia, and from Jesus and Mary Magdalene through the Franks and Merovingians to the hills of the Languedoc.

It should also be noted that Poussin made an earlier version of the *Et in Arcadia Ego* theme. This painting includes a skull with a slot cut into it and a bee resting on the cranium. The slot is in keeping with the ritualized slot that was cut into the skulls of Merovingian kings and the bee is a symbol of the royal line of Egyptian pharaohs, who saw the hive as a mirror for their society.

However, while many researchers focus on the *Et in Arcadia Ego* paintings there is a far more obvious work by Poussin regarding the relationship of Jesus and Mary Magdalene.

CHRIST AND THE WOMAN TAKEN IN ADULTERY

In the Louvre, in the adjacent room to the later of Poussin's *Et in Arcadia Ego* paintings, hangs his depiction of *Christ and the Woman taken in Adultery*, an episode recounted in the gospel of John (7.53–8.11). The gospel text does not actually name the woman, but a long artistic tradition identified the adultress with Mary Magdalene – a tradition ultimately based on the false allegation that Mary was a sexual sinner whom Jesus forgave (*see* page 206). In this painting Jesus and Mary Magdalene stand facing each other in the foreground. Between them, in the background, is a woman holding a child and clearly pregnant with a second. As Jesus points to the adulteress his finger rests on the mother in the background, who is at the centre of the painting. The clothes of the mother are blue and white in the style of the Virgin Mary, which as mentioned previously, also appeared in art worn by Mary Magdalene until the Church forbade it. It is unlikely that the mother figure is a symbol of moral correctness with which we should compare the adulteress, since the purpose of this biblical scene was to teach people not to judge others. An alternative is that by having Jesus point at both the mother and the Magdalene he is telling us that they are one and the same. It is further evidence that Poussin was party to the secret of the bloodline and gives credibility to his place in the Rennes-le-Château mystery.

ST ANTHONY AND ST PAUL IN THE DESERT

The painting *St Anthony and St Paul in the Desert* by David Teniers the Younger (1610–90) was mentioned in the chapter on the Temple. Like Poussin's second *Et in Arcadia Ego* it was alluded to in the parchments released by Sion during the 1960s. The painting works on many levels and although Poussin's work has been made synonymous with the Rennes affair the Teniers work is equally revealing.

The original painting is believed to be in a private collection in Spain, having been sold at auction in 1923 and subsequently hidden from public view. A search for this work will bring up references to a poor copy at Shugborough Hall in England (*see* below). The only accurate copy known to exist is a bromide that the Priory of Sion owned for a number of years, having instructed Nic Haywood to procure it. Nic loaned the bromide to me and it is reproduced in the plates section of this book.

Even though the painting clearly shows a crucifix on the table, the bromide was wrongly catalogued as *Elijah and Elisha being fed by the Raven*, a scene from the Old Testament. This mislabelling would appear to have been a deliberate attempt to hide the work from the public eye. What it actually shows is St Paul the Hermit (not Paul the apostle) and St Anthony beside a table in the foreground with a raven that is bringing them bread. On and around the table are objects such as a skull, a book and an hourglass. In the background are a hilltop town and a shepherdess.

A skull and an hourglass are recorded as being present on tables during Rosicrucian meetings in the 17th century (as referred to by Christopher McIntosh in *The Rosicrucians*), and with the cross and book form the requirements for a 'chamber of reflection' like the one in the church at Rennes-le-Château (*see* page 101). As the painting pre-dates the Masonic Rose+Croix Degree it can be seen as an authentic reference to an earlier Rosicrucian movement.

Like Poussin's Arcadian shepherds, the figures in Teniers' painting are set against the backdrop of a real location in the region of Rennes-le-Château. Nic Haywood drew my attention to 'the clifftop building in the Teniers composition'. One possible candidate is L'Hermitage ('The Hermitage'), to the south of Rennes-les-Bains, but the clifftop town is more in keeping with Rennes-le-Château itself. This would place the painting to the southwest of the village.

Looking across the landscape this would form the southwest corner of the hidden temple, while Poussin's painting shows the northeast corner.

The account of a raven bringing bread to feed a hermit exists in the Bible, where a raven feeds Elijah in the Old Testament (1 Kings 17.4–5). This image appears again in St Jerome's *The Life of St Paul the Hermit*, his account of St Paul and St Anthony the Great in the desert. The prophets Elijah and Elisha are said by Sion to have had an alchemical teacher–pupil relationship that mirrors that of Paul and Anthony. A statue of St Anthony the Great appears in the church at Rennes-le-Château and his feast day is January 17. The raven is a symbol of the opening stage of the alchemical process, *nigredo* or blackening.

Through the gift of bread, Teniers performs an interesting sleight of hand by linking the scene to a saint who took bread to feed a hermit. The saint is depicted as a shepherdess in the background of Teniers' and her name is St Roseline.

ST ROSELINE

St Roseline or Rosilyn de Villeneuve was born in 1263 at Arcs in southeast Provence. Her feast day is January 17 and roses are her symbol. Sion recounted her legend and her symbolic importance:

> 'The name Rosilyn has been a Kabbalistic godsend, for the fact
> that [her name encodes] the 'Line of Secret Places' [the 'Rose
> Line'] and that this saint was local to the Languedoc region.
> Having secretly given bread to a cave-dwelling hermit, she was
> challenged by her father while en route with more supplies
> concealed in her folded apron. On surrendering she allowed the
> apron to fall open but, as the legend informs us, no bread dropped
> to the ground, only a cascade of fresh roses!'

Recognizing this to be a miracle, her father, the lord of Arcs, instructed his kitchen staff to provide food for the poor from that day onward. In adult life Roseline became a nun and was known for having visions. When her brother, a Crusader knight, escaped his captors he claimed to have followed visions of Roseline surrounded by roses to find his way home. She died on January 17, 1329, and her body is said to remain uncorrupted.

Roseline was a nobleman's daughter, but her depiction as a shepherdess in Teniers' painting links it thematically to Poussin's Arcadian shepherds.

There are a number of statues of St Roseline in the Rennes-le-Château region including one at the church of Espéraza, which is in the same style as the statues at Rennes-le-Château. Father Boudet, the incumbent of Rennes-les-Bains at the end of the 19th century, placed Espéraza at the centre of a circle of churches in his book *The True Language of the Celts and the Stone Circle of Rennes-les-Bains* (*see* page 110). The name Roseline also represents the 'Rose Line' that runs parallel to the Paris Meridian and passes near Rennes-le-Château.

POUSSIN AND TENIERS HOLD THE KEY

Both Poussin's and Teniers' paintings work on many levels and relate to more than one aspect of the Rennes-le-Château mystery. Their presence can be clearly discerned in the Rose+Croix Degree of Freemasonry and therefore relate to the idea of initiation through the landscape. The pentagram structure of Poussin's later *Et in Arcadia Ego* echoes Henry Lincoln's 'landscape geometry' and the composition also evokes the bloodline and the Arcadian links to Mary Magdalene's tribe. The presence of Mary as the shepherdess in the company of her family also alludes to the bloodline by challenging us to question who lies in the tomb and to consider the meaning of 'the place where the underground stream emerges'.

SHUGBOROUGH HALL

It is not by chance that both the Poussin and Teniers paintings are represented at Shugborough Hall in Staffordshire, England. Shugborough brings together many of the themes in this mystery and it is also the home of the Anson family, earls of Lichfield.

Patrick Anson, fifth earl of Lichfield, a renowned photographer and cousin of Queen Elizabeth II, agreed to meet me and Bruce Burgess in 2005 during the making of the documentary *Bloodline*. Sadly, before the meeting could take place, Lord Lichfield died suddenly of what was diagnosed as a cerebral haemorrhage. The meeting had been arranged by a representative of the Priory of Sion, who later suggested that a toxin might have been used to induce such an event. During our research we discovered that four other members of the Priory of Sion were thought to have died in the same manner.

The Shugborough estate has so many works of art and sculpture that pertain to the mysteries of Rennes-le-Château and the Priory of Sion that this is unlikely to be a coincidence. In the grounds of Shugborough Hall stands a stone monument representing Poussin's *Et in Arcadia Ego* in reverse and, as I mentioned, the house is also home to a copy of *St Anthony and St Paul in the Desert* by Teniers the Younger.

The 'shepherds' monument was added to an existing stone archway along with a number of other structures in the gardens that give the impression of being part of a wider design, such as a route of initiation. The monument depicts an identical scene to the one in Poussin's painting with the figures standing beside a tomb but in reverse, an effect that appears in alchemy as mirroring. It also bears this inscription, which has so far managed to elude definitive translation:

O.U.S.A.V.V.A.V.
D.   M.

The full stops clearly give the impression that we are reading a set of initials. According to Jocelyn Godwin's analysis of the *Hypnerotimachia Poliphili*, a 15th-century romance, the initials D. M. on sculptures of this kind generally stand for *Dis Manibus* ('to the Shades'), an old Roman devotional statement.

This is also a standard code format for Freemasons who have long employed the use of *verbum dismissum*, the blanking of words following the first letter. Many Masonic books, for example, use the term G.A.O.T.U. in place of their title for God, the 'Grand Architect Of The Universe'.

According to Nic Haywood the code on the monument is still in use at this time so cannot be revealed. I doubt it exists in everyday Freemasonry or it would long ago have leaked into the public domain. According to Nic,

> 'The most important esoteric clue to the Shugborough monument
> is that of the ceiling design of the dining room, built at the same
> time depicts Isis and Serapis (a late form of Osiris) in roundels,
> clearly identified by their attributes, a sistrum and a corn-measure
> or shibboleth.'

A sistrum is a kind of metal rattle used in rituals, while the 'shibboleth' is a sheath of corn. But it is also a word used to mean a secret password in Masonic rituals.

The elements of the mystery at Shugborough Hall can be drawn together as a complete understanding of the bloodline in art and architecture.

The exiled tribe of Benjamin came to Arcadia in Greece, a place depicted by Poussin's painting. Arcadia was also the ancient home of the Sicambrian Franks, the ethnic group from which the Merovingians emerged, and through the clues in the art and architecture of Shugborough Hall we are expected to link the two.

In the tomb of the Merovingian king Childeric a golden bull's head was discovered. According to the Bible, the tribe of Benjamin also idolatrously worshipped the Golden Calf, as depicted in Poussin's painting *The Adoration of the Golden Calf*. This includes dancers who are a mirror images of those in his *Dance to the Music of Time*, which itself is based upon Guido Reni's *Aurora*, as is the ceiling of Shugborough Hall.

SYMBOLISM AND MEANING

We have begun to see how the many forms of symbols can be used to transmit information. They form a universal language used by secret societies and artists to convey messages to those who can read them.

Symbols must be contemplated to reveal their inner nature.

Just as a poet reduces a vast concept to a few lines, a complex idea can be reduced to a single symbol or geometrical shape. Symbols can also appear on the cusp of the conscious and unconscious. They form the boundaries of language, where the most complex concept is transformed into the simplest of images.

The images we are examining reverberate through the many levels of consciousness and lead us toward the inner teachings of Sion: alchemy and, ultimately, gnosis.

CHAPTER 17

ALCHEMY
AND GNOSIS

The vital thing is not the transmutation of metals,
but that of the person.

The Priory of Sion

INTRODUCTION

Alchemy has been many things throughout history. It has been the property of the 'puffers' attempting to make gold; a symbolic path; the key to immortality; and a map of Jungian individuation. Some even link its process to nuclear transmutation.

It is not possible to summarize alchemy in the short space of one chapter, and some would argue that the application of alchemy could never adequately be expressed in language. Like enlightenment or love, no amount of words can convey the experience except to those who have already tasted it.

The practice of alchemy is the thread that links the modern Priory of Sion to the adepts of the past. Alchemy pervades the mysteries of Rennes-le-Château and is at the heart of the Western occult tradition. We must endeavour to approach the core secrets of alchemy as it has the potential to transform people, objects, science and art toward perfection.

In an interview, Nic Haywood affirmed that 'there are many alchemists among Priory of Sion ranks'. Sion holds these alchemists in high esteem and it is at this level that Sion serves to effect change:

> 'Such work is of little use unless the individual can ultimately set his sights on assisting in the worldly journey of his fellow man,

facilitating changes and shifts in the collective consciousness. It is to this "underground stream" that such energies are directed.'

There are a number of common misconceptions concerning the *Ars Magna*, the 'Great Art' that is alchemy. Some think that it is entirely concerned with making gold, others that it can be reduced to Jungian individuation or Freudian psychology. A third common interpretation is that alchemy is like the process of meditation or tantra. All of these are correct as aspects of the application of alchemy but none of them encompasses the complete Art.

Alchemy speaks of the search for the 'Philosopher's Stone', yet it seems that many fail to appreciate the 'philosophical' element inherent in this term. The fact that it is not a chemist or a scientist but a philosopher who discovers the 'stone' tells us something of its nature. The philosophical aspect of the process indicates that it takes places internally first. It begins within the deeper considerations of a philosophical mind.

The risk at this stage is to think that the alchemical process is entirely a symbolic account of internal processes, but this is a valid approach to begin with.

Following this route we move toward the psychology of ritual and the transformational work of Jung's individuation and Assagioli's psychosynthesis. The book *Alchemy* by Johannes Fabricius and the beautifully illustrated *Transformation of the Psyche* (2003) by Henderson and Sherwood provide excellent starting points for the path of self-contemplation and for many this will be journey enough.

But in Golden Lane in Prague a surprise awaits us in the White Tower, where the emperor Rudolf II once imprisoned the English alchemist Edward Kelley (1555–97). Here we find the remains of an alchemical workshop with kiln, glass alembics, 'masculine' and 'feminine' jars and all manner of chemistry apparatus. It is a revelation that takes us beyond the limits of psychology and deep into metallurgy. Alchemists actually did attempt literally to make gold from base metals by chemical distillation. We should not be surprised at this, the process of transmutation, both material or spiritual, is universal and can map perfectly onto psychology, physics, chemistry, art and architecture, in both making gold and synthesizing sub-personalities. These are all aspects of alchemy. It is the *Ars Magna* of transformation.

The theory and practice of the Western tradition of alchemy have roots in both ancient Greece and ancient Egypt. The Arabic term for alchemy, *al-Kimia*, means 'process', which is also relevant, but the term itself is said to stem from the ancient name of Egypt: *Kemet*, the Black Land, named from the dark alluvial soil deposited by the inundations of the Nile. From this primary matter life springs forth.

Here we find alchemy at the beginning of creation; it is the source, the seed and the starting point from which all life develops. It concerns itself with the energy of transformation through every stage of life and every aspect of existence. Philosophically, alchemy brings to fruition Platonic idealism. In this, the archetypes of nature are perfect and the goal of alchemy is to accelerate evolution toward that perfection. This is Arcadia waiting to be discovered. Sion affirms that 'alchemy does in a lifetime what nature takes a thousand years to complete.'

Success at achieving the *Magnum Opus*, the Great Work of alchemy, affords a view of reality from all sides and to achieve this one must reverberate on all levels: physical, psychological, emotional, chemical and philosophical. All these levels are found in *Le Serpent Rouge* and in the Rennes-le-Château mystery in general. These can be identified as living works of Hermetic perfection as they mirror the both the process and the individual who seeks to unravel their secrets.

THE BOOK OF THE HOLY TRINITY

Sion has claimed among its ranks the French artist Jean Cocteau (1889–1963), whose work is imbued with esoteric thought and symbols. As mentioned in previous chapters, Cocteau's mural in the French church in Leicester Place, off London's Leicester Square draws upon the 15th-century alchemical treatise *Das Buch der heiligen Dreifaltigkeit (The Book of the Holy Trinity)* attributed to the German monk Ulmannus. Nic Haywood had recommended that I should locate a copy as it contains ideas important to my quest.

Over time I have tracked down a number of editions of this rare manuscript. It seems that fewer than 20 copies exist in the world and there are no reprints or facsimile copies available. It is a fascinating work, combining alchemical symbolism with heraldic devices and Christian iconography. There are early versions of this text at the Wellcome Institute library in London and in the Glasgow University library in Scotland.

The edition in the Glasgow University library seemed the most complete. It is a beautiful item of perfectly legible and surprisingly readable calligraphy, and 37 glorious plates. This rare old manuscript may be the key to many aspects of the mystery.

At first glance I was instantly struck by how much heraldry pervades the alchemical images. With copious crowns and heraldic shields throughout the work it would seem to allude to the bloodline and the idea of royal secrets reminded me that alchemy is sometimes called the 'Royal Art'. Also, in terms of the alchemical process, blood has always been symbolic of the smelting of sulphur, which creates a blood-like red fluid when molten.

The most striking plate in the *Book of the Holy Trinity* is the crucifixion scene with the blue lily (fleur-de-lys) in the background and the Virgin Mary surmounting a sublime crescent moon in the foreground.

I have compared four examples of this plate and certain details common to all four can be considered core to the scene's meaning.

The Virgin Mary is shown in all four images with long hair past her waist. This feature is usually associated with Mary Magdalene, following the gospel of Luke where an unnamed woman uses her hair to wash the feet of Jesus. Mary Magdalene has waist-length hair in art from the 15th century onward, and long hair was also a symbol of the Merovingians. In the Wellcome Institute version of this image, the figure's fingers criss-cross in an identical manner to the Magdalene in the altar painting at Rennes-le-Château. This provides a further hint that in this plate the two Marys have been combined into a single figure.

The text states:

> 'Man is created out of the twofold sun. The inward, spiritual
> sun embodies the divine hermaphrodite. He is the personifi-
> cation of unselfish alchemy, consisting of Jesus, the male stone of
> purity (Mercurius/Spirit) and Mary, the female stone of loveliness
> (Luna/Body). Their unity with God the Father (Sol/Soul), the
> petrolith, which strengthens against all the devil's temptations.'

The 'inward sun', or 'black sun', is also present in the Cocteau mural, but the fleur-de-lys is replaced with a rose, signifying that the Rosicrucians are the present keepers of this philosophy. According to French legend the fleur-de-lys, or lily flower, was delivered by angels to the Merovingian king, Clovis, at his baptism as a gift from the Virgin Mary. It denotes that the lineage of these kings is considered divine. The link between the fleur-de-lys and French nobility can be seen as early as King Robert of the Franks in the fifth century. A lily can also represent the lineage of the pharaohs.

Here, both alchemy and the bloodline can act as metaphors for each other. We see it in the heraldic devices and in the kings and queens of alchemical manuscripts such as the *Splendor Solis* or the image of Mary beneath the cross in the *Book of the Holy Trinity*. This is both the royal art and royal descent. In terms of consciousness they are both descended from the Christ. The key theme of the crucifixion is resurrection and this is of great interest to alchemists.

The resurrection is aptly illustrated by the Tarot card 'Judgment', which shows the dead rise up from the earth summoned by the heavenly call of an angel's trumpet. Like the metals at work in his crucible, the alchemist allows himself to die and be resurrected *while still alive*. This is the deepest meaning of the Third Degree in Freemasonry and the essence of baptism in all religions: a path to the perfection of human nature. Psychologists see this as the redemption of our darkest unconscious material – our personal 'demons' rising up to become angels.

ALCHEMY AND PSYCHOLOGY

The psychological approach to alchemy is important because it is the most available and readily understandable experience of the Great Work. Transpersonal psychology in particular aims to understand all inner experiences, from the deepest trauma to the heights of religious experience, and, as Jung discovered, this process maps easily onto the archaic illustrations of alchemy. Jung and his followers, such as Marie-Louise von Franz, have even made the bold assertion that we create the world around us and attract those who act out our unconscious issues.

Traditional alchemy often includes a stage of 'integration'. The integration into the whole of all the parts of the psyche is the work of psychologists, and one application of the science of alchemy. As progress is made toward an integrated personality we begin to experience synchronicities, through which 'the effectiveness of the self increases', as von Franz put it in *Alchemical Active Imagination*. Synchronicity requires the individual to have some influence over their environment through remote manipulation. This is no small revelation.

In alchemy, synchronicity can also be termed 'correspondence'. It equates with the Hermetic axiom 'as above, so below' and with the idea of pilgrimage. With the right psychological attitude it is a means to evolve the self so that it is repeated in the physical world.

Once the evolution of the self is complete, it takes what von Franz refers to as a 'pure form'. This attracts other pure forms in the physical world, as when the spirit of the individual is pure and the spirit of the object is pure – gold being considered by alchemists the purest — the spirits can converse. Alike spirits are drawn to each other, creating synchronicity.

The perfection of the 'inner' and 'outer' gold must occur at the same time and results in both the 'Philosopher's Stone' and the flash of gnosis or illumination.

THE STONE OF THE WISE

The goal of alchemy is to attain the 'Philosopher's Stone', a stone that according to Nic Haywood 'comes from heaven, created by man'. The stone is balanced between the physical and spiritual spheres. We find this represented by the physical Philosopher's Stone, the symbolic ashlar of Freemasonry (see page 160), and by the underlying philosophy of Platonic idealism. As Sion says: 'Everything ethereal has its physical counterpart (as above, so below, etc.)'.

This allows the application of the stone to any aspect of life and is recognized by other adepts as a reflection of spirit in matter. As Sion describes it:

'The Philosopher's Stone is a semi-physical, partly corporeal,
partly ethereal matter, cohered, realized and concentrated by the
successful alchemist by means of complex methods of distillation.
The "flash" of revelation, the Gnostic vision, is captured for all
time and may then be applied to any subject matter.'

This is reminiscent of the 'soul of inanimate objects' in occult traditions.

'The fact that the term "making a Golden Head" — essentially a
Sufi expression — refers to actively labouring toward discovering
the stone is in itself telling.'

The Golden Head comes in many forms but can generally be seen as a reference to the enlightened state of gnosis: direct communication with the divine.

GNOSIS

We all experience moments of being connected to something greater than ourselves. For some this manifests as moments of mental clarity or a deep sense of peace; for others something breaks through into their awareness and deep insights about their nature are revealed. When fear subsides we are revealed, our old self breaks open briefly, and in this moment we become closer to the divine. In terms of psychology such moments manifest in 'peak experiences', personal revelations that broaden our perception of ourselves and the world around us.

These are simple, often humbling, experiences. But the intention is similar to alchemy: to be open and fearless in our quest for contact with the divine, the experience of gnosis.

The idea of gnosis in its most accessible and available form is that of exploring the feminine intuition that resides in all our hearts. Here we can find our own path to God by experiencing a deeper level of meaning to life and perhaps an experience of the divine.

The development of many of the major religions in the West has led to outward-facing constructs that focus on power and control. They emphasize, and claim ownership of, the external aspects of divinity. Access to the divine can only be via their rules or they cease to be of any value. Parallel to this, the mystery schools of the Western esoteric tradition have developed under constant threat of persecution. These are seen as a challenge by religions as they focus on the internal process; self-discovery of the divine spark that resides in all of us.

Spiritual renewal often requires the collapse of old structures, both externally and internally. These constructs give way to allow a deeper experience, closer to the core of our being.

* Faith has its uses but the closer we get to the truth of Jesus, the closer he comes to us. Much can be gleaned from reading the Gnostic scriptures, such as the *Gospel of Thomas*, which is in the form of a series of 114 sayings attributed to Jesus, for example: 'Those who lead you say to you, "See, the Kingdom is in the sky".... [But] it is within you.' (*Gospel of Thomas* 3.)

This gospel was discovered at Nag Hammadi in 1945 and, unsurprisingly, has not been accepted by the Vatican. The idea that heaven is within us hands the power of the Church to the individual. That is not to say that organized religions have no purpose: they may guide and support people in their spiritual practice. But they are a barrier to God because they offer a simplified deity for us to relate *to*, rather than an abstract, experiential phenomenon we can relate *with*.

Nic Haywood tells us that he is 'deeply involved with the underlying spirituality that underpins the order and would inevitably replace a dissolved Christianity.'

The Priory of Sion is not a religion. It has core spiritual truths but we must not confuse this with religion. Whereas religions are mostly human constructs and incompatible with one another, spirituality is inherent within all of us; it is compatible with all true expressions of itself and entirely at ease in any time or location.

It is not easy to understand this as an adult after our lives have already been conditioned by Christianity. For most who were exposed from an early age to Christian culture in any form, the idea of God brings to mind the image of an old man. It comes as no surprise that by adulthood many people will have turned their backs on religion and allowed their spirit to go to sleep. By having an image of God that is of no symbolic value, we no longer need to wonder or think about God.

To undo this mindset and remove this block, we have to kill our preconceived idea of God in order to rediscover what God really is. It is necessary to create a space for the divine to manifest through us.

There are other paths, such as meditation and the breathing techniques of yoga. Nature also holds further routes to the true Kingdom. Richard Dawkins may rail against Santa Claus, but does he stop to look up at the stars, or stare out across the ocean? And if so, does this move him in some deep and resonant place, like the stir of a primitive belonging? There is an old saying that 'man looks through a microscope to see how great he is in relation to everything, he looks through a telescope to see how small and insignificant he is'. I would add that man looks to science to *forget* who he is. There are moments of wonder to be had by contemplating the stars or standing in a forest or watching the waves arrive from a distant shore. When we open ourselves to being moved at some deep level as the scale and beauty of nature overwhelm the ego, in the deep sense of peace that follows deep spiritual insights may come. This potential to awaken is always present, like a background hum, as we are haunted by the ghost of our true selves. The Gnostics experienced 'the Self within the self'. Revelation is the Self revealed to the self. Here is how Nic Haywood describes it:

'Gnosis: that single divine spark or flash that is revelation. This is the goal of every aspirant. The gift from God which raises steward into master, knight into king, pilgrim into saint or neophyte into adept. It is a moment that lasts for an aeon in which and after which all things make perfect sense. Harmony is rendered visible, taste is acquired, and the roots of all matter are perceived and that which was mutable is made fixed. Spirit is made substance, fixed for eternity. This is the "Stone of the Wise", the sparkle of which is but one's own reflection in the eyes of Isis, Mother of the Eternal Sea or Source. One finally sees oneself in the mirror that is creation.'

'To become illumined is an experience which, when the
moment occurs, is the most beautiful and divine gift from oneself
to oneself. At that moment the word: "I" has a wholly new, but
not totally unexpected meaning.'

We have each had moments that embody this. Psychologist Abraham Maslow
describes them as 'peak experiences': spontaneous experiences of something
greater than ourselves.

TOWARD A WHOLE

In the *Gospel of Thomas* (saying 61), Jesus makes the following statement:

'For this reason I say, if one is whole, one will be filled with light,
but if one is divided, one will be filled with darkness.'

We are born whole but atheists, with no more knowledge of God than we have
knowledge of the sun and moon. Over time our personalities fragment and
as these parts rule us from our unconscious we become polytheistic, like the
ancient Greeks and Egyptians. We harbour a pantheon of influences to appease
and express, each fighting for control. Only those few born whole, transcendent
or brave enough to take the heroic journey to unify their fragmented psyche
will move beyond this.

The Egyptians and Greeks understood their pantheons of archetypal gods
and beings as valuable to humanity's development. They drew these mythical
beings on the stars to remind of us of the influence of archetypes.

To resolve the gods and integrate them back into the psyche is of the utmost
importance to human development. Using tools such as meditation, psycho-
therapy or alchemy we might evolve toward synthesis, a whole and unified self,
at which point we naturally become monotheistic.

The spiritual path is a strange undertaking that appears in all societies dating
back to the dawn of man. This can be seen as an argument for the importance
of religion within society, but equally it could be interpreted as a primitive urge
that should be understood and allowed to develop unencumbered by organized
religion.

If your religion does not help you to achieve a direct experience of the
divine then it is an obstacle. We can all take issue with the Catholic Church
for its treatment of women, its homophobia and its history of persecution, but

its real crime is that it has become a placebo to millions. It has no intention of allowing people to find their own path to God, or of helping them to experience the divine. It exists merely to perpetuate its own power and control.

Ultimately everything that is a barrier to God, be it religions, secret societies or individual human pride, must be allowed to fall away. But for this to happen, there must be a mass revelation, no less: an event on a vast scale that is seen and recognized by all. There is another word for such a revelation, from which it might appear that the end is nigh: apocalypse.

PART 4

OUTCOME

CHAPTER 18

THE APOCALYPSE

And I John saw the holy city, New Jerusalem, coming down from God out of heaven, prepared as a bride adorned for her husband.

Revelation 21.2

THE MILLENNIUM MENTALITY

There are many themes running through the mythos of the Priory of Sion and the Rennes-le-Château mystery. Amid all the secrets and spiritual meanderings we stumble, time and again, across the same unspoken tradition, a concept that lurks in the shadows of Western civilization. We of the Western mindset are chained to certain religious ideas. Whatever our spiritual leanings, we were born into a 'millennium mentality', with its fixation on the 'End Times' and the promise of apocalypse.

Although not a Christian, like many in the West I was exposed to ideas from the Book of Revelation throughout my early life, via both education and cultural references. With the millennium looming large for my generation there was an unspoken expectation, even among the agnostics, that *something* would happen as the Gregorian calendar crept into the 21st century. We went about our daily lives ignoring the subtle expectation that quietly haunted our thoughts with images of destruction. The millennium passed. Nothing happened. Those sweeping the floor to earn a living in 1999 continued to sweep the floor in 2000 and beyond. As ever, any major change in circumstances arose from individuals taking responsibility for their lives instead of waiting for divine intervention.

Admittedly the 'year 2000' date does not come directly from scripture, but so many churches had capitalized on the millennium that they significantly added to the sense of expectation. Lifting headlines from the press about wars and climate change as signs and evidence, like the biblical prophets they cashed in on the spirit of the age with fluorescent posters demanding that we repent before it was too late. The posters have long since surrendered to the seasons or been covered by numerous new slogans attempting to bury the painful truth.

The Christian faiths have failed to make good on their promises so we can now turn our backs on the myth of the apocalypse. Unless, perhaps, it is left to others to make a revelation.

The Priory of Sion had previously made little or no reference to the apocalypse, although there are direct references to it in alchemy, Rosicrucianism and Freemasonry. We have also seen how the Templars attempted to create another element of the Book of Revelation with their designs for a 'New Jerusalem' based at Rennes-le-Château. We also know the Cathars held the Book of Revelation to be a key text. They believed that the Vatican was the 'harlot' of the apocalypse (*see* Edward Peters, ed., *Heresy and Authority in Medieval Europe*) and that the evil of the world would eventually be judged by fire.

In the depths of alchemy, the esoteric path that imbues the language and designs of the Priory of Sion, there is a strong millennialist tradition often called 'chiliasm'. We also note that the red serpent of Sion's call to the wise, *Le Serpent Rouge*, echoes the red dragon uncoiling from the pages of St John's revelation.

More examples will follow as I make the case for the apocalyptic theme underpinning many of the traditions at work here. But first we must examine Sion's opinion on the subject.

WHAT THE PRIORY OF SION TELLS US

During one interview with Nic Haywood he revealed that Sion upholds a belief that the apocalypse is a very real event and that it will happen sometime soon:

> 'Yes, there is an event that nobody will fail to recognize. We are as a race reaching a point of cessation of time itself, seasons merging. This cannot happen without the collapse of certain structures in nature; time will dissolve. The Qur'an speaks of the end of this cycle as commencing with stone-swept winds.'

The tradition of apocalyptic scripture has a long history in many religious movements. As well as the Christian Book of Revelation, Judaism and Islam have their own eschatology, or belief in the End Times.

Zoroastrianism, which dates from c 6000–4000 BCE, has a doctrine of 1,000-year periods that end with cataclysm and heresy. This continues until the final millennium, estimated to be around the year 2000, when good conquers evil in a final battle and a king is restored. The Zoroastrian sacred book, the Zend Avesta, also speaks of how Zoroaster's seed will be dormant 'in the lake' for 3,000 years before awakening. The Zend Avesta is thought to be around 3,000 years old, so this 'awakening of the seed' would be due around now. This seed has ties to the bloodline and we will return to it later.

Zoroastrianism may have been the source of apocalyptic thinking in Judaism and Islam and also a major influence on Christianity, but the idea of the end of the world is not limited to the religious traditions originating in the Middle East. Buddhism and Hinduism also speak of cycles of creation and destruction, with Buddhism in particular predicting its own 'second coming' in the form of Maitreya, the Buddha of the future. The Maya are also well known for their calendar of cycles that spiral down toward a single date as are the Chinese. This rhythmic return appears in other myths, like the returning king of French tradition.

The Bible is littered with apocalyptic insights and prophecies. I asked Nic if Sion's understanding of the apocalypse is linked to biblical prophecy, and he replied: 'Yes, to the Revelation of John the Divine.'

THE BOOK OF REVELATION

The main source of the apocalyptic theme in Western thought is the Apocalypse of St John the Divine, perhaps better known as the Book of Revelation. Attributed to the same St John who wrote the gospel, this book was held in high esteem by such luminaries among Sion's associates as Sir Isaac Newton, who was fascinated by prophecies and visions of the future. It also features heavily in Freemasonry as part of the Rose+Croix rituals covered earlier.

The term 'apocalypse' is another word for 'revelation' and comes from the Greek word *apokalyptein* meaning 'to uncover' or 'to reveal'. In biblical terms the 'revelation' is often either of God's will or a prophecy of cataclysm and coming events. There are other apocalypses in the Bible, such as the visions of the prophets Ezekiel and Daniel in the Old Testament, which represent the apocalyptic traditions of Judaism. The Book of Revelation draws on these earlier biblical texts but its vision of the 'End Times' is unique in being a distinctly Christian apocalypse.

The Book of Revelation is the most outlandish text in the New Testament, for which reason it was the last book to be accepted as part of the Christian

Bible. It is a visionary and highly symbolic journey through the past, the present and the future as predicted by St John. The future aspect of the text is what concerns us.

At the time St John was writing (believed to be c 90CE), many Christian groups expected that after 2,000 years Jesus would return and herald a new 'Golden Age', the Eden/Arcadia of which humankind was disinherited by Adam's desire for knowledge. According to Revelation, the Golden Age would last for 1,000 years and then be followed by a period under the rule of Satan, the Anti-Christ. This would lead to a final battle in which Christ would return in a blaze of majesty to preside over the defeat of evil, the Last Judgment and, ultimately, the end of the world.

THE SEVEN SEALS

At the core of the Book of Revelation is the opening of the seven seals on a great book (Revelation chapters 6–8). The Lamb (Christ) takes the book from the right hand of God and opens the seals one by one, unleashing the chain of events that herald the final cataclysm. The imagery is fantastical and on the face of it describes events that would destroy much of the population of the earth and render a fair portion of the planet uninhabitable. But in among this vivid account there are clues that the descriptions may hold some hidden meanings.

The ritual of the 18th (Rose+Croix) Degree of the Ancient and Accepted Scottish Rite of Freemasonry (referred to in the Stations of the Cross at Rennes-le-Château by the boy in a tartan sash; *see* page 97) includes the enacting of the opening of the seven seals. The seven seals of the book of Revelation also appear in alchemy in a number of Rosicrucian documents (*see Secret Symbols of the Rosicrucians of the 16th and 17th Centuries,* published by AMORC), which also includes the 'by this sign you will conquer' motif on the earth, air, fire, water diagram that matches the water stoup in the church at Rennes-le-Château.

The author of the Bacstrom Manuscript of Rosicrucian initiation (*see* page 48) declares:

> 'I will leave public affairs and arrangements to the Government of
> God, who will bring about the events foretold in the Revelation
> of St John, which are fast accomplishing.'

The opening of the seven seals reveals events that escalate toward a worldwide catastrophe. Here are a few examples and how they have been interpreted.

The first seal depicts the rise of a military leader, a man on a white horse who gains control of ten nations. He is described as being represented by two semi-precious stones, jasper and carnelian. The priests of ancient Israel wore breastplates during ceremonies that had 12 semi-precious stones embedded in them to represent the 12 tribes of Israel. Carnelian represented the tribe of Benjamin, to which Mary Magdalene belonged, and would therefore denote a link to this tribe. Historically this figure has been linked to Napoleon, who was famously depicted by Jacques-Louis David astride his rearing white horse.

On the opening of the first seal we witness four animals surrounding the throne. One Christian tradition holds that these creatures, which first appear in the Book of Ezekiel in the Old Testament, symbolize the four gospel authors. However, they can be traced back to Babylonian astrology, where they were signs of the zodiac.

The opening of the second and third seals brings visions of wars and famine that ravage the world. I asked Sion if a war could be contrived to suit an apocalyptic agenda. The response was a solemn 'It wouldn't be the first time'.

Wars are so common in recent world history that it would be difficult to use this as a measure of anything other than humanity's idea of 'business as usual'.

When the fourth seal is broken death is unleashed on one quarter of the world. In current terms, that would mean 1.5 billion people would 'die'. This might be a symbolic death of some kind, such as a loss of faith in the major religions. This idea is given weight with the opening of the fifth seal, which describes the 'dead' receiving robes and being told to wait. As even theologians agree, the dead have no bodies and therefore nothing to hang their robes upon.

The opening of the sixth seal brings a vision of a cataclysmic event, with stars falling from the sky and a great earthquake. The sun is seen to turn black, which is a prevailing image in alchemy and represents the first stage of the alchemical process, *nigredo* or blackening. An example of the black sun can be seen in Jean Cocteau's mural in the French Church in London.

The opening of the seventh seal heralds more destruction. Blood and hail rain from the skies, a third of the earth is burned and a third of sea life dies. A burning mountain is hurled into the sea. A blazing star called Wormwood falls from the sky, opening the abyss and producing black cloud that obscures a quarter of light from the sun. At the time of the Chernobyl disaster in 1986 it was pointed out that *chernobyl* means 'wormwood' in Russian, but the significance of this remains inconclusive. The seventh seal appears to describe the arrival of a comet or an asteroid, with the appearance of shooting stars heralding a major impact.

St John goes on to describe a plague of locusts coming out of the earth and attacking anyone who does not have the seal of God on their forehead. The locusts are described as each having a gold crown, a woman's hair, a human face, a lion's teeth, breastplates of iron and wings that sound like thunder. Their tails contain a sting. Some interpret the locusts as helicopters or fighter planes, the impact and poisoning of the sea and burning of the land as nuclear war. Terms such as 'horses that breathe fire' can easily be interpreted as tanks, which have replaced cavalry on the battlefield. But this is a modern view that fits our narrow timeframe of technology.

Until the arrival of a comet or another major cataclysm, it is difficult to pin these events on any specific point in history. Sion needs to be in possession of other information if they are to justify their expectation that the End Times, as described in Revelation, are imminent.

A WINDOW ON THE FUTURE

It is important to realize that Sion's knowledge of the apocalypse is less significant than how they come to have it, as Nic Haywood says:

'To Sion the method by which this information is known is more important than the event ... Gnosis, timing of events, signposts to watch, passed down.'

The bloodline could potentially provide two distinct sources of information.

The first would be an oral tradition, whereby past events of a cyclic nature – such as the return of a comet that affected the Earth's eco-systems – were recorded and passed down through the bloodline. A good example is the biblical tale of the Deluge, as we find similar accounts in many myths and stories across the globe, which suggests that there is likely to be an underlying truth to it. If this event did take place it is possible that there were signs predicting its arrival and that these were recorded in a form such as ritual, to be passed down through noble families to allow them to prepare for and capitalize on further events in the future. Added to this I am aware that Sion takes a great interest in the capture and transmission of knowledge in early civilizations.

A second possibility is race memory, or as it is termed today, genetic memory. There may be a clue to this in the *Serpent Rouge* reference to the 'blood that cries from the soil' and its use of the labyrinth. The labyrinth in this context would act as a route back to the 'source', a path tracing the origin of the underground stream of knowledge. It would act as a tool for those who are equipped to access information beyond the constraints of linear time. The recurring notion of something dormant in the blood to be awakened at a specific time was covered earlier (*see* page 237) but the power afforded to those with true race memory would be immense. It would immediately elevate an individual above those of us to whom being born is like waking in the middle of the night without truly knowing what came before. It would provide the only clear perspective on the past.

PROPHECY

Outside of the bloodline there are other means to future knowledge (beyond the popular tabloid horoscopes and various other gimmicks for divination) that retain some credibility. The most widespread form of prediction has historically been prophetic vision, be it from the Bible or relatively recent historical figures such as Nostradamus, whose utterances (such as 'The first and last of his sons will shine again in France') are ambiguous enough to fit many of the bloodline claims.

To prophesy is to know and to communicate a future event. This requires access to information beyond the present, which we perceive as part of linear time. This knowledge may arrive in many forms, such as flashes of insight, visions, dreams, journeys of active imagination, meditation, trance and mystical states. There can also be visitations in the form of guides and angels or through mediums, channels and diviners.

Historically prophecy was an integral part of religious life, with prophets believing or at least claiming that their messages come from a higher source such as God or other divine inspiration. More recent trends have seen these sources identified as spirit guides, angelic forces and even alien intelligences. Obviously the receiver may be mistaken in assuming that the source is speaking from an informed perspective, or at least with authority.

At first sight prophecy and prediction would appear to be the domain of cranks and the gullible, but as quantum science and transpersonal psychology begin to encroach into this area our view of time as a cord, along which events are strung like knots on a rope, begins to unravel. Like dreams and *déjà vu* another time is available here and now.

VISIONS

In and around the church of Mary Magdalene at Rennes-le-Château there are many references to visions. As we have seen, the inscription above the church door states 'This place is terrible', a quotation from the vision of Jacob on seeing the ladder with angels ascending and descending. In the garden stands a mock Visigothic pillar that has the Alpha and Omega suspended beneath the limbs of a cross as described in the Emperor Constantine's vision of the cross. Constantine's vision was accompanied by the phrase 'By this sign you will conquer', which is repeated above the water stoup within the church.

The garden of the church's priest, Father Saunière, was consecrated to Our Lady of Lourdes after a vision of the Virgin Mary that appeared there in 1858, and her statue surmounts the Visigothic pillar. Saunière himself visited Lourdes on a number of occasions to partake of the healing waters so must have had some faith in these matters.

Saunière is quoted at one point as likening Rennes-le-Château to a second Lourdes, to which many people would flock. Just prior to his appointment a similar event had occurred at Pontmain in southern France on January 17, 1871. Witnesses claimed to have seen an apparition of the Virgin Mary hovering in the sky for three hours. The vision was approved by the Catholic Church and the site became a pilgrimage location.

VIRGIN MARY APPARITIONS

The phenomenon of Virgin Mary apparitions has many links to our story. The apparitions are difficult to explain away as entirely imaginary, because Our Lady often appears to groups for prolonged periods of time. This does not mean that they can be taken at face value, however, as they remain unexplained and religious convictions may paint them with a Catholic veneer. It may be that these are somehow manifestations of the feminine archetype surfacing as group hallucinations.

The figures seen in these visitations seem predisposed to make prophecies. That they often choose to make them to a child in some lonely spot rather than to a Pope or another world leader has much in common with the problem of alleged UFO eyewitness accounts. But none of these concerns need devalue the quality of the information provided by the 'vision'. Unlike most forms of prophecy, Virgin Mary visitations tend to be very specific in the information they impart.

THE MESSAGE OF OUR LADY OF FATIMA

The most famous prophecy, and the most pertinent to our enquiries are the words ascribed to the Virgin Mary apparition at Fatima in Portugal. In 1917 a figure described as 'brighter than the sun' appeared to three children in Fatima and imparted three secrets to them in the form of predictions. The visitations continued for six months drawing ever increasing crowds of witnesses. The first of the prophecies was an image of hell, of people trapped in fire among demons. The second prediction stated that although the First World War would end, if people did not mend their ways a second war would occur, far worse than the first. The accuracy of this prediction is of course a matter of history. The vision also asked that Russia be consecrated to the sacred heart and that this happened in 1952 is evidence that the Vatican takes these messages very seriously.

The third secret was only to be revealed by the Pope after 1960. One of the three children who witnessed the vision was Lúcia Santos, later Sister Lúcia (1907–2005). She recorded the secret and stated in her memoirs that it began with the words: 'In Portugal, the dogma of the Faith will always be preserved.' In the event the Vatican withheld the prophecy until the year 2000, when it released a version that has no such beginning and is clearly not the same message.

There are clues to the actual nature of the third secret. Sister Lúcia also wrote for a number of Catholic publications, referring enquirers to chapters 8 to 13 in the Book of Revelation. This covers everything from the opening of the seven seals to the rise of the red dragon. Cardinal Joseph Ratzinger, later Pope Benedict XVI, said in November 1984 that the third secret of Fatima dealt with the 'End Times'. In the same year Ratzinger also stated in the Pauline Catholic magazine *Jesus*:

> 'It adds nothing to what Christians must know respecting what is stated in the Book of Revelation.'

Pope John Paul II is also reported as commenting on the third secret:

> 'If you read that the oceans will inundate continents, and millions of people will die suddenly in a few minutes, once this is known, then in reality it is not necessary to insist on the publication of this secret.'

We could dismiss this as scaremongering to attract people back to Catholicism and I would tend to agree, were it not for the fact that Dr Grant Beardmore, a theologian and former Catholic priest who had studied in the Vatican, once told me something of great significance.

According to Dr Beardmore, there was a great deal of interest in Rennes-le-Château within the Vatican. He claimed that this was in part due to a rumour that the third secret of Fatima related to the apocalypse, and mentioned Rennes-le-Château.

Dr Beardmore told me that the third secret was said to contain the following:

1. The actual date of the apocalypse. Apparently the Pope to whom this was passed on kept it a secret and took it with him to his grave.
2. The prediction that a plague of pandemic proportions would sweep the globe prior to this event.
3. The revelation that Rennes-le-Château is key to the apocalypse.

With regard to pandemics, AIDS is an example that we are all aware of, and the possibility of a swine flu or avian flu outbreak that could decimate the world's population is all too real.

Dr Beardmore also warned me to be careful of what I said about the Vatican while in the Rennes-le-Château area. He said they have important work to do down there and should not be obstructed. It is public knowledge that the Vatican funded a ground radar scan of the church and its grounds in the mid-1990s.

I questioned my Priory of Sion contact, Nic Haywood, on the matter and asked: does the apocalypse relate to Rennes-le-Château? He replied: 'In a way it is coded in Rennes-le-Château.'

A RETURN TO RENNES-LE-CHÂTEAU

The apocalypse has also been linked to Rennes-le-Château by authors such as David Wood and Elizabeth Van Buren. Each found their own route to this conclusion, Wood through geometry and cometary impact and Van Buren through alchemy and astrology.

The Sermon on the Mount scene within the church at Rennes-le-Château may have some relevance to this, as during the sermon (Matthew 24.37) Jesus foretells the coming of the end of the world: 'But as the days of Noah were, so shall also the coming of the Son of man be.'

I asked Sion if they were using Rennes-le-Château as a way to warn people of a coming event. Their somewhat ambiguous response was: 'We do not want to "get a message out", as people will have enough to contend with.'

Author Elizabeth Van Buren has written an entire book of apocalyptic links, including the 'cyclic cross of Hendaye', a stone cross with cryptic inscriptions and carvings on it that stands in a churchyard of Hendaye in the southwest of France on the Spanish border. Van Buren puts forward the idea that Rennes-le-Château will act as a refuge from the apocalypse. Her work is wildly speculative as she 'channels' a fair amount of her information, but Sion concurs:

'Rennes is a refuge, and certainly withstood it [a previous
cataclysm] before, but it's unlikely it was used as such at the time.'

Elizabeth Van Buren believes that the cross of Hendaye points to Rennes-le-Château. In his book *The Mysteries of the Cathedrals*, the alchemist Fulcanelli interpreted the cross as being both alchemical and apocalyptic, and he decodes the Latin inscription on it as stating: 'All life takes refuge in a single space.' Van Buren believes this 'space' to be at Rennes-le-Château. She interpreted the Latin to mean that there was a doorway at Rennes-le-Château that would allow people to escape the cataclysm by stepping out of time. The idea of this doorway was covered in the chapter on Emerging Themes (*see* page 129).

It became apparent during my research that Sion believes that at some earlier point in history the cataclysmic 'event' was expected but failed to materialize. Nic Haywood mentioned that the stone igloos, or *capitales*, on the hillside surrounding Rennes-le-Château (*see* page 109) were built for witnessing such an event.

This implies that whatever the 'event' is, it will be visual and will occur in the region in or around Rennes-le-Château, as that is what these structures face.

THE DELUGE

The Priory of Sion does not expect the event to entirely destroy life on earth but they seem convinced, in terms of Europe at least, that it will reduce the population dramatically. Excluding impact from a massive asteroid it is unlikely that any single natural event would render the earth completely devoid of life. There is an expectation that humankind will continue in some form. When I asked Nic about the nature of the event, he replied:

'A deluge perhaps. Most climatologists and scientists are aware of
the imminence of such events. The next sign is the speeding up
of environmental change. This is not unique to the current history
of the globe, it has happened many times.'

Knowledge can be passed down in the form of myths, as with the story of a great flood, which is recounted in many of the earliest myths from around the world.

For those who doubt the veracity of prediction or the accuracy of cultural memory, there is another route to knowledge of the future. Geology and archaeology should be clear as to what events have ravaged the earth in the past. If a cataclysmic event has occurred periodically in the earth's history – such as a recurring glaciation or the near miss of a returning comet – these events would then be supported by physical evidence.

In its long and troubled history the earth has suffered major meteor impacts, floods, ice ages, and volcanic and seismic upheavals. Considering that the dust cloud from the eruption of the Mount St Helens volcano in 1980 took three years to dissipate, should a volcano of, for example, the magnitude of the Yellowstone Caldera erupt, much of the northern hemisphere would experience several years of winter, with too little sunlight for crops to grow. The much smaller eruption of Krakatoa in 1883 was heard 3,000 miles (5000km) away and led to what was described as a 'year without sun' causing crops to fail worldwide. It is hard to ignore the long history of cataclysm in the earth's geological record when mass extinctions have committed entire species to the fossil record.

In conversation Nic Haywood once referred to the loss of life during the event as a 'great cull'. This term can be found in the works of climate scientist James Lovelock. Lovelock's view is also of a natural event exacerbated by humankind's abuse of natural resources and subsequent pollution. His recent book *The Revenge of Gaia* explains future scenarios of massive 'climate refugee' migrations and wars caused by starvation and displacement.

Lovelock is often seen as on the fringe of science but the 'sixth natural extinction' or 'Holocene extinction event' is a term used by environmental scientists to describe the predicted effects of current global climate change on plant, animal and human life. This is predicted as a deluge that will occur within the next 30 years (*see Six Degrees* by Mark Lynas for an excellent summary of current research in this area).

If there is a place of refuge at Rennes-le-Château, why is it here in this region and not elsewhere? One possibility is that water is the key. If the event is driven by climate change then one possible scenario would be a deluge followed by a brief ice age. This is a natural cyclical event and the pollution we have caused since the industrial revolution is thought to have accelerated the process. A flooding then freezing of the land would be catastrophic. The region of the Languedoc has the highest water table in France and Rennes-les-Bains in particular has seven hot springs surfacing nearby. These springs penetrate down to the earth's magma so are heated volcanically, and hence they would remain impervious to falling temperatures. But this is only one possibility.

If the environmental destruction caused by the onset of the next cycle of cataclysm were to begin with a worldwide deluge, it would not be the first time civilizations have survived this kind of event, as recorded in many of the oldest world myths. Should a safe location be known, would this information not come down to us through history in some encoded form?

The story of Noah has kept this idea in mind for generations but the figure of Noah has links to Sion in that each head of Sion is referred to as a *Nautonnier* or 'Helmsman'. This term is taken from the Royal Arch of Freemasonry, and Nic confirms the connection with Noah: 'The Royal Arch is sometimes known as the Royal *Ark*, thus we liken the Helmsman to Noah.'

The idea that the Rennes-le-Château region survived the last flood has caused some to speculate that Pech Cardou is the actual site where Noah's ark came to rest. According to the document *The Cave of Treasures*, a sixth-century apocryphon, a mountain called 'Cardo', not Ararat, was the final resting place of Noah's ark.

There also exists a certain amount of peripheral evidence for links between the biblical deluge and the Rennes-le-Château mystery. Father Saunière's menagerie would seem to suggest a homage to the ark of Noah. The artist Poussin's personal seal was of a man holding a model ark and *Le Serpent Rouge* makes mention of Noah standing impassively on the rocks opposite Pech Cardou.

It is also possible that the notion of a 'sacred mountain' was attached to Pech Cardou. Once a location becomes viewed as important or sacred it tends to be subject to a certain amount of mythologizing and Rennes-le-Château is itself an excellent example of this. Cardou may be a symbolic Ararat, singled out by myths and stories to transmit the location through history, to keep it in the minds of people. The Paris Meridian, for example, passes through Cardou, denoting it as a place where time and space are linked. But more importantly, it was the place chosen by the Knights Templar to fulfil the prophecy of the New Jerusalem in Revelation 21.2: 'I saw the Holy City, the New Jerusalem, coming down out of heaven from God.'

THE NEW JERUSALEM

The landscape of Rennes-le-Château would appear to have been modified to represent the New Jerusalem from at least the time of the Templars. There are place names and locations that mirror old Jerusalem and it has been used to re-enact the route of Jesus as he laboured under the cross on the Via Dolorosa. This journey is also the central theme of the Rose+Croix degree. These threads converge to give weight to the idea that the New Jerusalem was in fact contrived and constructed in the Languedoc, and that it may have been based upon a far earlier tradition dating back to the time of the arrival of Mary Magdalene in this region.

The underground structure said to be at the heart of this landscape (*see* page 183) acts as both a tomb and a temple, and there is also a strong apocalyptic resonance to this as it has 12 gates that are open at different times. This was foretold in the Book of Revelation (21.10–13):

> 'And he carried me away in the Spirit to a mountain great and
> high, and showed me the Holy City, Jerusalem, coming down out
> of heaven from God.... It had a great, high wall with twelve gates
> and with twelve angels at the gates. On the gates were written the
> names of the twelve tribes of Israel.'

This idea is supported by Sion, who affirms that the temple is linked to revelation and the apocalypse. The entrances are four sets of three, the 12 entrances to the underground temple. There is a perfect symmetry and geometric importance to the design, which is explored in depth in John Michell's *City of Revelation*.

Contemporaneous with the Templars, the Cathars of the Languedoc were symbolized by the Toulouse cross, originating with the medieval counts of Toulouse and seen on the regional flag. The design is of an equal-armed cross with three gold spheres on each branch. The spheres are interpreted by French researcher Gérard Thome as representing the 12 gates of the New Jerusalem.

The presence of relics in the underground temple, and the uncovering of a tomb that includes the body of Mary Magdalene, and possibly also of Jesus, may set the stage for the next development, as set out in Revelation 21.9–10:

> 'Come hither, I will shew thee the bride, the Lamb's wife. And he
> carried me away in the spirit to a great and high mountain, and
> shewed me that great city, the holy Jerusalem, descending out of
> heaven from God.'

The Lamb is a title always associated with Jesus and as this passage illustrates, not only is there a 'bride' of Jesus to be revealed but this is linked to the New Jerusalem. If we accept that a New Jerusalem is located in the vicinity of Rennes-le-Château and that the body of Mary Magdalene, thought to be the bride of Jesus, is buried there, we have a very accurate, albeit contrived, enactment of this part of Revelation.

THE SECOND COMING

With a New Jerusalem rising from the receding floodwaters, the stage will be set for the Second Coming, the final act of St John's prophecy: the return of a priest-king who is universally accepted as ruler and will be expected to lead humankind toward a new golden age.

As reincarnation is not part of Catholic doctrine and divine intervention seems unlikely, the only real option for a Second Coming would be through hereditary means. If Jesus had a bride then there may well also have been children, as explained to me by Sion and covered in the chapter on Mary Magdalene. From these children would descend the modern-day bloodline families, into which the priest-king – heir to the holy family of Jesus – would be born.

The timing of this would be crucial.

Sion, we must remember, chose to go public in the spiritual vacuum created by the Second World War. As church attendance declined and the faith of millions was challenged by the death and destruction of a world war, Sion began to disseminate the alternative ideas of Jesus as a husband and father.

An event such as an apocalypse would further diminish the hold of organized religions on people's spiritual lives. As a natural disaster would not discriminate between church, mosque, synagogue or temple, but would destroy everything in its path, it will be hard for anyone to consider themselves the 'chosen ones'. The many religions that currently hide behind elaborate and complex structures of dogma that have eclipsed such simple questions as 'Who are we?' and 'Why are we here?' will be swept aside as they fail to protect their followers from the indiscriminate power that is nature.

A post-apocalypse civilization will need a uniting leader, and having been simmering in the background for 2,000 years it is here that the bloodline will find its purpose. In the aftermath of the 'great cull', anarchy and a new Dark Age will consume the West unless a leader quickly takes the reins. According to the bloodline tradition, the once and future king will be born of a union between two noble families. At this point in time the likely candidates are the Hapsburgs and the House of Lorraine.

Into this space comes a new way of being, led by one who is both a spiritual and a political ruler, a priest-king, like the priest-kings, or Hyksos, of ancient Egypt of the Order of Melchizedek. It will be a return of the Christ figure that is understood and recognized by all. Sadly, he cannot last a thousand years, because his role demands that he be sacrificed, either symbolically or literally, like the pagan gods of yore. However, his rule and his impact on society should live on.

The idea of the return of a 'Grand Monarch' or national saviour is very much a part of French tradition, with its historic mysteries of the 'survival' of the Merovingians, Louis XVII and even Charles de Gaulle. It is also a common theme of French myths such as Perrault's *Sleeping Beauty*, where the dormant kingdom is reawoken by a single gallant knight.

The myth of the returning king has also seeped into the religions and myths of other countries and cultures. In England for example, Arthur, 'the once and future king', is reputed to sleep beneath a hill with his knights, to awake when the nation is threatened. The Arthurian legends give us the image of the great sword Excalibur returning to the lake, where it remains hidden until a king appears that is fit to wield it. This echoes the idea of the seed of Zoroaster that lies dormant in a lake for 3,000 years, and the legend of Isis' reassembly of all the parts of the dismembered Osiris – except for his penis, which Seth threw into the Nile, never to be found.

CONCLUSION

Like many of the subjects that we have covered, the apocalypse can work on more than one level. On a personal level the opening of the seven seals could be seen to correlate with the 'opening' or activation of the seven chakras, or energy centres, along the spine, which represents a process of ascent from the primal and purely physical at the base of the spine to the enlightened and purely spiritual at the highest chakra, the crown of the head. When the chakras are open, we attain a perfect balance of physical and spiritual. While this idea first came to Western attention through non-Christian disciplines of Indian origin, such as yoga and tantra, the fact remains that it has always been present and available as a phenomenon of human experience.

At another level the apocalypse symbolizes the downfall of the Church as Jesus is rediscovered as a personal experience: the freedom to be who you really are and the ability to communicate directly with God as the Gnostics have maintained over the centuries.

In the light of this, the need for the mediation of priests would quickly dissolve.

But with all I have seen and heard I must conclude that there is something more to the idea of apocalypse than just personal spiritual development. There are many clues to a widespread, physically destructive event of some magnitude in the near future.

The world as it is cannot go on indefinitely, as any geologist or climatologist will tell you. And history tells us that the world has been destroyed many times. It has withstood comet impacts such as the one that created the Yucatan Peninsula and the Woodleigh crater in Australia; cycles of ice ages; magnetic pole shifts; and great earthquakes and seismic upheavals. A coming event of similar magnitude is not a case of 'if' but merely 'when'.

But even a flood, while devastating, will eventually recede.

Spirituality exists in every culture, at every stage of history, at every level of society. It is a constant, unlike scientific thinking, philosophical fashions and adopted ignorance. Spirituality has always fulfilled a need in the conscious development of humanity, so it will continue beyond the cataclysmic event. Sadly, it will take such a major event to bring about a widespread shift in consciousness. Should much of the world and its myriad of beliefs be swept into the sea, tragic though that would be, in the long term it may help to force humanity into a more balanced existence.

The universal shock caused by the destruction of a random third of life on earth being destroyed in a senseless cataclysmic event, as stated in the Book of Revelation, may help humanity come to realize that its gods are absent, or dead and lost to the world – or at least that its understanding of them has been distorted beyond repair.

In the aftermath perhaps there will be a shift in control from the will of established religions back to the will of the individual. The uncomfortable space of uncertainty and the pain of not belonging is a useful experience. It creates a space in us for the divine to occupy.

Ultimately, I think we have to let our gods die in order to rediscover them for ourselves. The final word on this subject belongs to Nic Haywood. During an informal discussion, when asked if he knew when the Event would happen, Nic declined to give an accurate date but stated:

'It will happen within your lifetime.'

CHAPTER 19

FINAL THOUGHTS

Lux Veritatis Alet Altare Templi –
'May the Light of Truth Sustain
the Temple Altar'

Like *Le Serpent Rouge* our journey began in darkness as I set about gathering the evidence for the Priory of Sion and their actions as they move through the shadows of history. With the help of Nicolas Haywood and other members of the order we have shone a light into the darkest corners of this mysterious organization. The aims and influence of Sion have been seen to be far-reaching and with Sion's help we have navigated through secret societies, religious mysteries, the arts, bloodlines, Rennes-le-Château, alchemy and the apocalypse.

As we have immersed ourselves in this myriad of esoteric subjects there remained a purity to their message, a clear stream of knowledge that flows in all directions from the centre of a rose. My role was to communicate it, to bring it into the light.

The clearest channel of release used by Sion was to make use of the mysteries of Rennes-le-Château as their vehicle to disseminate beliefs and ideals – like a mystic spiral reaching from a distant past, via the present, and into the future. It began as a small mystery – a wayward French priest at Rennes-le-Château – yet from such a speck of grit grows a pearl of immense value. Over time this mystery has coalesced into a complex system of beliefs and ideas seeped into the public domain in order to influence society. It has slowly revealed to us many secrets, and this was the Priory of Sion's intention:

> 'What if alternative history, a release that would be shocking whole, is let out piecemeal?'

If Sion has achieved one thing it has revealed to us the importance of the role of Mary Magdalene as a lost feminine archetype. If she were accepted as the bride of Jesus and the mother of his child or children it would redress a central and glaring imbalance in Christianity, and particularly in Catholicism.

The role of Mary Magdalene, as recognized among the 'heretics' and adepts, is that of a priestess, capable of elevating the role of women within the Church. As an archetype Mary Magdalene is important even for those millions in the West to whom the Church is no longer particularly relevant. Owing to the historical influence of orthodox Christianity on our culture, the figure of a sexually active, empowered young woman as a positive archetype is still so lacking in modern society that many still regard such a figure with suspicion as morally wayward or worse.

Symbolically, Mary is the repressed feminine aspect within man.

Human nature, diverse and fascinating, cannot be diverted or repressed without causing harm to the individual. Repression is rife in many religions and one measure of religious teachings is often their attitude to sexuality. But sexuality and spirituality are not mutually exclusive, as Christianity has often seemed to suggest. The path of tantra, for example, is of particular interest to those in this regard. Like the twin serpents on the staff of Hermes, tantra has the effect of opening the chakras and releasing an undeniable force of energy that bridges the spiritual and physical realms.

Mary Magdalene is also a symbol of an alternative Christianity, passed down through the ages as secret teachings. We have seen how symbolism was used to protect and pass on these secrets. They are encapsulated in documents and rituals and circulated among secret societies and heretical priests to protect an unorthodox spiritual path. As the Rose+Croix Degree of the Rosicrucians found its way into Freemasonry (and *Le Serpent Rouge*) this unorthodox path also embraced the path of alchemy.

Alchemy – the complete science of transformation and individual evolution toward gnosis – offers a direct experience of the divine. It is tied in some ways to the knowledge of future events, including the apocalypse, and how the bloodline of Jesus and Mary Magdalene will produce a 'Second Coming' in the aftermath.

As the apocalypse sets the scene for a new Messiah, the orthodox view would have us believe that Jesus will be returning, literally from heaven. But Jesus will not return in person, for in all likelihood he is dead and buried in the Arcadian landscape of Rennes-le-Château. If this were fully understood, none would take offence as the life and teachings of Jesus would then be seen in a different light. If Jesus is made to be solely human, to be truly 'Christ-like' becomes more attainable to every living person. It is entirely possible for anyone to be humble and compassionate, tolerant and forgiving, wholly accepting of difference to the point of complete equality. This is true Christianity.

JOURNEY'S END

In undertaking to find the truth we have stumbled upon what appears to be the greatest lie in history: that Jesus was without a wife and an heir, and that he died upon the Cross. In revealing this lie we are responsible in part for where such a revelation will lead. You have joined me on this strange pilgrimage and in the end all that stands is faith and truth. Sometimes they are the same but if we are to sacrifice one then it is truth that must remain. The truth is more important.

My intention in writing this book has been both to do justice to the material provided by Sion and to move things forward. If, as the previous chapter explores, the coming of knowledge coincides with the coming of a cataclysmic event then I have taken part in preparing the ground for this.

When the time is right, more of the mystery will be revealed. The underground stream has yet to truly surface for all to see. There are secrets that have the power to impact upon the world, to fundamentally challenge many core beliefs in religion, science and history. Therefore they cannot be revealed lightly. This journey attempts to create an awareness that there are more revelations yet to come.

Change is coming and, as the Priory of Sion tells us time and again:

'Everything is going according to plan.'

Rob Howells
January 17, 2011

APPENDIX

DOCUMENTATION

How strange they are, the manuscripts of this Friend,
great traveller through the unknown.

Le Serpent Rouge

THE PRIORY OF SION AND RENNES-LE-CHÂTEAU DOCUMENTS

Many aspects of the mysteries of the Priory of Sion and Rennes-le-Château have revolved around parchments and other documents. Sion's first line of contact with individuals is often to send them a document, until recently *Le Serpent Rouge*, for example (*see* Chapter 10).

It would seem that Sion's 'archives' are hidden among existing libraries, some public but many in private collections, a dispersed model of security much like the system that Umberto Eco writes of in *Foucault's Pendulum*. Without permission or the correct bibliographical details the archives are impossible to locate.

In recent years Sion has provided, promised and directed me to numerous works. Below is a list of the important Rennes-le-Château documents, and the items promised or sent to me.

During the 1960s the Priory of Sion made public a number of documents relating to Rennes-le-Château. These included parchments that were said to have belonged to Father Bérenger Saunière and the *Dossiers Secrets* (*Secret Dossiers*), a collection of cuttings and notes relating to the mystery. The manuscripts and other documentary items passed to me by Sion are listed below:

Parchments

The two parchments first published in Gérard de Sède's *The Accursed Treasure of Rennes-le-Château* and later in Baigent, Lincoln and Leigh's *The Holy Blood and the Holy Grail* were said to have been discovered by Bérenger Saunière when he excavated the church at Rennes-le-Château.

Henry Lincoln discovered that there were codes hidden within the parchments and deciphered them. The encoded messages are:

'To Dagobert II, King, and to Sion is this treasure and he is there dead.'

'Shepherdess no temptation. Poussin and Teniers hold the key. Peace 681. By the cross and this horse of God. I conquer this demon guardian at midday. Blue apples.'

De Sède had already linked the parchments to Rennes-le-Château so the content of these manuscripts further acts as signposts to the mystery. They mention the Poussin and Teniers paintings explored in Chapter 16 and the Asmodeus statue from the church, while 'blue apples' is a Masonic term.

The 'horse of God' reference may be to the painting *Heliodorus Expelled from the Temple* by Delacroix which is situated in the Chapel of Angels in Saint-Sulpice church, Paris, as supported by Sion's *Serpent Rouge* text.

The manuscripts circulated by de Sède were eventually discovered to be modern fabrications and many researchers quickly dismissed them out of hand. They were produced in support of Pierre Plantard's mission in what was described to me as a 'cottage industry' outside Paris in the 1960s, but Sion maintains that they were based on authentic originals discovered by Saunière.

It is said that Saunière travelled to Saint-Sulpice to have the parchments decoded. This would have been done by Emile Hoffet, a leading member of the researchers based there. According to Sion,

'It is likely that these four parchments were, in reality, handed over – traded if you will – for the whereabouts of another document by an inner circle of very powerful clerics at Saint-Sulpice: the group referred to as "Hoffet's Workgroup".'

Author Jean Markale claims that Hoffet had a secret library at Saint-Sulpice. This was confirmed by Sion as a small archive within the church library. I was granted access to this but the documents were removed before I could view them.

Dossiers Secrets

Sion sent me a copy of the *Dossiers Secrets* (*Secret Dossiers*) as a matter of historical reference. It should be noted that these and other documents that Sion sent are stamped with two Masonic (Grand Lodge Alpina) insignia that confirm that they were permitted for release and circulation. This is said to be standard policy for any document released outside of a Sion 'campaign' (of information) and has been in place since 1985 to prevent the circulation of inappropriate or doctored material.

When Pierre Plantard was tasked with gathering the scattered adepts of post-war Europe, one of his methods was to use the Bibliothèque Nationale de France in Paris as a 'noticeboard'. The *Dossiers Secrets* was a file of news clippings and documents to or from which items could be added or removed. Of course, this required a 'friend' of Sion within the library to facilitate the storage and retrieval of uncatalogued material. I can confirm that such a person still exists today but I am not at liberty to reveal their identity.

The secret dossiers were not meant for the public and have caused a certain amount of confusion for researchers. As Sion puts it,

> '*Les Dossiers Secrets* were originally contrived as a noticeboard of sorts, but later became a vehicle for deliberate, purposeful mystification and also acted as both a public record and a means of verification.'

The purpose they served was as a means to communicate between different factions. They included a copy of *Le Serpent Rouge* and this was used to attract the interest of people whom Sion considered to be aligned with their cause.

The content of the *Dossiers* evolved constantly as items were added and removed over time, and they are still updated as a matter of tradition, although they do not appear in any cataloguing system within the library.

Teniers' painting *St Anthony and St Paul in the Desert*

Aside from the above I was also sent a number of other items including a bromide copy of the Teniers painting mentioned above. On loan from Sion and passed to me by Nicolas Haywood, this is the only known accurate copy to exist of the original, which has been in private hands for nearly 80 years. The bromide is included in the plates section of this book.

Splendor Solis plates

I also received several plates from an original manuscript of the *Splendor Solis* that belongs to Nic Haywood's private collection of alchemical manuscripts. I have included Plate VIII as an example as it illustrates the quote 'Deliver me out of the mire and let me not sink' as referred to in both the church at Rennes-le-Château and *Le Serpent Rouge*.

Among the plates I received was Plate III, which shows a knight standing over a fountain where the light and dark fluid mix from two water sources. This can be found in the Rennes-le-Château landscape at the place where the rivers 'White' (Blanc) and 'Salt' (Sals) meet. Locally this place is known as 'Le Bénitier' or holy water stoup, such as the one held aloft by Asmodeus within Rennes-le-Château church. It is one example of how an initiation based on the alchemical process was built into the landscape and the church.

Tarot designs

Sion sent me five designs for Tarot cards. They stated that artist and filmmaker Jean Cocteau either influenced the designs or possibly even devised them. Cocteau was said to be a member of Sion and the Hermit card included in the plates section shows the word ZION in the shape of a key hanging from the hermit's necklace. The second card included is the *Papesse* (High Priestess), which features the alchemical axiom VITRIOL written between two lines at a single point perspective. A similar design can be seen on a publication called *Vaincre*, published by Pierre Plantard in 1946 advocating the creation of a United States of the West.

The letter of intent

During the making of the Bloodline documentary Sion sent a letter to me and the producers dated 17th January 2006 that set out their intention to support the project. But what was really interesting was that it had a number of signatures and seals attached to it.

Signatures on Priory of Sion documents are not to be taken at face value for two reasons. It is my understanding that the order maintains a series of stamps of signatures allowing for the co-signing of documents in the absence, and even after the death, of certain key members. Also, the use of stamps does not require items to be in physical circulation – sent to and fro between signatories, with the attendant risks of going astray or falling into the 'wrong hands' – prior to official release. Stamps also mean that a number of variations of documents in

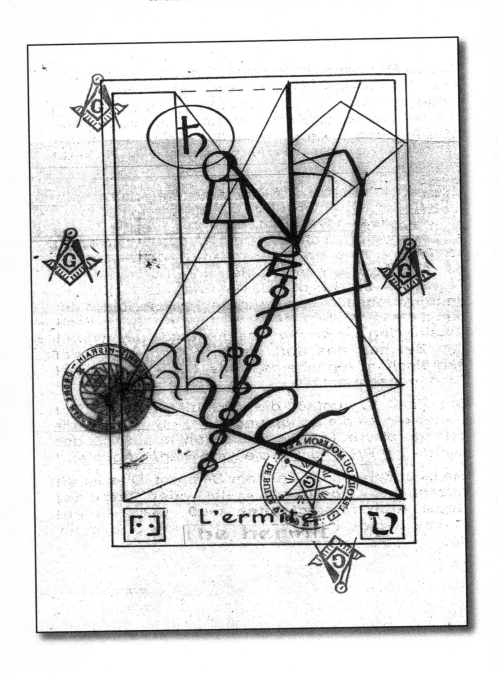

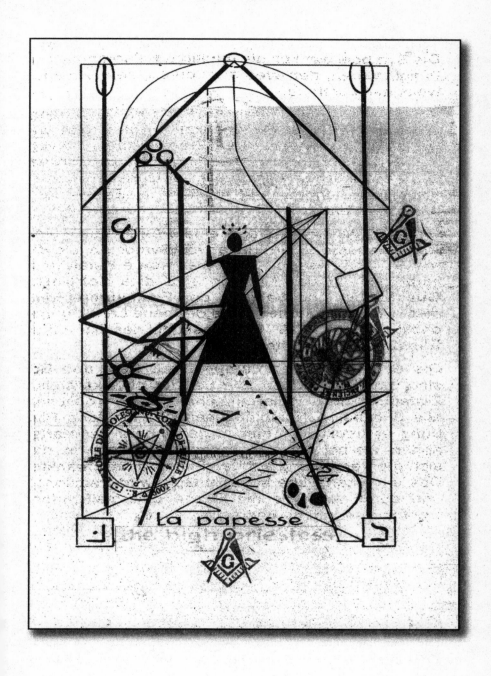

terms of language can be produced and collated accordingly into a single item, depending on the recipient. These variant copies can then be 'signed' without the signatory needing to be present.

With this in mind I can make no claim that the signatures appended to the letter of intent were by the hand of those to whom they are attributed. The first signature is by Nicolas Haywood, using his old family name of St Aubyn, and has the stamp of the 'Children of Isis'. I can find no record of this group but they may be linked to the alchemical lodges of European Freemasonry. It may be a subset of the Hermetic lodge of which Nic is a member but again this is not conclusive.

Alongside this is the signature of Thomas Plantard, son of Pierre Plantard and current Grand Master of the Priory of Sion, although his position is disputed. His signature and stamp appear to bear the words *Ordre de Morges*. Morges is a Swiss town where two European Masonic lodges, Lux in Tenebris ('Light in the Dark') and Saint-Jean du Léman ('St John of Lake Geneva'), are based. But I cannot conclusively link Thomas Plantard to either.

Next is the signature of Raphael Sauvage, whom I believe to be the great-grandson of Gaston Sauvage, who was known to be part of the alchemist Fulcanelli's inner circle. Raphael's stamp appears like that of the Misraim-Memphis Masonic lodge that appears on many of Sion's publicly released documents.

The final signature is unknown to me and also difficult to discern. It appears to be 'A. Sewole'. Beneath Sewole's signature is the stamp of the REAA, the *Grand Orient de France Suprême Conseil Grand Collège du Rite Ecossais Ancien Accepté*. This is a known Masonic order based in France.

Priory of Sion frontispiece

This Sion design (*see* page 38) is said by Nic Haywood to be of 'little literary merit' but of 'geo-mathematical and esoteric relevance'. The design is a geometrical image with two arrows passing through the centre, flanked by the letters alpha and omega. This closely resembles the badge of the Order of the Secret Monitor (OSM), a well established Masonic lodge under the United Grand Lodge of England. There are variations to the design but in sending it to me Sion are clearly indicating a link between the two orders. Like the Rosicrucians, the OSM have been known to claim that their order can be traced back to ancient Egypt.

The badge of the Secret Monitor consists of arrows within a six-pointed star and often contains the letters D and J and is surmounted by a crown. The badge represents the friendship between David and King Saul's son Jonathan in the Old Testament (Samuel 1). Their covenant of love and friendship mirrors the Masonic ideal of brotherly love.

Bacstrom's seal
The alchemist Sigismund Bacstrom was initiated into the Rosicrucians by the Comte de Chazal in 1794 (*see* page 51). The Bacstrom seal is a small image that contains an eagle, and a serpent looking down on a toad. The first two elements are key to *Le Serpent Rouge*, whereas the toad generally signifies base qualities to be redeemed. These creatures also signify the three main phases of alchemy: black toad = *nigredo* (blackening); white eagle = *albedo* (whitening); serpent or dragon = red tincture/Philosopher's Stone.

Essay on fire
Nic also submitted a copy of his essay on the esoteric nature of fire, which is the most thorough explanation I have ever seen. Among Sigismund Bacstrom's letters is a note stating that if he should meet another claiming to be a Rosicrucian he would challenge them to explain the esoteric nature of fire. Nic's essay is ample evidence of his qualification as a member. It was not included here for reasons of space but it is available on my website (http://www.robhowells.co.uk).

Rennes-le-Château cemetery map
A copy of a hand-drawn map of the graveyard at Rennes-le-Château with a key to who is buried where was sent to me as the book was going to press. I am aware that it is an immensely important item to researchers but I have chosen not to include it in this book, because unfortunately the cemetery has been subject to vandalism by treasure hunters and amateur archaeologists for a number of years. The map in no way indicates any need to excavate the area but relates to a reference in *Le Serpent Rouge* and I hope to expand on this at a later date.

The secret of the Templars
This is a selection of pages from a self-published work by mathematician Patricia Villiers-Stuart. It includes a geometrical analysis of Poussin's *Et in Arcadia Ego* (*The Shepherds of Arcadia*) linked to the Golden Section and the geometry of occultist Dr John Dee. Dee was an influence on the Rosicrucian grades

circulating in Paris in the 19th century. The 'words of power' conveyed by Rosicrucian masters to initiates were drawn from Dee's writings.

The geometry overlaid on the Poussin canvas contains a circle segmented into 12 parts. The same geometrical design is overlaid on a map of the area near Rennes-le-Château and centres on the place called L'Homme Mort (The Dead Man). The 12 segments of a circle are symbolic of both the rose (as in cathedral rose windows) and the 'Rose Line' that passes close to this area.

There are said to be two pages missing from this work that were to be sent at a later date but as yet they have not arrived.

Outstanding items

It may be of interest to researchers that there are a number of other items that Sion was due to send me but remain outstanding. These include photographs of two documents said to date from the 14th and 17th centuries. The latter is a 'palimpsest', that is, it is written over a much older document that has had the words partially erased. This is by design and it is likely that the two texts interact in some way. I have seen a small photo of this manuscript so I know that it does at least exist in some form.

Sion also mentioned notes and diagrams by a former archaeologist and member of Sion, some of which are said to be in code. These would provide guidance on the cave systems close to Rennes-le-Château, such as where specific underground locations and hidden entrances can be found in the area to the east of the village. It is unlikely that I would have published these if they had come into my possession but they could be used to support the hypothesis of underground tombs and temples (*see* Chapter 11).

Finally, I should note that Sion aso directed me to seek out the Chinon Parchment in the Vatican Secret Archive (*see* Chapters 2 and 8), and alchemical texts such as the *Splendor Solis* and the *Book of the Holy Trinity* (*see* Chapter 17).

SELECT
BIBLIOGRAPHY

For a full list of related books and recommended further reading, visit the author's website www.robhowells.co.uk.

Abraham, L, *A Dictionary of Alchemical Imagery*, Cambridge University Press, 2001

Agrippa, C, *Three Books of Occult Philosophy*, Llewellyn Publications, US, 1993

Allen, T G (trans), *The Book of The Dead*, University of Chicago Press, 1974

AMORC, *Secret Symbols of the Rosicrucians of the 16th and 17th Centuries*, AMORC, 1987

Assagioli, R, *Psychosynthesis*, Thorsons, 1999

Attwater, D, *The Penguin Dictionary of Saints*, Penguin Books, 1983

Baigent, M, H Lincoln and R Leigh, *The Holy Blood and the Holy Grail* (published in the US as *Holy Blood, Holy Grail*)

Baigent, M, H Lincoln and R Leigh, *The Messianic Legacy*, Arrow, 2006

Baigent, M, *The Jesus Papers*, Element Books, 2006

Byrne, P, *Templar Gold*, Symposium, 2001

Batschman, O, *Nicolas Poussin*, Reaktion Books, 1990

Barnstone, W (Ed), *The Other Bible*, HarperCollins, 2005

Bertaulet, J, *De verloren koning en de bronnen van de graallegende* (*The Lost King and the Sources of the Grail Legends*), Stichting Mens en Kultuur, 1991

Blake, W, *Jerusalem* (poem)

Blunt, A, *Poussin*, Pallas Athene Arts, 1995

Brunes, T, *Sacred Geometry*, Rhodos, 1967

Byrne, P, *Templar Gold*, Blue Dolphin Publishing, 2001

Boudet, H, *La Vraie Langue Celtique et le Cromlech de Rennes-les-Bains* (*The Language of the Celts and the Stone Circle of Rennes-les-Bains*), Bélisane, 1984 facsimile of 1886 edition

Bulfinch, T, *Bulfinch's Mythology*, Modern Library Inc, 1998

Butler, A, *Lives of the Saints*, Paraclete Press, 2005

Chaplin, P, *City of Secrets,* Robinson Publishing, 2007

Charpentier, L, *Mysteries of Chartres Cathedral,* Research into Lost Knowledge Organisation Trust, 1997

Cooper, J C, *An Illustrated Encyclopaedia of Symbols,* Thames and Hudson, 1978

Clarke, R B, *An Order Outside Time,* Hampton Roads, 2005

Cruz, J C, *Relics,* Our Sunday Visitor Inc, 1984

Cirlot, J E, *A Dictionary of Symbols,* Routledge, 1983

Dawood, N A, trans, *The Koran,* Penguin Classics, 2003

de Sède, G, *The Accursed Treasure of Rennes-le-Château,* DEK Publishing, 2001

de Sède, G, *Rennes-le-Château,* Robert Laffont, 1988

Dee, Dr J, *The Hieroglyphic Monad,* Weiser, 2001

Codex Rosa Crucis D.O.M.A., Philosophical Research Society, 1974

Douzet, A, and P Coppens, *The Secret Vault,* Adventures Unlimited Publishing, 2006

Dunn–Mascetti, M, *Saints: The Chosen Few,* Boxtree, 1994

Eschenbach, Wolfram von, *Parzival,* Penguin, 2004

Fabricius, J, *Alchemy,* Aquarian Press, 1989

Fanthorpe, L, *Rennes-le-Château,* Bellevue Books, 1991

Frale, B, *Templar Book,*

Fulcanelli, *The Dwellings of the Philosophers,* Archive Pr & Communications 1999

Fulcanelli, *Le Mystère des Cathédrales,* Brotherhood of Life Inc 1987

Gaines, H F, *Cryptanalysis,* Dover Publications, 2000

Gardner, L, *Genesis of the Grail Kings,* Bantam, 2009

Gettings, F, *The Secret Zodiac,* Routledge, 1987

Gilbert, R A, *Freemasonry and Esoteric Movements,* lecture, Canonbury Masonic Research Institute (CMRC), 2000

Godwin, J (trans), *Hypnorotermachia Poliphilia,* Thames & Hudson, 2005

Hall, M P, *The Secret Teachings of All Ages,* Forgotten Books, 2008

Hancock, *The Sign and the Seal,* Arrow, 1993

Hancox, J, *The Queen's Chameleon,* Jonathan Cape Ltd, 1994

Harris, L, *The Secret Heresy of Hieronymus Bosch,* Floris Books, 1995

Henderson and Sherwood, *Transformation of the Psyche,* Routledge, 2003

Hulse, D A, *The Key of it All. Book 2: The Western Mysteries,* Llewellyn Publications, 1994

Jackson, A F C, *Rose Croix: A History of the Ancient and Accepted Rite,* Lewis Masonic, 1980

Jung, C G, *Psychology and Alchemy*, Routledge, 1980

King, K L, *What is Gnosticism?*, Belknap, Harvard, 2005

Knight, G, *A Practical Guide to Cabalistic Symbolism*, Helios, 1966

Lincoln, H, *The Holy Place*, Corgi, 1992

Lynas, M, *Six Degrees*, Harper Perennial, 2008

Markale, J, *The Church of Mary Magdalene*, Inner Traditions, 2004

MacGregor Mathers, S L, *The Book of the Sacred Magic of Abra-Melin the Mage*, Dover Publications, 1976

Leloup, J (trans), *The Gospel of Mary Magdalene*, Inner Traditions, 2002

Leloup, J (trans), *The Gospel of Philip*, Inner Traditions, 2004

Metford, J C J, *The Christian Year*, Thames and Hudson, 1991

Moreux, *Alchimie Moderne*, Gaston Doin, 1924

Michelle, J, *City of Revelation*, Sphere, 1973

Muller, M (trans), *Zend Avesta* (3 vols), Adamant Media Corporation 2001

Mackintosh, C, *The Rosicrucians*, Weiser, 1998

Moore, T *Care of the Soul*, Piatkus Books, 1992

Newton, J F, *The Men's House*, Macoy, 1969

Post, E, *Saints, Signs and Symbols*, SPCK Publishing, 2002

Perrault, C, *Fairy Tales*, Dover Publications Inc, 2000

Porter, J R, *The Lost Bible: Forgotten Scriptures Revealed*, Duncan Baird/Chicago University Press, 2001

Rappaport, A S, *Myths of Ancient Israel*, Avenel, 1988

Robinson, (ed), *The Nag Hammadi Library*, HarperOne, 2000

Rigby, G, *On Earth as it is in Heaven*, Rhaedus Publications, 1996

Robison, J, *Proofs of a Conspiracy*, Forgotten Books, 2008

Rowan, J, *Subpersonalities*, Routledge, 1989

Ryan, F, *Vincent de Paul and Louise de Marillac*, Paulist Press International, 1996

Shanks, H, *Understanding the Dead Sea Scrolls*, Random House Inc , 1998

Sismonde, J C L S de, *History of the Crusades against the Cathars in the 13th Century*, Gazarü Libris, 1826

St Germain, Comte de, *The Most Holy Trinosophia*, Forgotten Books, 2008

Starbird, M, *The Woman with the Alabaster Jar*, Bear and Co, 1993

Starbird, M, *The Goddess in the Gospels*, Bear & Company, 1998

Steinbrecher, *Inner Guide Meditation*, Weiser, 1994

Street, C E, *Earthstars*, Earthstars Publishing, 2001

Stoyanov, Y, *The Other God*, Yale University Press, 2000

Suzuki, S, *Zen Mind, Beginner's Mind*, Shambhala Publications Inc, 2005

Thierring, B, *Jesus the Man*, Corgi Books, 1993

Thierring, B, *Jesus of the Apocalypse*, Doubleday, 1996

Trismosin, S, *Splendor Solis*, Phanes Press, 1994

Ulmannus, *Buch der Heiligen Dreifaltigkeit (The Book of the Holy Trinity)*, c 1415–19

Van Buren, E, *Refuge from the Apocalypse*, CW Daniel, 1986

Vermes, G (ed), *The Complete Dead Sea Scrolls in English*, Penguin, 2004

Villiers Stuart, P, *The Secret of the Templars*, Self published, 1983

Von Franz, M L, *The Alchemical Active Imagination*, Shambhala, 1997

Voragine, J de, *The Golden Legend*, Princeton, 1993

Waite, A E, *Brotherhood of the Rosy Cross*, Kessinger, 1992

Walvoords, *The Prophecy Knowledge Handbook*, Victor Books, 1998

Wind, J E, *Pagan Mysteries in the Renaissance*, WW Norton, 1968

Wood, D, *Genisis*, Baton Press, 1985

Wood, D, and I Campbell, *Geneset*, Bellevue Books, 1994

Wakefield and Evans, *Heresies of the High Middle Ages*, Columbia University Press, 1991

Wright, T *Original Theory of the Universe*, The Book Service Ltd, 1971

Walsh, M (ed), *Butler's Lives of the Saints*, Burns and Oates, 1995

Watkins, J, *The Old Straight Track*, Abacus, 1994

Winwood Reade, R, *The Veil of Isis or Mysteries of the Druids*, General Books LLC, 2010

Whone, *Church Monastery Cathedral*, Element Books, 1991

Yates, F A, *Giordano Bruno and the Hermetic Tradition*, University Of Chicago Press, 1991

Yates, F A, *Rosicrucian Enlightenment*, Paladin, 1972

INDEX

INDEX

as depiction of Jesus' family 190, 247
and *Le Serpent Rouge* 166
and Rennes-le-Château 105, 126, 128, 155, 182, 244–5, 293–4
see also Shugborough Hall
European Union xi, 23
Eye of Providence 112, 163

F

Fama Fraternitatis Rosae Crucis 32–3, 145
Fatima, Our Lady of 274
feminine aspect 134, 158, 164–6, 168, 177
of Christianity 210–11, 212–13, 284
of God 165–6
Holy Grail as 197–8
Féral, Alain 96
Ficino, Marsillio 152
fish symbolism 235
Flamel, Nicolas 132, 133, 140, 171
and *Le Serpent Rouge* 144–5, 146, 154, 163, 164, 169, 172–3, 175–6
fleur-de-lys symbolism 257
Fleury, de, family 100, 123, 173
Fleury, Paul-Urbain Vincent de 114, 173, 230–31
foot-washing 115, 142, 175, 206–7
Foucault's Pendulum (Eco) 128
fountain symbolism 105, 246
Frale, Barbara 30
France:
Catholic Church in 50–52
as Gaul 66–7
Jewish community in 67, 68, 174
kings of 228–9
Franks 66–7, 228, 248
Freemasonry 18, 35–9
Ancient and Accepted Scottish Rite 39, 97
Grand Pontiff (19th) Degree 234
Knight of the Brazen Serpent (25th) Degree 174
Rose+Croix (18th) Degree 89, 101, 102, 114, 120, 231, 251
Ancient and Honourable Fraternity of Royal Ark Mariner 105
and church of Rennes-le-Château 91, 93, 97, 99, 102, 105, 119–21
Co-Freemasonry 211
Grand Lodge Alpina 17, 36, 37, 39
and Knights Templar 25, 35, 37–9, 121
and Priory of Sion 20–21, 23, 120
Rite of Memphis 96, 120
and Rosicrucianism 34, 119–21
symbols of 88–9, 93, 112, 160, 161, 165–6
and Temple of Solomon 35, 119, 121, 163, 205, 231
United Grand Lodge of England (UGLE) 35, 36, 37, 39

and use of code 252
York (American) Rite:
Royal Arch Degree 35, 121, 154, 156, 231, 278
French Church mural, London (Cocteau) 98, 106, 126–7, 256, 270
French Revolution 69

G

garden, closed, and fountain, symbolism of 105
Gélis, Father Antoine 75–6, 78, 119
geometry, sacred 124–7
George III, king of United Kingdom of Great Britain and Ireland 233, 238
Germaine de Pibrac, St 99, 133
'gesture of horror' 172
giants 235–6
Gibeah, battle of 205
Giscard, Bernard 93, 95, 99
Gisors 58
treasure of 103
gnosis 136, 158, 178, 202, 259–62
and Jesus' 'inner teachings' 209–12
Golden Head 30, 49, 259
Golden Legend, The (de Voragine) 207, 208, 223, 228
Golden Rule (Section) 12
Golgotha 113, 128
Gospel of Mary 207, 209, 210–11, 212
Gospel of Philip 212–13, 219–20, 224
Gospel of Thomas 198, 210, 260, 262
Gregory (the Great), Pope 206
gryphon symbolism 95–6

H

Hammott, Ben 183–4, 196–8, 204
Hancox, Joy 46
Hapsburg dynasty 229, 230, 231, 281
Haywood, Nicolas 6–10, 111, 292, 293
head symbolism 113
Helena, St 193, 197
Heliodorus Expelled from the Temple (Delacroix) 167, 287
Hendaye, cyclic cross of 276
Henry IV, king of France 50
Hercules 162–3
Hermaphrodite (alchemy) 168, 172
Herod the Great 195
hexagram symbolism 156
Hinduism 268
Hiram Abiff 156, 205
Hoffet, Emile 73, 287
Holy Blood and the Holy Grail, The (Baigent, Leigh and Lincoln) 1–2, 11, 15, 58, 59, 70, 227
Holy Grail 68, 197
symbolism of 98–9, 158, 197–8, 234